Strategies
for business
and
technical
writing

DISCARDED-LIBRARY
CAL POLY HUMBOLDT

W9-CRR-185

HF 5721 .H37

Harty, Kevin J.

Strategies for business and
technical writing /

SUBJECT TO LATE FINE

THE LIBRARY
HUMBOLDT STATE UNIVERSITY
ARCATA, CALIFORNIA 95521

DEMCO

Strategies for business and technical writing

KEVIN J. HARTY

Temple University

HARCOURT BRACE JOVANOVICH, INC.

New York   San Diego   Chicago   San Francisco   Atlanta
London   Sydney   Toronto

Copyright © 1980 by Harcourt Brace Jovanovich, Inc.

All rights reserved. No part of this publication may be
reproduced or transmitted in any form or by any means,
electronic or mechanical, including photocopy, recording,
or any information storage and retrieval system, without
permission in writing from the publisher.

ISBN: 0-15-583924-1

Library of Congress Catalog Card Number: 79-91442

Printed in the United States of America

In loving memory of Edna M. Harty

Preface

In general, writing courses are taken with reluctance and taught with difficulty. Courses in business and technical writing have managed to overcome these problems, mainly by emphasizing to both students and instructors that this kind of writing is closely related to the "real world" of work. For this reason, *Strategies for Business and Technical Writing* should appeal to practical-minded instructors and students. Most of the contributors to this anthology write from a sense of purpose and understanding that can result only from a career in business communications. The twenty-five essays in this anthology—some of them classics—not only teach professional writing but also offer themselves as fine professional examples. In so doing, they pick up where many standard business and technical writing textbooks leave off.

The standard business and technical writing textbooks are limited in their treatment of particular writing problems. Where problems are treated, the point of view is usually restrictive. For instance, a textbook may tell students to use proper diction and avoid jargon, and provide simple instructions to accomplish these tasks; but as J. Harold Janis points out in Part 2, jargon is often appropriate to, if not necessary for, effective business and technical communication. Even where business and technical writing textbooks provide more than just simple instructions, this anthology may offer a different point of view.

Strategies for Business and Technical Writing includes comprehensive discussions of specific points—resumes and letters of employment, letters that sell (a product or the producer), letters that say *no*, memoranda, formal reports. Such broader issues as problems of style, jargon, audience analysis are also treated in detail. Students can learn of the various strategies employed by people in business and industry who are required to communicate information as part of their job. These are strategies devised after years of experience. In Part 1, for example, Herbert Popper describes six guidelines that all professional writers should follow in their work—six guidelines only, reduced from countless other possibilities. In Part 4, Martin Swift recreates the process by which a manager composes a routine memorandum—a process that eliminates a number of wasteful motions a manager might go through.

Courses in business and technical writing should instill at least one notion in students' minds: Although there is no one way to write a memorandum, letter, or report—individual and corporate practices differ—all professional writing must consist of clear and effective prose. Students should be taught to recognize that business and technical writing differs in essential aspects from the expository prose taught in freshman composition courses. Business and technical writers communicate with different audiences and for different (and varying) purposes. Learning to write well for business and industry, then, might involve some adjustments by students.

Finally, at the end of *Strategies,* I have compiled an extensive annotated bibliography of sources of information on business and technical writing. Teachers and students should find this bibliography helpful in locating information on more specific topics. This bibliography also can be used for library research assignments. For example, students could be required to prepare abstracts and summaries of reading—just two forms of business and technical writing.

The arrangement of the essays in this anthology is intended to run parallel to a possible syllabus for courses on the subject. This allows for three distinct but equally reasonable choices: (1) *Strategies* may be used to supplement a standard business or technical writing textbook; (2) it may be used along with a standard composition textbook to introduce students to the writing problems and demands of business and industry; (3) it may very satisfactorily be used alone. In any case, *Strategies* may be kept as a handy reference book.

I offer these suggestions in lieu of an instructor's manual or a series of questions at the end of each selection. The essays speak for themselves, I think, and an instructor's manual or a series of questions for study and review would be more appropriate to a less specialized anthology. In my own classroom discussions of business and technical writing, I find such questions either stress the obvious or steal fire from my dialogue with students.

All the essays collected here have survived the most rigorous kind of scrutiny—that of my students, in courses and seminars on business and technical writing at Rhode Island College, Temple University, the Federal Reserve Bank of Philadelphia, and Gino's, Inc.

I would like to thank a number of people for their advice and assistance while this anthology was in the making. George Deaux, Alan Wilde, Monica Letzring, and Kenneth G. Schaefer—all of the Department of English at Temple University—offered many helpful suggestions. Wayne Maxson and the interlibrary loan staff of the Paley Library at Temple University cheerfully filled my many loan requests. My editors, Drake Bush and Bob Beitcher, encouraged me to see this project through and carefully supervised its publication.

I would be remiss if I failed to acknowledge some long-term debts to former teachers and colleagues who have taught me the virtue of patience and discipline and have set standards for scholarly and professional research that I have tried to live up to: Joseph Schwartz of Marquette University; R. M. Lumiansky of the American Council of Learned Societies; Ruth J. Dean, formerly of the University of Pennsylvania; Lee Morgan and Earle Labor of Centenary College of Louisiana; and Earl Stevens of Rhode Island College.

Finally, I owe my greatest debt to Jamie, who suffered through this project and countless others without complaint, and to whom I owe more than I can ever repay.

KEVIN J. HARTY
Temple University

Contents

2

The problem of jargon   67

3

Resumes and letters about employment 99

4

Letters and memoranda 137

5

Reports   187

6

Annotated bibliographies   269

Introduction

The essays in this anthology discuss professional writing—the writing done on the job by business men and women, scientists, technicians, and engineers. Professional writing differs from other kinds of writing in its emphasis on clarity, brevity, precision, and concreteness. It also differs from other kinds of writing in that its practitioners usually do not think of themselves as writers: they are managers, executives, and researchers whose jobs sometimes require them to write.

People in business and industry generally know enough about the mechanics of writing to produce reports, memoranda, and letters. But knowing just enough can be frustrating, because ineffective writing wastes time and money. According to the Darrell Institute of Business Research, the average business letter now costs $4.77 to produce. It costs more, of course, if the writing is poor or misdirected.

The essays in this book discuss ways in which professional writing can be made more effective. None of the selections, however, offers a quick cure for writing ills. There is no such cure. Like any other kind of writing, professional writing requires time and practice before it will improve. The essays in this anthology are the result of years of experience in business and professional writing. They are intended to guide students who are interested in learning about or improving their business and technical writing by providing a range of professional strategies that are employed in clear and effective reports, memoranda, and letters.

The best professional writing is the result of a three-part writing process: prewriting, writing, and rewriting. Any piece of writing that ignores the first or last part of this process is sure to fail. Prewriting requires thought before composing even a first draft. We must analyze our audience: Whom are we

1

writing to? Why to this person and not to someone else? What is our relation to this person? How does this person expect to be treated? We must examine the true purpose of the written communication we are about to compose: Why did our boss or client request this report? What objective will this memorandum fill? Is this a letter that says no in a considerate way? Are we asking for a job or for an interview? We must also clarify our ideas: What should be included in the piece of writing and what need not be there at all? Of course, to answer any one of these questions, a person in business or industry must have answers to some of the other questions.

Rewriting is equally complex. Rewriting is not simply a quick final check for correct punctuation, spelling, and form. Proofreading is an essential part of this process, but rewriting requires much more. The considerations that went into prewriting must be reviewed. In fact, we become our own editor at this stage: we pretend that we are the audience whom we are writing to; we examine our writing critically, inquiring into nuances of language and tone that we might have ignored in the initial drafts. It is at this stage that we ask ourselves whether or not our style and tone are appropriate.

We can see how this three-part process works by examining a piece of professional writing that fails to communicate effectively to its audience. The following two paragraphs are excerpted from the booklet "New York State Income Tax Forms and Instructions for Filing," published by the New York State Income Tax Bureau.

> The return for the period before the change of residence must include all items of income, gain, loss or deduction accrued to the taxpayer up to the time of his change of residence. This includes any amounts not otherwise includable in the return because of an election to report income on an installment basis.
>
> Stated another way, the return for the period prior to the change of residence must be made on the accrual basis whether or not that is the taxpayer's established method of reporting. However, in the case of a taxpayer changing from nonresident to resident status, these accruals need not be made with respect to items derived from or connected with New York sources.

How do we react to this information? If we are taxpayers in need of this information to solve one or another of our tax problems, we are sure to feel annoyed. Why must tax forms be so complicated? Was this written for a trained accountant or for the average taxpayer? Isn't it possible to present this information in plain English? These are the questions we all have asked about similar kinds of writing.

Further, whoever composed these two paragraphs for the New York State Income Tax Bureau would not have satisfied their supposed purpose: to inform taxpayers of how to adjust their tax returns in the case of changing residence. Although the grammar is correct and the style passable, the message certainly is not being communicated. Among other faults, this writer did not consider the particular audience this information is intended for. Unfamiliar words or usages like *includable, accrual basis,* and *election* are used without explanation. If the tax laws are not clear, taxpayers will not understand them. If taxpayers do not understand the tax laws, they will complete their forms incorrectly, and either cheat themselves or the government out of money. In the end, these two paragraphs will have missed their mark, and unnecessary complications will have resulted. Why? Because of poor writing.

The three-part process of prewriting, writing, and rewriting applies to all kinds of writing, not only to professional writing. But it is especially important to the person in business or industry who recognizes that any communication can win or lose a sale, a friend, or a job interview. Effective communication can mean a big sale (and maybe a promotion?), a pleased customer who will continue to share a business interest, an interview for a challenging new job (and a higher salary?).

For these reasons, good professional writing never requires restatement. Its message should be stated once, clearly and precisely. It should be understood on a first reading. In the second of the two paragraphs previously examined, the writer acknowledges in so many words that the first paragraph needs rewriting. Here is the first sign that prewriting was not properly done. Then there is the sign that rewriting also failed: the second paragraph, the restatement of the first, is no clearer, no more straightforward. As we might have decided after reading these two paragraphs for the first time, both writer and reader are in trouble.

The essays in this anthology suggest some ways of using the three-part process to insure effective professional writing in the three basic forms such writing takes: the letter, the memorandum, the report.

Before discussing the particular forms of professional writing, however, *Strategies for Business and Technical Writing* includes a series of essays, in Section One, on general principles of effective communication. John D. deButts, former chief executive of AT&T, sets the tone of these essays by discussing the importance of anticipating the customer's predicament and then following up on the customer's problem when dealing with a complaint. Behind deButts' comments lies a basic principle of effective professional writing: consider your readers and their needs first. Some additional principles basic to effective business communication are discussed by John S. Fielden, who addresses the problems of readability, appropriateness, concreteness, and clarity in professional writing. Fielden also provides a handy performance inventory for professional writers to use in analyzing the effectiveness of their written communication.

The next two essays in Section One teach by negative example. They show how to write poorly. Paul W. Merrill suggests ways to insure ineffective writing by ignoring the needs of readers. Morris Freedman lists "seven sins" of writing that have special significance to business and technical communication.

Herbert Popper reverses the method of instruction. In his essay, Popper provides six guidelines for professional writers to apply when they try to improve their writing. Mary C. Bromage offers a paradox about professional writers: they generally know how to write more effectively, but often fail to do so. Bromage suggests several possible explanations for this paradox. The first section ends with a selection from David Ogilvy's classic book *Confessions of an Advertising Man*. What Ogilvy has to say about writing advertising copy is certainly relevant to other kinds of writing as well.

The three essays in the second section present different views of the problems jargon can pose in professional writing. Jargon is simply specialized terminology; in many cases it is appropriate to, if not necessary for, effective professional writing—that is, as long as it is not overused or misused. Again, knowing the audience is essential to avoiding complications with jargon.

Stuart Chase's essay is satirical. His topic is linguistic "overkill" among government officials, lawyers, and academics. In a more reserved vein, William Gilman suggests ways of reducing the problems jargon causes readers rather than reducing jargon itself. His suggestions are echoed by J. Harold Janis, whose essay underscores the need for the use of jargon in certain kinds of business and technical writing.

While professional writing is generally writing done on the job, it can also be writing done to get a job. The two essays in the third section of this anthology suggest ways in which professional writers can sell themselves through their writing. Caroline Donnelly's suggestions about writing cover letters and resumes can help transform a job applicant into a job candidate. Because letters about employment involve more than simple cover letters, the essay by J. H. Menning, C. W. Wilkinson, and Peter B. Clarke offers a discussion of follow-up letters, thank-you letters, job refusal letters, and letters of resignation, as well as a discussion of letters of application.

A more detailed discussion of professional letters and memoranda can be found in the fourth section. James M. Reid, Jr., and Robert M. Wendlinger, whose essay is excerpted from a book written in collaboration with the New York Life Insurance Company, suggest ways of insuring the effectiveness of professional letters and memoranda. In a selection from one of their monthly newsletters, writers for the Royal Bank of Canada argue that the qualities of a good sales letter should be found in all professional correspondence. Letters that say *no* exercise any writer's abilities, and Kermit Rolland provides six tested methods for insuring the success of this kind of letter.

Companies usually generate more memoranda than reports and letters, and this anthology includes two essays on the writing of memoranda. Harold Mintz's discussion is the more general and offers an analysis of the organization, format, and literary qualities of well-written memoranda. Martin Swift takes a badly written memorandum and shows the steps writers should follow to clarify their message and make their memoranda more effective. Because any kind of business correspondence can present professional writers with legal problems, this section of the anthology concludes with an analysis of the legal aspects of business correspondence by Herta A. Murphy and Charles E. Peck.

The lengthiest forms of professional writing are reports, and as the essays in the fifth section of this anthology show, the process of prewriting, writing, and rewriting can be most helpful to professional writers with their reports. J. C. Mathes and Dwight W. Stevenson present a method for identifying and analyzing the backgrounds and needs of audiences for professional reports. Richard W. Dodge, reporting on the results of a study conducted on the reading habits of managers at Westinghouse, shows the increased importance that abstracts play in professional communication. Also noting this, Christian K. Arnold discusses the key elements of an effective abstract. Charles W. Strong and Donald Eidson present guidelines for the effective use of visual aids, while Darrell Huff humorously suggests ways in which professional writers can lie with statistics. In the last two essays, Vincent Vinci and Rändi S. Smith provide convenient checklists for professional writers to use in putting together reports.

The twenty-five essays in this anthology suggest ways in which professional writers can make their writing more effective. These essays also show how they can make it more enjoyable. As long as business men and women, scientists, technicians, and engineers view writing as a chore, the effectiveness of their written communication will be limited. But the more these professional writers get into the habit of carefully prewriting, writing, and rewriting, the easier, and perhaps the more enjoyable, writing will become for them.

1

Some general principles of effective business and technical writing

When we tell customers, "We hear you," we'd better be listening

JOHN D. deBUTTS

When he wrote this article, John deButts was Chairman of the Board of the American Telephone and Telegraph Company (AT&T); he has since retired.

If you were to sit at my desk and read and answer the mail I get about telephone service, you'd come to realize, if you don't already, how much "little things" mean; how sometimes lifelong impressions of the character of our business are formed on the basis of a single contact with just one employee. Rather significant, I'd say, when you consider that the Bell System employs more than a million men and women.

You know, it's only natural when a customer feels service is poor or when he thinks his bill is too high that he is going to register a complaint with someone. But in all my years in this business, I can't recall ever receiving a letter that complained solely about cost or service. No, the key element in all the letters of complaint I get is how the customer was treated by an employee of the company. As a matter of fact, I'm sometimes amazed at just how tolerant our customers are of situations that to me would seem intolerable, before poor treatment by an employee finally pushes them to write to me or to one of the other officers, or to a public utility commissioner.

So that I don't give the wrong impression, let me add that intermixed with those complaints are a goodly number of commendation letters. And commendation letters, of course, always talk about how an employee treated the customer in a manner so unusually satisfying that the customer felt compelled to write to me about it.

I'd like to share portions of some of those letters with you. Here's one from a man in New Jersey:

John D. deButts, "When We Tell Customers, 'We Hear You,' We'd Better Be Listening," reprinted from *Bell Telephone Magazine,* 52 (September–October, 1973), pp. 2-5, by permission of the American Telephone and Telegraph Company.

Today, Saturday, at approximately 9:30 a.m., my next door neighbor rang my door bell to advise me that either my power or telephone line had pulled loose from my home and was lying across the street where cars coming and going could have caused a serious problem.

I went out to investigate, when, at the same time, one of your New Jersey Telephone trucks was approaching. He immediately pulled his truck to the curb, hopped out and raised the line from the road. Without any words from me, he took his ladder down from the truck and proceeded to reinstall the line to the house and make necessary repairs.

I then spoke to him for the first time. He had been in the vicinity making a phone installation, and spotted the trouble . . . I thanked him . . . I feel that AT&T and New Jersey Bell should be mighty proud to have a man like that working for you.

The customer was right. We *are* proud to have such a man—the kind of employee who epitomizes the Spirit of Service we used to talk so much about in the old days, and who possesses that "sense of proprietorship" we've been talking about more recently. We wish all our employees showed the same sense of judgment and concern for a customer's problem. However, in an organization as large as ours, there are bound to be some weak links.

Here's a letter from a customer who also happens to be a share owner:

My telephone has been out of order for the past four days. On April 8, 1973 at 7:00 p.m., I made my fifth call to your service department and was told, as I had been told four times previously, 'We'll take care of it.' I asked for his name and he refused to give it. I asked for the identity of his supervisor and again was refused . . . I asked, 'Do I have to go to New York to get my phone service restored?' He retorted, 'You can call whoever the hell you want, but it won't get your service a damn minute sooner.' Further discussion was pointless and I hung up.

The policy of permitting employees that have contact with customers to retain anonymity from behind Ma Bell's skirts is poorly conceived and poor customer relations. I cannot imagine any other company operating with this policy.

Now, consider this letter for a moment. The customer had been without service going on five days when he wrote. Subsequent investigation showed that one of our own cable crews working in the area was causing the problem, and that the customer was without service for still another day. Repair had been diligently searching for the cause of the problem from the time of the customer's first call, but no one thought to tell the customer what was being done. Obviously, the customer has every right to complain about being without service, but what is it that he is really complaining about here? Not lack of service, but an apparent lack of concern for his predicament, and the rude treatment he received from an employee.

When you get right down to it, there's really nothing very complicated about maintaining good customer relations. The guideline has been around a long time. Just follow the Golden Rule. If we treat the customer as we ourselves would like to be treated under the same set of circumstances, our actions are bound to meet with his approval. When I look through the letters I get from customers, I simply ask myself, "How would I like to be treated if I were in that customer's shoes?" The answers are usually fairly obvious.

Back when I was president of Illinois Bell, we had a saying there that "You not only have to give good service, but you've got to convince the customer that he's getting it." Here's a letter to illustrate what I mean.

> I am sorry to bother you but you should know about the poor service I had on the weekend.
>
> Saturday, April 28, about noontime, I found I could not use my phone . . . I reported on my neighbor's phone, immediately. I asked them to please fix it right away as I am an elderly lady—83 years old— and live alone. They said they would come before 5 p.m. I waited for them all Saturday and at 6 p.m. a man came and said he would come back later. He never came into my home. I waited for him until 11 p.m. and then went to bed. This was very upsetting and frightening for me and I didn't sleep. After I called again, they finally came . . . at 3 p.m., Sunday. I have large telephone bills and want better service than this.

In this case, Repair dispatched a man to investigate, and he found a short circuit in a cable on a pole outside the home. He worked on the trouble from Saturday afternoon into the early evening but couldn't finish the job and told the lady he'd return. He came back the next day, completed the splicing by early afternoon and left. The lady, not realizing that the repair had been completed, called again from the neighbor's phone. Another man was sent to check the problem, found everything in order, and reported to the lady that her phone was back in service. At which point, the lady took up her pen to write and tell us how we had let her down.

Now, I'm entirely sympathetic with this lady and can understand how such a thing can occur. A colleague of mine had a similar experience with an air-conditioning repairman. The man came into the home, looked briefly at the air conditioner, put the cover back on, picked up his tools and left. My friend's wife thought he had gone to get something from his truck, but when she looked out, the truck was gone. She waited all day for him to return, but he never came back. A second call to the repair shop the next day brought the information that a new part had to be ordered and, until it was received, the repair couldn't be completed. How easy it would have been, in both of these cases, for the repairman to give the customer a progress report.

Here's an excerpt from a letter I received from another share owner, one who had recently moved, relating an experience he had in merely inquiring about the types and cost of phone service:

> . . . I encountered a faceless voice that first demanded answers to a long list of questions, many of them personal, very few of them that

could have any bearing at all on the answer to my inquiry. Rightly or wrongly, I became irritated by the manner of my interrogator and when I recognized she was more interested in obtaining answers than she was in being helpful, and the questions had become so absurdly irrelevant to my request . . . I terminated the interview.

Now service representatives, obviously, must ask some questions if they are to do their jobs properly. But they should be flexible enough to know when to draw the line. When a customer begins to show irritation, as this one did, it's time to put aside the set routine. Fewer customers would have to be put through such prolonged fact-gathering if we spent just a little more time listening to what it is that the customer wants from us.

Finally, in the interest of balance, here's a note with a happy ending— from a customer who had a disappointing experience with one operator, only to have her faith restored later by the patient, resourceful service she received from another operator.

In contrast to her experience with the first operator, the customer had this to say about the second:

> . . . [She] listened to me, investigated the situation and had the courtesy to call me and explain that the number was out of order, that no report had been made to that effect earlier, but that she had done so.

Note the key word in this letter. The operator *listened* to her. The operator not only heard a problem described, but recognized how important it was for this customer to determine why she could not complete this particular call. The second operator, like the first, could have let the matter drop, but didn't. She followed through, determined the phone was out of order and reported it to the appropriate people.

Getting away from the letters for a minute, far more of our customer contacts come by phone. And of course, a certain number are in person. Our Operations-Commercial group ran a check on some 200 business offices around the country recently to see how "reachable" the business office manager was to the customer.

Well, I'm happy to say that the calls placed were handled properly more than 80 per cent of the time. If the caller was not passed along, he was not only told why, but also informed when he could expect the manager to return the call. Although I'm happy that the majority of the calls did go through, I'm equally concerned about the 20 per cent that didn't, and I worry about why they didn't.

We've got to stop building walls around our managers. These are the people who have the authority to correct the things the customers are complaining about. In all my years in this business, I've always had my home telephone number published in the directory. I know this isn't generally true of executives in other industries, but I've always felt it was the right thing to do. Over the years, I've received my share of crank calls, but I've also gotten calls from people just seeking help with their phone service. I've always been more than happy to help solve their problems whenever I can.

The Pacific Company, one time, made a study of some 150 written customer complaints. These complaints had been mailed either to company executives at Pacific, or directly to a public utility commissioner. In tracing the complaints back to see what kind of treatment the customer got along the way, the company discovered that more than half of the letter writers, 58 per cent, as I recall, had contact with only one employee before taking up their pens.

Like the 20 per cent of the calls that didn't get through to the managers in the Operations test, these letter writers didn't get the chance to have their problems reviewed by supervisors or managers at the local level. Well, you can bet that, following the written complaint, the customer got the attention from the people who should have given it to him the first time.

Again, don't misunderstand. I'm not suggesting that we capitulate to unreasonable demands, simply to curtail the number of complaints this company receives. We have rules and regulations to live by, and generally they must be observed. What does concern me, though, is that too often our employees hide behind the rule book and fail to honor some very sound requests simply because they are afraid to risk doing what they know is right, because it's not covered by the rules. In the final analysis, rules are there to guide us, not to govern us.

Take the case of the man in Brainerd, Minnesota, one of the very few places left in the country where equipment shortages still require 8-party service. As he was a year-round resident in an area primarily inhabited by summer vacationists, he asked if it wouldn't be possible to tie his line in with some of theirs. He reasoned that for most of the year, at least, when they were gone, his telephone wouldn't be ringing as often. You can't fault the logic. But do you know what our initial response was—absolutely not! You know why? If the other permanent residents found out, they'd want similar consideration. By the way, once he took the trouble to write me about his suggestion, we took another look at the rule book and found no reason why we shouldn't honor his request. He's a much happier man, today. And thinks a little better of us, too.

On the other hand, a Brooklyn customer, an elderly man, wrote telling how upset he was that his local bank had decided not to act as a collection agency for the company, and that he would now be forced to spend 70 cents in subway fares to come into the business office to pay his bill. While we couldn't force the bank to continue collecting his bill, as he suggested, we did ask the local business office manager to look into what could be done. Since the customer didn't believe in checking accounts, there was no safe way the manager could advise mailing in payments which would not incur costs almost as high as the subway fare to which the customer objected. In looking over the customer's payment record, the manager observed that over many years he always paid his bill promptly, and in full. In addition to providing this customer with the addresses of two other collection points nearer his home than the business office, the manager suggested, in light of the customer's fine credit record, that he remit payment every other month. Here's a manager willing to take a collection risk in an effort to do the right thing by this customer. And I find that very commendable indeed.

If we want to encourage employees to take such independent action in response to specific customer needs and requests, we, as managers, must set the climate. We'll never convince our customer contact-employees that we are sincerely interested in having them use their own good judgment in dealing with customers if we force a strict adherence to the rules and require double-checking of the most trivial matters up the line for higher level approval. While it is a manager's responsibility to see that his staff is adequately trained and can be relied upon to use common sense in dealing with customers, once that task is accomplished, managers should not keep intruding their presence. Following the careful selection, training and placement of the most competent employees in positions of trust and responsibility, nothing ruins initiative faster than to have managers who insist on second-guessing every decision and require that everything be run by the book. Again, we shouldn't throw the book away, but, I reiterate, the rules are there to guide us, not to govern us.

Over the past year, I've held more than 30 large, formal, employee meetings around the country and quite a number of smaller, informal, higher-level management meetings. At these meetings, I've stressed that I know of nothing more important to providing top-notch service than the *sense of proprietorship* each Bell System employee brings to his or her job.

Just recently, we embarked on a major national advertising campaign built around the simple phrase, "We Hear You." Through these three words we hope to convey to customers our determination to be responsive to their needs and concerns. Customer opinion, of course, will not be swayed one hair's breadth by any advertising campaign unless it is backed up by people who are ready and willing not only to listen, but to follow through with a satisfactory performance from the customer's point of view. When we say "We Hear You," it carries the promise that we will listen. Employees who have that sense of proprietorship will see to it that the promise is kept.

I remind you that where that sense of proprietorship has been lost, you and I have no more important responsibility than to restore it; and where it has not, no more important responsibility than to see that it is maintained.

When that's done, the customer will know that we're listening.

"What do you mean I can't write?"

JOHN S. FIELDEN

John S. Fielden is the Dean of the School of
Business Administration at the University of
Alabama.

What do businessmen answer when
they are asked, "What's the most troublesome problem you have to live
with?" Frequently they reply, "People just can't write! What do they learn in
college now? When I was a boy . . . !"

There is no need to belabor this point; readers know well how true it is.
HBR subscribers, for example, recently rated the "ability to communicate" as
the prime requisite of a promotable executive (see Exhibit 1).[1] And, of all the
aspects of communication, the written form is the most troublesome, if only
because of its formal nature. It is received cold, without the communicator's
tone of voice or gesture to help. It is rigid; it cannot be adjusted to the recipients' reactions as it is being delivered. It stays "on the record," and cannot be
undone. Further, the reason it is in fact committed to paper is usually that its
subject is considered too crucial or significant to be entrusted to casual, short-
lived verbal form.

Businessmen know that the ability to write well is a highly valued asset in
a top executive. Consequently, they become ever more conscious of their
writing ability as they consider what qualities they need in order to rise in
their company.

They know that in big business today ideas are not exchanged exclusively
by word of mouth (as they might be in smaller businesses). And they know

---

[1] See also, C. Wilson Randle, "How to Identify Promotable Executives," HBR May–June 1956, p.
122.

Reprinted by permission of the *Harvard Business Review*. "What Do You Mean I Can't Write?"
by John S. Fielden (May–June 1964). Copyright © 1964 by the President and Fellows of Harvard
College; all rights reserved.

Exhibit 1. Qualities that characterize promotable executives

Source: Taken from Exhibit III, Garda W. Bowman, "What Helps or Harms Promotability?" (Problems in Review), HBR January–February 1964, p. 14.

that even if they get oral approval for something they wish to do, there will be the inevitable "give me a memo on it" concluding remark that will send them back to their office to oversee the writing of a carefully documented report.

They know, too, that as they rise in their company, they will have to be able to supervise the writing of subordinates—for so many of the memos, reports, and letters written by subordinates will go out over their signature, or be passed on to others in the company and thus reflect on the caliber of work done under their supervision.

Even the new data-processing machines will not make business any less dependent on words. For while the new machines are fine for handling tabular or computative work, someone must write up an eventual analysis of the findings in the common parlance of the everyday executive.

Time for action

Complaints about the inability of managers to write are a very common and justifiable refrain. But the problem this article poses—and seeks to solve—is that it is of very little use to complain about something and stop right there. I think it is about time for managers to begin to do something about it. And the first step is *to define what "it"—what good business writing—really is.*

Suppose you are a young managerial aspirant who has recently been told: "You simply can't write!" What would this mean to you? Naturally, you would be hurt, disappointed, perhaps even alarmed to have your *own* nagging doubts about your writing ability put uncomfortably on the line. "Of course," you say, "I know I'm no stylist. I don't even pretend to be a literarily inclined person. But how can I improve my writing on the job? Where do I begin? Exactly what *is* wrong with my writing?" But nobody tells you in specific, meaningful terms.

Does this mean that you can't spell or punctuate or that your grammar is disastrous? Does it mean that you can't think or organize your thoughts? Or does it mean that even though you are scrupulously correct in grammar and tightly organized in your thinking, a report or letter from you is always completely unreadable; that reading it, in effect, is like trying to butt one's head through a brick wall? Or does it mean that you are so tactless and boorish in the human relations aspect of communication that your messages actually build resentment and resistance? Do you talk "down" too much or do you talk "over your reader's head"? Just what do you do wrong?

Merely being told that you can't write is so basically meaningless and so damaging to your morale that you may end up writing more ineffectually than ever before. What you need to know is: "What are the elements of good business writing? And in which of these elements am I proficient? In which do I fall down?" If only the boss could break his complaint down into a more meaningful set of components, you could begin to do something about them.

Now let's shift and assume that you are a high-ranking manager whose job it is to supervise a staff of assistants. What can you do about upgrading the writing efforts of your men? You think of the time lost by having to do reports and letters over and over before they go out, the feasibility reports which did not look so feasible after having been befogged by an ineffectual writer, the letters presented for your signature that would have infuriated the receiver had you let them be mailed. But where are you to start?

Here is where the interests of superior and subordinte meet. Unless both arrive at a common understanding, a shared vocabulary that enables them to communicate with one another about the writing jobs that need to be done, nobody is going to get very far. No oversimplified, gimmicky slogans (such as, "Every letter is a sales letter"; "Accentuate the positive, eliminate the negative"; or "Write as you speak") are going to serve this purpose. No partial view is either—whether that of the English teacher, the logician, or the social scientist—since good business writing is not just grammar, or clear thinking, or winning friends and influencing people. It is some of each, the proportion depending on the purpose.

Total inventory

To know what effective business writing is, we need a total inventory of all its aspects, so that:

 • Top managers can say to their training people, "Are you sure our training efforts in written communications are not tackling just part of the problem? Are we covering all aspects of business writing?"

 • A superior can say to an assistant, "Here, look; this is where you are weak. See? It is one thing when you write letters that you sign, another when you write letters that I sign. The position and power of the person we are writing to make a lot of difference in *what* we say and *how* we say it."

 • The young manager can use the inventory as a guide to self-improvement (perhaps even ask his superior to go over his writing with him, using the writing inventory as a means of assuring a common critical vocabulary).

 • The superior may himself get a few hints about how he might improve his own performance.

Such an inventory appears in Exhibit 2. Notice that it contains four basic categories—*readability, correctness, appropriateness,* and *thought.* Considerable effort has gone into making these categories (and the subtopics under them) as mutually exclusive as possible, although some overlap is inevitable. But even if they are not completely exclusive, they are still far less general than an angry, critical remark, such as, "You cannot write."

Furthermore, you should understand that these four categories are not listed in order of importance, since their importance varies according to the abilities and the duties of each individual. The same thing is true of the subtopics; I shall make no attempt to treat each of them equally, but will simply try to do some practical, commonsense highlighting. I will begin with readability, and discuss it most fully, because this is an area where half-truths abound and need to be scotched before introducing the other topics.

Readability

What is *readability?* Nothing more than a clear style of writing. It does not result absolutely (as some readability experts would have you believe) from mathematical counts of syllables, of sentence length, or of abstract words. These inflexible approaches to readability assume that all writing is being addressed to a general audience. Consequently, their greatest use is in forming judgments about the readability of such things as mass magazine editorial copy, newspaper communications, and elementary textbooks.

To prove this point, all you need do is to pick up a beautifully edited magazine like the *New England Journal of Medicine* and try to read an article in it. You as a layman will probably have trouble. On the other hand, your physician will tell you that the article is a masterpiece of readable exposition. But, on second look, you will still find it completely unreadable. The reason, obviously, is that you do not have the background or the vocabulary necessary to understand it. The same thing would hold true if you were to take an article from a management science quarterly, say, one dealing with return on investment or statistical decision making, and give it to the physician. Now he is likely to judge this one to be completely incomprehensible, while you may find it the most valuable and clear discussion of the topic you have ever seen.

In situations like this, it does not make much difference whether the sentences are long or short; if the reader does not have the background to understand the material, he just doesn't. And writing such specialized articles according to the mathematical readability formulas is not going to make them clearer.

Nevertheless, it is true that unnecessarily long, rambling sentences are wearing to read. Hence you will find these stylistic shortcomings mentioned in Exhibit 2. The trick a writer has to learn is to judge the complexity and the abstractness of the material he is dealing with, and to cut his sentences down in those areas where the going is especially difficult. It also helps to stick to a direct subject-verb-object construction in sentences wherever it is important to communicate precisely. Flights of unusually dashing style should be reserved for those sections which are quite general in nature and concrete in subject matter.

What about paragraphs? The importance of "paragraph construction" is often overlooked in business communication, but few things are more certain to make the heart sink than the sight of page after page of unbroken type. One old grammar book rule would be especially wise to hark back to, and that is the topic sentence. Not only does placing a topic sentence at the beginning of each paragraph make it easier for the reader to grasp the content of the communication quickly; it also serves to discipline the writer into including only one main idea in each paragraph. Naturally, when a discussion of one idea means the expenditure of hundreds (or thousands) of words, paragraphs should be divided according to subdivisions of the main idea. In fact, an almost arbitrary division of paragraphs into units of four or five sentences is usually welcomed by the reader.

As for jargon, the only people who complain about it seriously are those who do not understand it. Moreover, it is fashionable for experts in a particular field to complain about their colleagues' use of jargon, but then to turn right around and use it themselves. The reason is that jargon is no more than shop talk. And when the person being addressed fully understands this private language, it is much more economical to use it than to go through laborious explanations of every idea that could be communicated in the shorthand of jargon. Naturally, when a writer knows that his message is going to be read by persons who are not familiar with the private language of his trade, he should be sure to translate as much of the jargon as he can into common terms.

The same thing holds true for simplicity of language. Simplicity is, I would think, always a "good." True, there is something lost from our language when interesting but unfamiliar words are no longer used. But isn't it true that the shrines in which these antiquities should be preserved lie in the domain of poetry or the novel, and not in business communications—which, after all, are not baroque cathedrals but functional edifices by which a job can be done?

The simplest way to say it, then, is invariably the best in business writing. But this fact the young executive does not always understand. Often he is eager to parade his vocabulary before his superiors, for fear his boss (who has never let him know that he admires simplicity, and may indeed adopt a pretentious and ponderous style himself) may think less of him.

Leading the reader

But perhaps the most important aspect of readability is the one listed under the subtopic "reader direction." The failure of writers to seize their reader by the nose and lead him carefully through the intricacies of his communication is like an epidemic. The job that the writer must do is to develop the "skeleton" of the document that he is preparing. And, at the very beginning of his communication, he should identify the skeletal structure of his paper; he should, in effect, frame the discussion which is to follow.

You will see many of these frames at the beginning of articles published in HBR, where the editors take great pains to tell the reader quickly what the

Exhibit 2. Written performance inventory

1. READABILITY

READER'S LEVEL

☐ Too specialized in approach

☐ Assumes too great a knowledge of subject

☐ So underestimates the reader that it belabors the obvious

SENTENCE CONSTRUCTION

☐ Unnecessarily long in difficult material

☐ Subject-verb-object word order too rarely used

☐ Choppy, overly simple style (in simple material)

PARAGRAPH CONSTRUCTION

☐ Lack of topic sentences

☐ Too many ideas in single paragraph

☐ Too long

FAMILIARITY OF WORDS

☐ Inappropriate jargon

☐ Pretentious language

☐ Unnecessarily abstract

READER DIRECTION

☐ Lack of "framing" (i.e., failure to tell the reader about purpose and direction of forthcoming discussion)

☐ Inadequate transitions between paragraphs

☐ Absence of subconclusions to summarize reader's progress at end of divisions in the discussion

FOCUS

☐ Unclear as to subject of communication

☐ Unclear as to purpose of message

2. CORRECTNESS

MECHANICS

☐ Shaky grammar

☐ Faulty punctuation

FORMAT

☐ Careless appearance of documents

☐ Failure to use accepted company form

COHERENCE

☐ Sentences seem awkward owing to illogical and ungrammatical yoking of unrelated ideas

☐ Failure to develop a logical progression of ideas through coherent, logically juxtaposed paragraphs

3. APPROPRIATENESS

A. UPWARD COMMUNICATIONS

TACT

☐ Failure to recognize differences in position between writer and receiver

☐ Impolitic tone — too brusk, argumentative, or insulting

SUPPORTING DETAIL

☐ Inadequate support for statements

☐ Too much undigested detail for busy superior

OPINION

☐ Adequate research but too great an intrusion of opinions

☐ Too few facts (and too little research) to entitle drawing of conclusions

- [ ] Presence of unasked for but clearly implied recommendations

ATTITUDE

- [ ] Too obvious a desire to please superior
- [ ] Too defensive in face of authority
- [ ] Too fearful of superior to be able to do best work

B. DOWNWARD COMMUNICATIONS

DIPLOMACY

- [ ] Overbearing attitude toward subordinates
- [ ] Insulting and/or personal references
- [ ] Unmindfulness that messages are representative of management group or even of company

CLARIFICATION OF DESIRES

- [ ] Confused, vague instructions
- [ ] Superior is not sure of what is wanted
- [ ] Withholding of information necessary to job at hand

MOTIVATIONAL ASPECTS

- [ ] Orders of superior seem arbitrary
- [ ] Superior's communications are manipulative and seemingly insincere

4. THOUGHT

PREPARATION

- [ ] Inadequate thought given to purpose of communication prior to its final completion

- [ ] Inadequate preparation or use of data known to be available

COMPETENCE

- [ ] Subject beyond intellectual capabilities of writer
- [ ] Subject beyond experience of writer

FIDELITY TO ASSIGNMENT

- [ ] Failure to stick to job assigned
- [ ] Too much made of routine assignment
- [ ] Too little made of assignment

ANALYSIS

- [ ] Superficial examination of data leading to unconscious overlooking of important pieces of evidence
- [ ] Failure to draw obvious conclusions from data presented
- [ ] Presentation of conclusions unjustified by evidence
- [ ] Failure to qualify tenuous assertions
- [ ] Failure to identify and justify assumptions used
- [ ] Bias, conscious or unconscious, which leads to distorted interpretation of data

PERSUASIVENESS

- [ ] Seems more convincing than facts warrant
- [ ] Seems less convincing than facts warrant
- [ ] Too obvious an attempt to sell ideas
- [ ] Lacks action-orientation and managerial viewpoint
- [ ] Too blunt an approach where subtlety and finesse called for

article is about and what specific areas will come under discussion during its progress. In every business document this initial frame, this statement of purpose and direction, should appear. Furthermore, in lengthy reports there should be many such frames; indeed, most major sections of business reports should begin with a new frame.

There should also be clear transitions between paragraphs. The goal should be that of having each element in a written message bear a close relationship to those elements which have preceded and those which follow it. Frequently a section should end with a brief summary, plus a sentence or two telling the reader the new direction of the article. These rather mechanical signposts, while frequently the bane of literary stylists, are always of valuable assistance to readers.

The final aspect of readability is the category that I call "focus." This term refers to the fact that many communications seem diffuse and out of focus, much like a picture on a television screen when the antennas are not properly directed. Sometimes in a report it seems as if one report has been superimposed on another, and that there are no clear and particular points the writer is trying to make. Thus the burden is put on the reader to ferret out the truly important points from the chaos.

If a writer wants to improve the readability of his writing, he must make sure that he has thought things through sufficiently, so that he can focus his readers' attention on the salient points.

Correctness

The one thing that flies to a writer's mind when he is told he cannot write is *correctness*. He immediately starts looking for gammar and punctuation mistakes in things that he has written.

But mistakes like these are hardly the most important aspects of business writing. The majority of executives are reasonably well educated and can, with a minimum of effort, make themselves adequately proficient in the "mechanics" of writing. Furthermore, as a man rises in his company, his typing (at least) will be done by a secretary, who can (and should) take the blame if a report is poorly punctuated and incorrect in grammar, not to mention being presented in an improper "format."

Then what is the most important point? Frequently, the insecure writer allows small mistakes in grammar and punctuation to become greatly magnified, and regards them as reflections on his education and, indeed, his social acceptability. A careless use of "he don't" may seem to be as large a disgrace in his mind as if he attended the company banquet in his shorts. And in some cases this is true. But he should also realize (as Exhibit 2 shows) that the ability to write *correctly* is not synonymous with the ability to write *well*. Hence, everyone should make sure that he does not become satisfied with the rather trivial act of mastering punctuation and grammar.

It is true, of course, that, in some instances, the inability to write correctly will cause a lack of clarity. We can all think of examples where a misplaced comma has caused serious confusion—although such instances, except in contracts and other legal documents, are fortunately rather rare.

A far more important aspect of correctness is "coherence." Coherence means the proper positioning of elements within a piece of writing so that it can be read clearly and sensibly. Take one example:

INCOHERENT: "I think it will rain. However, no clouds are showing yet. Therefore, I will take my umbrella."
COHERENT: "Although no clouds are showing, I think it will rain. Therefore, I will take my umbrella."

Once a person has mastered the art of placing related words and sentences as close as possible to each other, he will be amazed at how smooth his formerly awkward writing becomes. But that is just the beginning. He will still have to make sure that he has placed paragraphs which are related in thought next to one another, so that the ideas presented do not have to leapfrog over any intervening digressions.

Appropriateness

I have divided the category *appropriateness* into two sections reflecting the two main types of internal business communications—those going upward in the organization and those going downward. This distinction is one that cannot be found in textbooks on writing, although the ideas included here are commonplace in the human relations area.

There is an obvious difference between the type of communication that a boss writes to his subordinate and the type that the subordinate can get away with when he writes to his boss (or even the type that he drafts for his boss's signature). I suspect that many managers who have had their writing criticized had this unpleasant experience simply because of their failure to recognize the fact that messages are affected by the relative positions of the writer and the recipient in the organizational hierarchy.

Upward communications

Let us roughly follow the order of the subtopics included under upward communications in Exhibit 2. "Tact" is important. If a subordinate fails to recognize his role and writes in an argumentative or insulting tone, he is almost certain to reap trouble for himself (or for his boss if the document goes up under the boss's actual or implied signature). One of the perennially difficult problems facing any subordinate is how to tell a superior he is wrong. If the subordinate were the boss, most likely he *could* call a spade a spade; but since he is not, he has problems. And, in today's business world, bosses themselves spend much time figuring out how to handle problem communications with discretion. Often tender topics are best handled orally rather than in writing.

Two other subtopics—"supporting detail" and "opinion"—also require a distinction according to the writer's role. Since the communication is going upward, the writer will probably find it advisable to support his statements with considerable detail. On the other hand, he may run afoul of superiors who will be impatient if he gives too much detail and not enough generalization. Here is a classic instance where a word from above as to the amount of detail required in a particular assignment would be of inestimable value to the subordinate.

The same holds true for "opinion." In some cases, the subordinate may be criticized for introducing too many of his personal opinions—in fact, often for giving any recommendation at all. If the superior wishes the subordinate to make recommendations and to offer his own opinions, the burden is on the superior to tell him. If the superior fails to do so, the writer can at least try to make it clear where facts cease and opinions begin; then the superior can draw his own conclusions.

The writer's "attitude" is another important factor in upward communications. When a subordinate writes to his boss, it is almost impossible for him to communicate with the blandness that he might use if he were writing a letter to a friend. There may be many little things that he is doing throughout his writing that indicate either too great a desire to impress the boss or an insecurity which imparts a feeling of fearfulness, defensiveness, or truculence in the face of authority.

Downward communications

While the subordinate who writes upward in the organization must use "tact," the boss who writes down to his subordinates must use "diplomacy." If he is overbearing or insulting (even without meaning to be), he will find his effectiveness as a manager severely limited. Furthermore, it is the foolish manager who forgets that, when he communicates downward, he speaks as a representative of management or even of the entire company. Careless messages have often played an important part in strikes and other corporate human relations problems.

It is also important for the superior to make sure that he has clarified in his own mind just what it is he wishes to accomplish. If he does not, he may give confused or vague instructions. (In this event, it is unfair for him to blame a subordinate for presenting a poorly focused document in return.) Another requirement is that the superior must make sure that he has supplied any information which the subordinate needs but could not be expected to know, and that he has sufficiently explained any points which may be misleading.

Motivation is important, too. When a superior gives orders, he will find that over the long run he will not be able to rely on mere power to force compliance with his requests. It seems typically American for a subordinate to resent and resist what he considers to be arbitrary decisions made for unknown reasons. If at all possible, the superior not only should explain the reasons why he gives an order but should point out (if he can) why his decision can be interpreted as being in the best interests of those whom it affects.

I am not, however, suggesting farfetched explanations of future benefits. In the long run, those can have a boomerang effect. Straight talk, carefully and tactfully couched, is the only sensible policy. If, for example, a subordinate's request for a new assignment has been denied because he needs further experience in his present assignment, he should be told the facts. Then, if it is also true that getting more experience may prepare him for a better position in the future, there is no reason why this information should not be included to "buffer" the impact of the refusal of a new assignment.

Thought

Here—a most important area—the superior has a tremendous vested interest in the reporting done by his subordinates. There is no substitute for the thought content of a communication. What good is accomplished if a message is excellent in all the other respects we have discussed—if it is readable, correct, and appropriate—yet the content is faulty? It can even do harm if the other aspects succeed in disguising the fact that it is superficial, stupid, or biased. The superior receiving it may send it up through the organization with his signature, or, equally serious, he may make an important (and disastrous) decision based on it.

Here is the real *guts* of business writing—intelligent content, something most purveyors of business writing gimmicks conveniently forget. It is also something that most training programs shortchange. The discipline of translating thoughts into words and organizing these thoughts logically has no equal as intellectual training. For there is one slogan that is true: "Disorganized, illogical writing reflects a disorganized, illogical (and untrained) mind."

That is why the first topic in this section is "preparation." Much disorganized writing results from insufficient preparation, from a failure to think through and isolate the purpose and the aim of the writing job. Most writers tend to think as they write; in fact, most of us do not even know what it is we think until we have actually written it down. The inescapability of making a well-thought-out outline before dictating seems obvious.

A primary aspect of *thought*, consequently, is the intellectual "competence" of the writer. If a report is bad merely because the subject is far beyond the experience of the writer, it is not his fault. Thus his superior should be able to reject the analysis and at the same time accept the blame for having given his assistant a job that he simply could not do. But what about the many cases where the limiting factor *is* basically the intellectual capacity of the writer? It is foolish to tell a man that he cannot *write* if in effect he simply does not have the intellectual ability to do the job that has been assigned to him.

Another aspect of thought is "fidelity to the assignment." Obviously the finest performance in the world on a topic other than the one assigned is fruitless, but such violent distortions of the assignment fortunately are rare. Not so rare, unfortunately, are reports which subtly miss the point, or wander away from it. Any consistent tendency on the part of the writer to drag in his pet remedies or favorite villains should be pointed out quickly, as should persistent efforts to grind personal axes.

Another lapse of "fidelity" is far more forgivable. This occurs when an eager subordinate tends to make too much of a routine assignment and consistently turns memos into 50-page reports. On the other hand, some subordinates may consistently make too little of an assignment and tend to do superficial and poorly researched pieces of work.

Perhaps the most important aspect of thought is the component "analysis." Here is where the highly intelligent are separated from those less gifted, and those who will dig from those who content themselves with superficial work. Often subordinates who have not had the benefit of experience under a strict taskmaster (either in school or on the job) are at a loss to understand why their reports are considered less than highly effective. Such writers, for example, may fail to draw obvious conclusions from the data that they have presented. On the other hand, they may offer conclusions which are seemingly unjustified by the evidence contained in their reports.

Another difficulty is that many young managers (and old ones, too) are unsophisticated in their appreciation of just what constitutes evidence. For example, if they base an entire report on the fact that sales are going to go up the next year simply because one assistant sales manager thinks so, they should expect to have their conclusions thrown out of court. They may also find themselves in difficulty if they fail to identify and justify assumptions which have been forced on them by the absence of factual data. Assumptions, of course, are absolutely necessary in this world of imperfect knowledge—especially when we deal with future developments—but it is the writer's responsibility to point out that certain assumptions have been made and that the validity of his analysis depends on whether or not these assumptions prove to be justified.

Another serious error in "analysis" is that of bias. Few superiors will respect a communication which is consciously or unconsciously biased. A writer who is incapable of making an objective analysis of all sides of a question, or of all alternatives to action, will certainly find his path to the top to be a dead end. On the other hand, especially in many younger writers, bias enters unconsciously, and it is only by a patient identification of the bias that the superior will be able to help the subordinate develop a truly objective analytical ability.

Persuasiveness

This discussion of bias in reporting raises the question of "persuasiveness." "Every letter is a sales letter of some sort," goes the refrain. And it is true that persuasiveness in writing can range from the "con man" type of presentation to that which results from a happy blending of the four elements of business writing I have described. While it would be naive to suggest that it is not often necessary for executives to write things in manipulative ways to achieve their ends *in the short run,* it would be foolish to imply that this type of writing will be very effective with the same people (if they are reasonably intelligent) *over the long run.* Understandably, therefore, the "con man" approach will not be particularly effective in the large business organization.

On the other hand, persuasiveness is a necessary aspect of organizational writing. Yet it is difficult to describe the qualities which serve to make a communication persuasive. It could be a certain ring of conviction about the way recommendations are advanced; it could be enthusiasm, or an understanding of the reader's desires, and a playing up to them. One can persuade by hitting with the blunt edge of the axe or by cutting finely with the sharp edge to prepare the way. Persuasion could result from a fine sense of discretion, of hinting but not stating overtly things which are impolitic to mention; or it could result from an action-orientation that conveys top management's desire for results rather than a more philosophical approach to a subject. In fact, it could be many things.

In an organization, the best test to apply for the propriety of persuasiveness is to ask yourself whether you would care to take action on the basis of what your own communication presents. In the long run, it is dangerous to assume that everyone else is stupid and malleable; so, if you would be offended or damaged in the event that you were persuaded to take the action suggested, you should restate the communication. This test eliminates needless worry about slightly dishonest but well-meaning letters of congratulation, or routine progress reports written merely for a filing record, and the like. But it does bring into sharp focus those messages that cross the line from persuasiveness to bias; these are the ones that will injure others and so eventually injure you.

Conclusion

No one can honestly estimate the billions of dollars that are spent in U.S. industry on written communications, but the amount must be staggering. By contrast, the amount of thinking and effort that goes into improving the effectiveness of business writing is tiny—a mouse invading a continent. A written performance inventory (like Exhibit 2) in itself is not the answer. But a checklist of writing elements should enable executives to speak about writing in a common tongue and hence be a vehicle by which individual and group improvement in writing can take place.

By executives' own vote, no aspect of a manager's performance is of greater importance to his success than communication, particularly written communication. By the facts, however, no part of business practice receives less formal and intelligent attention. What this article asserts is that when an individual asks, "What do you mean I can't write?"—and has every desire to improve—his company owes him a sensible and concrete answer.

The principles of poor writing

PAUL W. MERRILL

Paul W. Merrill was an astrophysicist and editor for the Mount Wilson Observatory in Pasadena, California.

Books and articles on good writing are numerous, but where can you find sound, practical advice on how to write poorly? Poor writing is so common that every educated person ought to know something about it. Many scientists actually do write poorly, but they probably perform by ear without perceiving clearly how their results are achieved. An article on the principles of poor writing might help. The author considers himself well qualified to prepare such an article; he can write poorly without half trying.

The average student finds it surprisingly easy to acquire the usual tricks of poor writing. To do a consistently poor job, however, one must grasp a few essential principles:

    I. Ignore the reader.

    II. Be verbose, vague, and pompous.

    III. Do not revise.

Ignore the reader

The world is divided into two great camps: yourself and others. A little obscurity or indirection in writing will keep the others at a safe distance; if they get close, they may see too much.

Write as if for a diary. Keep your mind on a direct course between yourself and the subject; don't think of the reader—he makes a bad triangle. This

Paul W. Merrill, "The Principles of Poor Writing," reprinted from *Scientific Monthly,* 64 (January 1947), pp. 72-74, by permission of the American Association for the Advancement of Science.

is fundamental. Constant and alert consideration of the probable reaction of the reader is a serious menace to poor writing; moreover, it requires mental effort. A logical argument is that if you write poorly enough, your readers will be too few to merit any attention whatever.

Ignore the reader wherever possible. If the proposed title, for example, means something to you, stop right there; think no further. If the title baffles or misleads the reader, you have won the first round. Similarly, all the way through you must write for yourself, not for the reader. Practice a dead-pan technique, keeping your facts and ideas all on the same level of emphasis with no telltale hints of relative importance or logical sequence. Use long sentences containing many ideas loosely strung together. *And* is the connective most frequently employed in poor writing because it does not indicate cause and effect, nor does it distinguish major ideas from subordinate ones. *Because* seldom appears in poor writing, nor does the semicolon—both are replaced by *and*.

Camouflage transitions in thought. Avoid such connectives as *moreover, nevertheless, on the other hand*. If unable to resist the temptation to give some signal for a change in thought, use *however*. A poor sentence may well begin with *however* because to the reader, with no idea what comes next, *however* is too vague to be useful. A good sentence begins with the subject or with a phrase that needs emphasis.

The "hidden antecedent" is a common trick of poor writing. Use a pronoun to refer to a noun a long way back, or to one decidedly subordinate in thought or syntax; or the pronoun may refer to something not directly expressed. If you wish to play a little game with the reader, offer him the wrong antecedent as bait; you may be astonished how easy it is to catch the poor fish.

In ignoring the reader avoid parallel constructions which give the thought away too easily. I need not elaborate, for you probably employ inversion frequently. It must have been a naive soul who said, "When the thought is parallel, let the phrases be parallel."

In every technical paper omit a few items that most readers need to know. You had to discover these things the hard way; why make it easy for the reader? Avoid defining symbols; never specify the units in which data are presented. Of course it will be beneath your dignity to give numerical values of constants in formulae. With these omissions, some papers may be too short; lengthen them by explaining things that do not need explaining. In describing tables, give special attention to self-explanatory headings; let the reader hunt for the meaning of P^1r_0.

Be verbose, vague, and pompous

The cardinal sin of poor writing is to be concise and simple. Avoid being specific; it ties you down. Use plenty of deadwood: include many superfluous words and phrases. Wishful thinking suggests to a writer that verbosity somehow serves as a cloak or even as a mystic halo by which an idea may be glorified. A cloud of words may conceal defects in observation or analysis, either by opacity or by diverting the reader's attention. Introduce abstract nouns at the drop of a hat—even in those *cases* where the *magnitude* of the *motion* in a downward *direction* is inconsiderable. Make frequent use of the words *case, character, condition, former* and *latter, nature, such, very.*

Poor writing, like good football, is strong on razzle-dazzle, weak on information. Adjectives are frequently used to bewilder the reader. It isn't much trouble to make them gaudy or hyperbolic; at least they can be flowery and inexact.

Deadwood

BIBLE: Render to Caesar the things that are Caesar's.

POOR: In the case of Caesar it might well be considered appropriate from a moral or ethical point of view to render to that potentate all of those goods and materials of whatever character or quality which can be shown to have had their original source in any portion of the domain of the latter.

SHAKESPEARE: I am no orator as Brutus is.

POOR: The speaker is not what might be termed an adept in the profession of public speaking, as might be properly stated of Mr. Brutus. (Example from P. W. Swain. *Amer. J. Physics,* **13,** 318, 1945.)

CONCISE: The dates of several observations are in doubt.

POOR: It should be mentioned that in the case of several observations there is room for considerable doubt concerning the correctness of the dates on which they were made.

REASONABLE: Exceptionally rapid changes occur in the spectrum.

POOR: There occur in the spectrum changes which are quite exceptional in respect to the rapidity of their advent.

REASONABLE: Formidable difficulties, both mathematical and observational, stand in the way.

POOR: There are formidable difficulties of both a mathematical and an observational nature that stand in the way.

Case

REASONABLE: Two sunspots changed rapidly.

POOR: There are two cases where sunspots changed with considerable rapidity.

REASONABLE: Three stars are red.

POOR: In three cases the stars are red in color.

Razzle-dazzle

Immaculate precision of observation and extremely delicate calculations. . . .

It would prove at once a world imponderable, etherealized. Our actions would grow grandific.

Well for us that the pulsing energy of the great life-giving dynamo in the sky never ceases. Well, too, that we are at a safe distance from the flame-licked whirlpools into which our earth might drop like a pellet of waste fluff shaken into the live coals of a grate fire.

Do not revise

Write hurriedly, preferably when tired. Have no plan; write down items as they occur to you. The article will thus be spontaneous and poor. Hand in your manuscript the moment it is finished. Rereading a few days later might lead to revision—which seldom, if ever, makes the writing worse. If you submit your manuscript to colleagues (a bad practice), pay no attention to their criticisms or comments. Later resist firmly any editorial suggestions. Be strong and infallible; don't let anyone break down your personality. The critic may be trying to help you or he may have an ulterior motive, but the chance of his causing improvement in your writing is so great that you must be on guard. . . .

The seven sins of technical writing

MORRIS FREEDMAN

Morris Freedman is Professor of English and
Comparative Literature at the University of
Maryland.

Let me start by saying at once that I
do not come to you tonight just as a professor of English, for, frankly, I do not
think that I would have very much to say to you only as someone expert in the
history of the use—and misuse—of the language. And any remarks on literature might be confusing, at least without extensive elaboration, for the values
and objectives of literature seem so very different at first from those of technical writing—although fundamentally many of these values and objectives co-
incide. And I am sure that you are more than familiar with such things as
clichés, comma splices, fragmentary sentences, and the other abominations we
deal with in freshman composition. These obviously have nothing to do specifically with technical writing.

But I want to say, before anyone thinks that I class technical writing
entirely by itself, immune from rules and requirements of communication
that govern other kinds of writing, that technical writing calls for the same
kind of attention and must be judged by the same standards as any other kind
of writing; *indeed, it calls for a greater attention and for higher standards.* And
I say this as a former science and medical writer for the popular press; as a
former writer of procedure manuals and directives for the government; as a
former editor of technical studies in sociology, statistics, law, and psychology;
as a former general magazine editor; as a writer of fiction, essays, and scholarly articles; and, not least, as a professor of English. We can see at once why
technical writing must be measured by higher standards, or, at least, by different ones, if anyone will not grant me that they are higher. Technical writing is
so immediately functional. Confusing directions accompanying an essential

Morris Freedman, "The Seven Sins of Technical Writing," reprinted from *College Composition
and Communication*, 9 (February 1958). Copyright © 1958 by the National Council of Teachers of
English. Reprinted by permission of the publisher and the author.

device in a jet plane may result in disaster; bad writing elsewhere can have as its most extreme effect merely boredom.

Yet, while technical writing implicitly calls for great care, it differs from other kinds of writing in that its practitioners are, by and large, first technicians and only incidentally writers. And principally because of this arrangement, I think, technical writing has become characterized by a collection of sins peculiar to this discipline alone. I say the *collection* is peculiar to technical writing, not any one of the sins alone. Any newspaper, weekly magazine, encyclopedia, textbook, any piece of writing you might name, will contain one or another of these sins, in greater or lesser profusion. But I know of no kind of writing that contains as many different sins in such great number as technical writing, and with such great potential for danger. To repeat, the sins in the world at large—at least, of the sort I'm talking about—often don't matter much. And sometimes, too, they don't matter in technical writing. As my students argue when I correct them in informative writing: "You got the meaning, didn't you?" Yes, I did, and so do we all get the meaning when a newspaper, a magazine, a set of directions stammers out its message. And I suppose, too, we could travel by ox-cart, or dress in burlap, or drive around with rattling fenders, and still get through a day.

But technical writing in this age can no more afford widespread sloppiness of expression, confusion of meaning, rattletrap construction than a supersonic missile can afford to be made of the wrong materials, or be put together haphazardly with screws jutting out here and there, or have wiring circuits that may go off any way at all, or—have a self-destructive system that fails because of some fault along the way in construction. Technical writing today—as I need hardly reiterate to this audience—if it is much less than perfect in its streamlining and design may well result in machines that are less than trim, and in operation that is not exactly neat. This is at worst; at best, poor technical writing, when its effect is minimized by careful reading, hinders efficiency, wastes time. Let me remark too that the commission of any one of these sins, and of any one of many, many lesser ones, is really not likely alone to be fatal, just as one loose screw by itself is not likely to destroy a machine; but always, we know, sins come in bunches, the sin of avarice often links hands with the sin of gluttony, one loose screw may mean others, and, anyway, the ideal of no sins at all—especially in something like technical writing, where the pain of self-denial should be minimal—is always to be strived for.

A final word before I launch into the sins (whose parade, so long delayed, will prove, I hope, so much more edifying—like a medieval tableau). The seven I list might be described as cardinal ones, and as such they are broad and overlapping, perhaps, rather than specific and very clearly distinguished from one another. They all contribute to making technical writing less clear, concise, coherent, and correct than it should be.

Sin 1, then, might be described as that of **Indifference,** neglecting the reader. I do not mean anything so simple as writing down to an engineer or physicist, although this is all too common and may be considered part of this sin. This writing down—elaborating the obvious—is one reason the abstract or summary has become so indispensable a part of technical reports; very often, it is all the expert needs to read of the whole report, the rest being a matter of all too obvious detailing. Nor do I mean writing above the heads of your audience either, which is a defect likely to be taken care of by a thoughtful editor. Both writing over or under the heads of your reader, or to the side, are really matters of careless aiming and, as such, of indifference, too. But what I mean here by indifference are shortcuts of expression, elliptical diction, sloppy organization, bringing up points and letting them hang unresolved, improper or inadequate labelling of graphic material, and the like. This is communication by gutturals, grunts, shrugs, as though it were not worth the trouble to articulate carefully, as though the reader didn't matter—or didn't exist. This is basically an attitude of disrespect: *Caveat lector*—let the reader beware. Let the reader do his own work; the writer isn't going to help him.

Here is the concluding sentence from a quite respectable report, one most carefully edited and indeed presented as a model in a handbook for technical writers used by a great chemical firm. The sentence is relatively good, for it takes only a second reading to work out its meaning (perhaps only a slow first one for someone trained in reading this kind of writing):

> When it is assumed that all of the cellulose is converted to ethyl cellulose, **reaction conversion** of cellulose to ethyl cellulose, **per cent** of cellulose **reacted,** and **reaction yield** of ethyl cellulose based on cellulose are each equal to 100%.

This is admittedly a tough sentence to get across simply, considering that "cellulose" is repeated in several different contexts. Yet two guiding principles would have made it much clearer: 1. always put for your reader first things first (here, the meaning hangs on the final phrase, "each equal to 100%," which comes at the end of a complicated series); and 2. clearly separate items in a series. (The second rules seems to me one of the most important in technical writing where so many things have to be listed so often.) Here is the recast sentence:

> If all the cellulose is converted to ethyl cellulose, each of the following factors is then equal to 100%:
>
> 1. reaction conversion of cellulose to ethyl cellulose.
>
> 2. proportion of cellulose reacted.
>
> 3. reaction yield of ethyl cellulose based on cellulose.

The changes are not great, certainly, but in the process we have eliminated the indisputable notion of a percent being equal to a percent, and have arranged the series so that both the eye and the mind together can grasp the information immediately. Sin 1 then can be handled, one way, by cutting out indirect Rube Goldbergish contraptions and hitting your points directly on their heads, one, two, three.

The remaining sins I shall discuss are extensions of this primal one, disregard for the reader. Sin 2 may be designated as **Fuzziness,** that is, a general fuzziness of communication—vague words, meaningless words, wrong ones. The reader uses his own experience to supply the meaning in such writing; the writing itself acts only as a collection of clues. The military specializes in this sort of thing. I recall an eerie warning in an air force mess hall: "Anyone smoking in or around this mess hall will be dealt with accordingly." It still haunts me. Here is a caution in a handbook of technical writing with which you may be familiar: "Flowery, euphemistic protestations of gratitude are inappropriate." We know what this means, of course, but we ourselves supply the exact meaning. It happens that a "euphemism" is "the substitution of an inoffensive or mild expression for one that may offend or suggest something unpleasant." At least, that's what *Webster's Collegiate* says it is.

Here are some other examples: "The intrinsic labyrinth of wires must be first disentangled." The writer meant "network," not "labyrinth"; and I think he meant "internal" for "intrinsic" and "untangled" for "disentangled." Item: "The liquid contents of the container should then be disgorged via the spout by the operator." Translation: "The operator should then empty the container." Here is a final long one:

> When the element numbered one is brought into tactual contact with the element numbered two, when the appropriate conditions of temperature have been met above the previously determined safety point, then there will be exhibited a tendency for the appropriate circuit to be closed and consequently to serve the purpose of activating an audible warning device.

Translation:

> When the heat rises above the set safety point, element one touches element two, closing a circuit and setting off a bell.

Prescription to avoid Sin 2: use concrete, specific words and phrases whenever you can, and use only those words whose meaning you are sure of. (A dictionary, by the way, is only a partial help in determining the correct and *idiomatic* use of a word.) English is perhaps the richest of languages in offering a variety of alternatives for saying the same thing.

Sin 3 might be called the sin of **Emptiness.** It is the use of jargon and big words, pretentious ones, where perfectly appropriate and acceptable small and normal words are available. (There is nothing wrong with big words in themselves, provided they are the best ones for the job. A steam shovel is right for moving a boulder, ridiculous for picking up a handkerchief.) We may want to connect this sin with the larger, more universal one of pride, the general desire to seem important and impressive. During World War II a high government official devoted much time to composing an effective warning for a sticker to be put above light switches. He emerged with "Illumination is required to be extinguished on these premises on the termination of daily activities," or something of the sort. He meant "Put the lights out when you go home."

The jargon I'm talking about is not the technical language you use normally and necessarily for efficient communication. I have in mind only the use of a big word or a jumble of words for something that can be said more efficiently with familiar words and straightforward expressions. I have in mind also a kind of code language used to show that you're an insider, somewhere or other: "Production-wise, that's a high-type machine that can be used to finalize procedure. The organization is enthused." There is rarely any functional justification for saying "utilize" or "utilization" for "use," "prior to" for "before," "the answer is in the affirmative or negative" for "yes or no," or for using any of the "operators, or false verbal limbs," as George Orwell called them, like "render inoperative," "prove unacceptable," "exhibit a tendency to," "serve the purpose of," and so on and on.

Again, one can handle this sin simply by overcoming a reluctance to saying things directly; the most complex things in the world can be said in simple words, often of one syllable. Consider propositions in higher math or logic, the Supreme Court decisions of men like Brandeis and Holmes, the poetry of Shakespeare. I cannot resist quoting here Sir Arthur Quiller-Couch's rendition in jargon of Hamlet's "To be or not to be, that is the question." I am sure you all know the full jargon rendition of the soliloquy. "To be, or the contrary? Whether the former or the latter be preferable would seem to admit of some difference of opinion."

Sin 4 is an extension of 3: just plain **Wordiness.** The principle here is that if you can say anything with more words than necessary for the job, then by all means do so. I've already cited examples of this sin above, but compounded with other sins. Here is a purer example, the opening of a sentence in a technical writing handbook: "Material to be contained on the cover of the technical report includes . . ." This can be reduced to "The cover of the technical report should include . . ." Another example, less pure: "The front-mounted blade of the bull-dozer is employed for earth moving operations on road construction jobs." Translation: "The bull-dozer's front blade moves earth in road building." Item: "There is another way of accomplishing this purpose, and that is by evaporation." Translation: "Evaporation is another way of doing this." Instead of saying simply that "the bull-dozer's front blade moves earth," you say it "is employed for earth moving operations," throwing in "employed" and "operations," as though "moves" alone is too weak to do this tremendous job. The cure for this sin? Simply reverse the mechanism: say what you have to in the fewest words.

Sin 5, once again an extension of the immediately preceding sin, is a matter of **Bad Habits,** the use of pat phrases, awkward expressions, confusing sentence structure, that have, unfortunately, become second nature. Again, I'm not alluding to the perfectly natural use of familiar technical expressions, which may literally be called clichés, but which are not efficiently replaceable. Sin 5 is a matter of just not paying attention to what you say, with the result that when you do suddenly pay attention, you see the pointlessness or even humor of what you have set down. Perhaps the most common example of this sin is what has been called "deadwood," or what may be called "writing for the simple minded." Examples: "red in color," "three in number," "square in shape," "the month of January," "the year 1956," "ten miles in distance," and the like. What else is red but a color, three but a number, square but a shape, January but a month, 1956 but a year, ten miles but a distance? To say that something is "two inches wide and three inches long" is to assume that your reader can't figure out length and width from the simple dimensions "two inches by three inches." I once read that a certain machine was 18 feet high, "vertically," the writer made sure to add; and another time that a certain knob should be turned "right, in direction."

A caution is needed here. There are many obvious instances when qualification is necessary. To say that something is "light," for example, is plainly mysterious unless you add "in color" or "in weight" or, perhaps, "in density" (unless the context makes such addition "deadwood").

I would include under Sin 5 the locutions "as far as that is concerned" (lately shortened to "as far as that"), "as regards," "with regard to," "in the case of" ("In the case of the case enclosing the instrument, the case is being studied"). These are all too often just lazy ways of making transitions (and, thus, incidentally, quite justifiable when speed of writing is a factor).

Sin 6 is the **Deadly Passive,** or, better, deadening passive; it takes the life out of writing, making everything impersonal, eternal, remote and dead. The deadly passive is guaranteed to make any reading matter more difficult to understand, to get through, and to retain. Textbook writers in certain fields have long ago learned to use the deadly passive to create difficulties where none exist; this makes their subject seem weightier, and their accomplishment more impressive. (And, of course, if this is ever what you have in mind on an assignment, then by all means use the deadly passive.) Sin 6 is rarely found alone; it is almost indispensable for fully carrying out the sins of wordiness and jargon. Frequently, of course, the passive is not a sin and not deadly, for there simply is no active agent and the material must be put impersonally.

Examples of this sin are so easy to come by, it is difficult to find one better than another. Here is a relatively mild example of Sin 6.

> The standardization of procedure in print finishing can be a very important factor in the efficient production of service pictures. In so far as possible, the smallest number of types and sizes of paper should be employed, and the recommended processing followed. The fewer paper grades and processing procedures used, the fewer errors and make-overs that are likely. Make-overs are time-consuming and costly.

Here it is with the deadly passive out and some other changes made:

> To produce service pictures efficiently, a standard way of finishing prints can be very important. You should use as few types and sizes of paper as

possible, and you should follow the recommended procedure for processing. In this way, you will make fewer errors, and have to re-do less work. You will save time and money.

Associated with the deadly passive, as you might see from the two passages above, is the use of abstract nouns and adjectives for verbs. Verbs always live; nouns and adjectives just sit there, and abstract nouns aren't even there. Of course, there are a number of other ways of undoing the passivity of the passage I quoted, and of making other improvements, just as there were other ways of handling any of the specimens I have cited in the train of horrors accompanying my pageant of sins.

Finally we come to Sin 7, the one considered the deadliest by many, and not only by teachers of English but by technical writers and technologists of various sorts: **Mechanical Errors.** I don't think this sin the deadliest of all. It does happen to be the easiest one to recognize, the one easiest to deal with "quantitatively," so to speak, and the easiest one to resist. I suppose it is considered deadliest because then those who avoid it can so quickly feel virtuous. It can promptly be handled by good works alone. Actually most technical writing happens to be mechanically impeccable; not one of the examples I have used tonight had very much mechanically wrong with it. If anything, technical people tend to make too much of formal mechanics. I remember working with a physicist who had much trouble saying anything in writing. While his general incapacity to write was almost total, one thing he did know, and know firmly, and that was that a split infinitive was to be abhorred. That, and using a preposition to end a sentence with. He could never communicate the simplest notion coherently, but he never split an infinitive or left a preposition at the end of a sentence. If Nobel Prizes were to be awarded for never splitting infinitives or for encapsulating prepositions within sentences, he would be a leading candidate.

There are a handful of mechanical errors which are relevant to technical writing, and these are important because they are so common, especially in combination with other sins. (Split infinitives or sentence-ending prepositions, need I say, are not among them.) These are dangling participles and other types of poorly placed modifiers, and ambiguous references. There are others, a good number of others, but the ones I mention creep in most insidiously and most often.

Here are some examples stripped down to emphasize the errors:

Raising the temperature, the thermostat failed to function.
Who or what raised the temperature? Not the thermostat, I presume; and if it did somehow, as the result of current flowing in its wiring, then this ought to be said quite plainly.
The apparatus is inappropriately situated in the corner since it is too small.
What is too small? Apparatus or corner?

Every element in the device must not be considered to be subject to abnormal stress.

What is meant here is that "Not every element in the apparatus must be considered subject to abnormal stress," almost the opposite of the original taken literally.

I should like to conclude by emphasizing something I glanced at in my introduction, that the seven sins of technical writing are to be avoided not so much by a specific awareness of each, accompanied by specific penance for each, as by a much more general awareness, by an attitude toward subject matter, writing process, and reader that can best be described only as "respectful." You will not help yourself very much if you rely on such purely mechanical aids as Rudolph Flesch's formulas for "readable writing," or on slide rules measuring readability, much as you may be tempted to do so. These can be devil's snares, ways to make you think you are avoiding sin. There are no general texts, either, at present that will help you in more than very minor ways. The only aids you can safely depend on are the good book itself, that is, a good dictionary (there are many poor ones), any of the several volumes by H. W. Fowler, and occasional essays, here and there, by George Orwell, Jacques Barzun, Herbert Read, Somerset Maugham, and others. And these, I stress, can ony be *aids*. What is most important in eliminating sin in technical writing is general attitude—as it may well be in eliminating sin anywhere.

I repeat that technical writing must be as rationally shaped as a technical object. A piece of technical writing, after all, is something that is shaped into being for a special purpose, much as a technical object. The design engineer should be guided in his work by the requirements of function almost alone. (Of course, if he happens to have a boss who likes to embellish the object with useless doo-dads, why then he may have to modify his work accordingly to keep his job—as automobile designers do every day; but we try never to have in mind unreasonable situations of this sort). It is as pointless for the design engineer to use three bolts where one would do (both for safety and function), to make an object square when its use dictates it should be round, to take the long way through a process when there is a short way, as it is for the technical writer to commit any of the sins I have mentioned. Technical writing—informative writing of any sort—should be as clean, as functional, as inevitable as any modern machine designed to do a job well. If I will not be misunderstood in throwing out this thought, I should like to suggest to you that good technical writing should be like good poetry—every word in its exact place for maximum effect, no word readily replaceable by another, not a word too many or too few, and the whole combination, so to speak, invisible, not calling attention to its structure, seemingly effortless, perfectly adapted to its subject.

If one takes this general approach to the shaping of a piece of technical writing, and there really can't be much excuse for any other, then there is no need to worry about any of the sins I mention. Virtue may not come at once or automatically, for good writing never comes without effort, however fine one's intentions, but it will certainly come, and perhaps even bring with it that same satisfaction the creative engineer experiences. Technical writing cleansed of its sins is no less worthy, no less impressive, an enterprise than good engineering itself. Like mathematics to physics, technical writing is a handmaid to technology, but like mathematics, too, it can be a helpmate, that is, an equal partner. But it can achieve this reward of virtue only by emphasizing the virtues of writing equally with those of technology.

Six guidelines for fast, functional writing

HERBERT POPPER

Herbert Popper is a senior editor of the journal *Chemical Engineering.*

Some types of improvement in the quality of one's writing can only be achieved at the expense of quantity—for instance, by spending more time on the editing of drafts. However, regardless of whether you use longhand or some form of dictation, there are several areas where quantity and quality go hand in hand, and where it can actually take less time to produce an effective piece of communication than an ineffective one. The six guidelines that follow take aim at that area.

Because writing problems vary in kind and degree from person to person, you may find that some of these suggestions either don't apply to you or appear self-evident. However, "fast, functional" writing skills are so important to most engineers and technical managers that even if you only find one or two of the suggestions really useful, this should more than repay you for your reading time.

1. Know what your audience expects

A vice-president of operations was making his annual tour of the company's outlying facilities. At one plant, he chatted with the assistant manager about the upcoming labor negotiations with the local union.

"I wish you'd send me a fairly detailed report of those negotiations," asked the vice-president. Flattered by this request, the assistant plant manager

Herbert Popper, "Six Guidelines for Fast, Functional Writing," reprinted by special permission from *Chemical Engineering,* June 30, 1969. Copyright © 1969, by McGraw-Hill, Inc., New York, N.Y. 10020.

resolved to do an outstanding job of reporting. By the time negotiations were over, he had more than 50 pages of handwritten notes, which he decided to amplify with background information on some of the points the union or the management team had raised.

It took him two weeks after the close of negotiations to organize this material into a rough handwritten draft. Because of a secretarial bottleneck, it took him two more weeks to get this draft typed and edited, and then another two weeks to get the massive document typed up in final form. Nevertheless, as he signed the letter of transmittal in which he apologized for imperfections in the typing and commented on the shortage of good secretarial help, he felt rather proud of himself: The report read like a courtroom drama, and had a great degree of polish.

Unfortunately, before the report could even reach headquarters, the vice-president had made an acid phone call to the plant manager. Apparently, what the vice-president had really wanted was brief, day-by-day reports that he could review while negotiations were still in progress, and that he could pass on to another plant that started negotiations a week later. When he finally got the assistant plant manager's monumental opus, a lot of the information was old hat, the key points having been already passed along by the plant manager in a lengthy, long-distance phone call just before the close of negotiations.

Next year, the plant manager decided to handle the job of reporting himself; at the close of each day's session, he dictated his notes into a recorder—his secretary would type them up on the next day, so that he could ink in some comments and send them out as soon as he finished that day's negotiating. Since he didn't use a draft, his daily reports were not particularly polished; the inked-in comments and corrections looked rather informal—and yet these reports were acclaimed by the vice-president.

Moral of the story: Make sure you know what the audience wants. Don't be afraid to ask. There are times when speed, rather than quality or quantity, may be of the essence. In the example above, which is based on an actual situation, the assistant plant manager could have saved himself hours of toil by finding out what sort of details the vice-president did or did not want to know about, and whether quick dictation without a draft was acceptable.

Failure to find out or to really understand the audience's expectations is perhaps the single biggest time-waster in technical writing. An example of such inefficiency involves the engineer who uses exactly the same writing approach regardless of whether his report is primarily intended for the departmental archives, his immediate supervisor, or a financial executive on the appropriations committee.

If the report is just intended for a supervisor, for instance, there is nothing wrong with using technical jargon, and for keeping background information very brief. But if the report is to go to a financial executive—particularly one who lacks any sort of technical background—the engineer must avoid technical jargon, and explain some things that he would not need to explain to his boss, while leaving out technical details. In such a report, it is particularly important to make the first page or two tell the bulk of the story, in terms that are meaningful to the administrator.

If you are writing a dual-function report—say, one intended for both a financial executive and your boss—by all means get squared away with the latter on how the two approaches can be reconciled (e.g., by eventually giving your boss additional sections or informal notes that are omitted from the administrator's copy, by coming up with a preliminary version of the first two pages that you and your boss can review jointly before finalization, etc.).

When writing for publication, rather than for internal use, finding out the audience's expectations can be an equally great timesaver. Many magazines have booklets that discuss their "expectations" in regard to such things as writing style, quality of drawings, compatibility with readers' interests[1]—and are further prepared to conserve the author's time by reviewing outlines in some detail so as to minimize the need for revision of the final manuscript.

2. Mobilize your subconscious

Legend has it that on the day the opera "The Magic Flute" was scheduled to get its first performance, someone reminded Mozart that there still wasn't any overture, whereupon the composer calmly sat down and dashed off the magnificent overture just in time to give the score to the orchestra before the curtain went up. Actually, I think if this legend is true, the chances are that Mozart must have "precomposed" the overture in his mind days before he set it down on paper, so that leaving the actual writing until just before the deadline may not have been as risky as it seemed to others at the time.

Unfortunately, many of us tend to display a Mozart-like confidence in being able to meet a last-minute deadline regardless of whether we have done any precomposing or not.

If you have a writing project with a far-off deadline, and you don't feel like starting the actual writing right away, then don't. But I would still suggest that you draw up a rough outline as soon as you can, see how much information you already have available and how much more you will have to dig out, decide when you should start this digging out so that the information will be available at the proper time, and discuss the outline for the project with your boss or with a colleague. That way, you will not only get a feel for the emphasis needed (as discussed in the previous section), but you will be giving your subconscious mind a chance to come up with ideas while the project is incubating.

To come up with useful ideas, your subconscious should have some sort of framework—that way, perhaps some of the framework will be filled in for you while you shave in the morning. But if you wait till the last minute, even to prepare an outline or think about an approach, all your subconscious can do is to provide you with a feeling of anxiety.

Another constructive use for the prewriting period is to do some preselling. People hate shocks—which is what may happen when your recommendations based on a full year's work are coldly dropped on your department head's desk. It is fairer to him, and kinder to you and your writing time, to use the "let's let him in on part of the secret" technique. So, give your boss some inkling of what your report is going to recommend. Don't try to do a complete job of selling, but do give him a chance to get some exposure to your ideas. From his initial comments, you may also be able to obtain pointers on how to best link your ideas to his, and to the current objectives of the department. This can save a great deal of writing time in the long run, and will often let you get the constructive involvement of the reader much sooner than if you use the "This may come as a shock, but . . ." approach.

3. Build up and exploit your momentum

"I sit down with a fountain pen and paper and the story pours out. However lousy a section is, I let it go. I write on to the end. Then the subconscious mind has done what it can . . . The rest is simple effort . . . going over a chapter time and time again until, though you know it isn't right, it is the best you can do." That's how W. Somerset Maugham said he got his thoughts down on paper. If you have trouble getting started and building up momentum on a writing project, then the Maugham approach of putting down your thoughts in any old undisciplined way and eventually going back to polish them up, has a lot to recommend it. . . .

What do you do if you still don't succeed in unplugging your thoughts, regardless of whether you are using pen, pencil, stenographer or dictating machine? Here are a few additional pointers:

• Go over your outline . . . and pretend a good friend asked you to explain each point to him. If he were to ask questions such as "Why don't we just stick with the old process?" or "How does this gimmick work?," the chances are you wouldn't be at a loss for words—you would just say it like it is. So, pretend your friend is asking you questions that correspond to your outline, and write it like it is.

• Pretend that this is an examination, and that you have five minutes to get something down on paper for each thought on your outline— i.e., that if after five minutes you have nothing down on paper on the first point, you have nothing that you can be graded on, and you would thus get zero. (A couple of years ago, I took an aptitude test in which I was given a cast of two or three characters and had to shape them into a plot for a short story within ten minutes; then stop and shape another cast of characters into a new plot; then do this a few more times. Not considering myself a really fast writer, I was amazed at how much I could get down in ten minutes when the pressure was on, and when I knew I would be graded on content rather than style. It occurred to me that if I could pretend that I was in a similar situation when starting on a writing job, it would get me going—and it works!)

• Pick the best time to get started on a tough writing project. For most people, this may be the very beginning of the day, before things have come up to distract them. Others work best right after lunch. Still others find that the best time to unlock their thoughts is after dinner at home, and that once they get started that way, they can continue the project at work without much difficulty. If you haven't already done so, try to find a time pattern in the daily periods during which you feel sharpest and loosest; then exploit these periods to get started on tough projects.

Of course, getting started does not necessarily mean writing a brilliant beginning; it means getting started on the "meat" of the project. Very often a meaty fact-filled beginning is the most brilliant one anyway. But if you do feel the urge to think up something particularly striking or original, you may be better off doing this after most of the project is down on paper, rather than letting it be an initial stumbling block.

Once you have built up your momentum, how do you keep it?

First of all, try not to stop. Let someone take your phone messages. If you see a chance to finish the project by working late, do so. Resist the temptation to take a break until you start slowing down. (Personally, I find that sipping coffee or puffing on a cigar while doing difficult writing is preferable to running the risk of getting sidetracked by taking an unnecessary break.) Putting it into industrial engineering terminology, make sure you have a long enough production run to justify the setup time.

If you can't finish the project by working late, then it is usually better to leave it in the middle of a paragraph than to try and finish the particular section or thought. Finishing the thought the next day will be relatively easy, and this will serve to prime the pump for the next thought. I used to make the mistake of staying up until whatever hour was necessary to get a major section finished, only to find that it would take me all the next morning to stop resting on my laurels and to uncork my thoughts for the next section. Conversely, when I don't try so hard to come to a logical stopping place, I can usually continue the section without any difficulty the next morning and then launch right into the next section. (I can't take full credit for this approach; someone named Hemingway recommended it in a book called "A Movable Feast.")

4. Watch out for time-wasting verbosity

Not everybody has the uncoiling problems dealt with in the previous section. In fact, some people who can uncoil most of the time at the drop of a pencil encounter the opposite type of problem: How to avoid the verbosity that wastes their own time as well as that of the reader, so that they can make the most of their fluency as writers.

The first section in the 1966 "Efficient, Effective Writing" report[2] gave good advice on ways of recognizing and avoiding destructive verbosity. Although that section was aimed at making writing more informative, most of the suggestions can also lead to faster writing. For instance, the writer can usually save time by cutting down on passive verbs, abstract nouns, and prepositional phrases. (Obviously, it would have taken me longer to write the previous sentence had I said "Time can be saved by the writer if proper consideration is given to a reduction in the use of passive verbs, etc.")

Here are a few additional suggestions:

- Don't be legalistic in a nonlegal piece of writing. Lawyers have to be extremely careful to cover every possible contingency—hence they may feel justified in using strings of words that may differ only very slightly in meaning (e.g., null, void, of no legal force, etc.). But engineers are seldom justified in coming up with a phrase like "The *development, establishment,* and *implementation* of process-control *philosophies* and *policies* must take place at an *early* or *incipient* stage in a project." There just isn't enough difference between the italicized words to warrant using more than one of each; if you say "philosophies," 99 out of 100 readers will assume that this includes "policies."

- Don't waste time on excess hedging. For instance, when you say "Based on bench-scale experiments run at ten different temperatures, 300 F. produces the best yield," you have clearly indicated on what you base your conclusion, and there is no need to add hedge phrases such as ". . . 300 F. may tend to produce the best yields, assuming that these bench-scale results are freely applicable to commercial conditions . . ." Putting it another way, readers generally realize that almost any technical, business or philosophical statement that can be made is subject to limitations and qualifications; if you insist on pointing out limitations that are either obvious or unimportant, you are wasting time (and probably producing dull writing). Particularly wasteful and deadly is the "triple hedge"—e.g., ". . . may, under some circumstances, tend to . . ."

- Use more tables, illustrations and in-text listings to cut down on verbosity. . . . An item-by-item approach can result in tighter writing of all kinds, including the body of the report. (At the risk of appearing to disregard my own "hedging" caveat, I should point out that itemization can be carried to dull extremes, particularly once the triple sub-indentation stage is reached. But if you haven't been doing much itemizing, the technique can save you a lot of words in reducing generalities to specifics.)

- Consider leaving out some details altogether. Resist the temptation to tell the reader everything you know about the subject—just tell him what you think he needs to know. The latter is quite different from just telling him what you think he would like to hear—or from using a dual standard whereby you exclude all unfavorable details while including all those that are favorable. The memo or report that burdens the reader with every conceivable detail has not only taken the writer much more time than necessary, but suggests that the writer was unsure of himself because he left it to the reader to decide which of the details were significant. (If you are afraid that a short report won't adequately reflect the work that went into a particular study, you can always indicate the *type* of additional data that can be supplied on request.)

Of course, the classic example of detail elimination involves the man who got a letter from his landlord asking if he intended to vacate his apartment. The answer consisted of "Dear Sir: I remain, Yours Truly, Henry Smith."

Unfortunately, it's not always that easy to combine succinctness with politeness in handling one's correspondence, particularly when one is dictating it. Things that can waste the dictator's (and the reader's) time include:

- Marathon sentences. An occasional long sentence can supply useful variety, and may be needed in order to relate ideas to each other, but strings of runaway sentences impede efficient communication.

- Ditto for marathon paragraphs.

- Shotgun or overkill attacks on the topic, whereby the dictator, not being sure he has said what he really wanted to say, goes on to re-attack the topic in several other, equally roundabout, ways.

- Tendencies to throw in cliches and meaningless phrases just to keep the dictation process going. It is less wasteful to keep your secretary waiting for a minute while you find the right phrase than to dictate a phrase that adds nothing.

5. Save time via the "example" technique

Most of us find the going slow when we write on an abstract, philosophic level for any length of time. True, the amount of such writing can be minimized by translating abstract concepts into dollars and cents, but this cannot always be done. For instance, if you are trying to change the attitudes of foremen towards some community or labor-relations problem, neither payout time nor discounted cash flow is going to be of much help to you. But this does not mean that your communications with the foremen must be entirely on an abstract philosophic, level.

Good philosophy is hard to write. There are all sorts of pitfalls: failure to define terms, or to relate them to the reader's frame of mind, failure to avoid either oversimplification or obtuseness, etc. But fortunately, you can write about an abstract topic—e.g., a desired change in attitude—without staying on the abstract level for very long. The idea here is to translate the abstract into the specific by using analogies, miniature case histories (either actual or hypothetical), projections of what might happen if the status quo were maintained, etc.

Of course, this "example" technique is not limited to communications that deal with corporate philosophy but should also be used when generalities and abstract concepts crop up in technical writing. Here, a one-sentence "for instance" can often take the place of a much longer explanation; a liberal sprinkling of such sentences can keep the discussion on the ground, and can result in an easier-to-write yet more-informative communication than one in which all abstract technical concepts are explained or promoted in only theoretical terms.

6. Know thyself, and thy writing

The difficulty in many articles dealing with improving your writing is their generality; they presuppose that all writers have the same problems. This report has tried to be more specific—for instance, by showing how *less* discipline can be a timesaver for the engineer who has trouble uncoiling, whereas *more* discipline can be an eventual timesaver for someone whose problem is verbosity or poor organization rather than lack of writing fluency.

Where do you fall within these two extremes? Should your prime emphasis be on boosting your writing output or on boosting its quality? If you have difficulty answering that question, you can get help quite readily.

For example, the 1966 "Efficient, Effective Writing" report[2] supplied some simple tests whereby you can evaluate the informative quality of your writing. If your score is low, perhaps your prime goal should be to make your writing more informative. At the beginning, this may reduce your page output because you will be spending more time on editing and rewriting. However, if you try to learn from your editing, you will find that output will eventually increase along with quality. This means spending a few minutes reviewing an edited draft to see what type of corrections are prevalent, and to think about ways of minimizing the need for these types of corrections in subsequent writing.

Discuss your writing with your boss. Some bosses are reluctant to initiate such a discussion because they have found that it takes almost as much tact to constructively criticize a subordinate's writing as it would to constructively criticize his wife or family. But if you initiate such a discussion (I mean about your writing, not your wife), the chances are that overly defensive postures can be avoided, and that you and your boss will both gain a better insight into problem areas.

Ask your boss whether he thinks you are spending too much or too little time on writing. For instance, based on samples, would he settle for draftless dictation on some reports in order to give you more time for engineering?

If one of your writing problems is that interruptions are always breaking your train of thought, ask your boss about ways of getting more privacy, or about occasionally working at home to make headway on difficult writing chores.

In order to discuss other aspects of your writing, you may want to go over a sort of writing-inventory checklist, such as the one published in the *Harvard Business Review* article "What Do You Mean I Can't Write?"[3] This can be a good starting point in getting your supervisor's views on such matters as whether you sometimes present too many opinions and not enough supporting data (or vice versa), whether you tend to under- or overestimate his familiarity with your work, etc.

A concluding thought: The engineer who progresses in his company tends to do more writing every year. Eventually, he may also have to supervise the writing of subordinates; many of their reports and memos will go out over his signature and will reflect on the caliber of the work done under his supervision. Thus the engineer who becomes adept at fast, functional writing is in an enviable position—he can save a significant and increasing amount of time, establish his credentials as an efficient communicator, and eventually help his subordinates solve their own communication problems. We hope that the suggestions in various sections of this report will help point the way, and will let you apply the "work smarter, not harder" principle to your communicating.

Acknowledgement

Some of the ideas in this final section stem from various members of *Chemical Engineering*'s editorial staff, and also from Manny Meyers of Picatinny Arsenal, and Peter J. Rankin of Basford Inc.

References

1. See, for instance, "How to Write for *Chemical Engineering*," a booklet available from *Chemical Engineering*, 330 W. 42 St., New York City.
2. Johnson, Thomas P., How Well Do You Inform?, *Chem. Eng.*, Mar. 14, 1966 (Reprint No. 295).
3. Fielden, J., *Harvard Bus. Rev.*, May–June 1964, p. 147. [See also pages 14–28 in this book.]

Defensive writing

MARY C. BROMAGE

Mary C. Bromage is Professor of Written
Communication at the Graduate School of
Business Administration at the University of
Michigan.

As a rule, the best English is written by people without literary preten-
sions, who have responsible executive jobs. . . . Though often letters,
speeches and reports must be written in a hurry and, because of the
countless considerations that clear writing involves, are bound in some
way to fall short of the full intended meaning, conscientious people will
always regret this necessity. . . .[1]

Good functional writing means be-
ing aware of more than syntax and sequence. Intangible factors lying in the
changing pressures of the "office" may becloud issues and befuddle readers.
The writer's particular situation calls for as much self-awareness as does his
style and organization. It is relatively easy for the practical writer to free
himself from "sins" like mismated modifiers or pronouns with absentee own-
ership, and to find a logical pathway, but what about the "countless considerations," those less obvious sources of possible interference with the sense of
his reports, letters, memos, procedures, summaries or analyses? Writing is a
form of human behavior, both individual and corporate, and as much stands
between the lines as on them.

Mary C. Bromage, "Defensive Writing," © 1970 by the Regents of the University of California.
Reprinted from *California Management Review*, volume XIII, number 4, pp. 45 to 56, by permission of the Regents.

Stated aims

What, first of all, are the guiding aims of a businessman when he takes pencil or dictaphone in hand? A candid answer, currently arrived at, will enable him to measure for himself his success or failure as he copes with the daily demands that he "communicate." Industry nowadays takes for granted the establishment of production goals and quality controls. In an attempt to apply the same approach to writing, 450 management men (between 35 and 45 years of age) in one large industrial corporation have been asked during the past two years to respond to this question: "What qualities do you consider most desirable in business communications?"

Three qualities outnumber all the rest in the answers to that question: **clarity, brevity,** and **directness.** Yet when samples of the writing done by these same respondents are examined, the results are often at variance with the proclaimed preferences.

Paradox of results

Consider this sentence from a new marketing manager's report to his vice president: "Moreover, the anticipated introduction of new competitive products with more modern appearance and/or superior lasting characteristics will make particularly vulnerable that portion of the sales volume of the lines which is derived from customers intending their purchase for use primarily for a short period." Presumably, the writer meant (but hesitated to say): "Some of our customers now buy our product primarily for short-term use. They may be won away by competitive products that look more modern and last longer." Vagueness, wordiness, and indirectness are not always attributable to poor grammar, as the original quotation (which is grammatically correct) suggests. The fact was that the newcomer may have had mental reservations, perhaps unacknowledged, about emphasizing a forecast both uncertain and unwelcome in an upward-directed report.

The real question is this: how clear, how concise, how direct does the sender of a particular communication really want to be? Businessmen, as readers, may avow one thing and, as writers, practice another.

For unplanned ambiguity, there is no basis: for the carefully qualified safeguarded sentence, there is a use. Auditors accompany their reports with the statement that: "Our examination was made in accordance with generally accepted auditing standards, and accordingly included such tests of the accounting records and such other auditing procedures as we considered necessary in the circumstances."[2] As far as the recipient is concerned, the meaning is open-ended, but one accountant explained the long sentence with its built-in qualifications by the understandable reasoning that there is justification for linguistic leeway in presenting a certification.

Factors that may not be consciously recognized often control the hand behind the pencil. George Eliot, the nineteenth century writer of special prescience, once said that one's words reveal one's less conscious purposes. **The real question is this: is a writer conscious of his purpose and thereby in control of it?**

What price clarity?

As to clarity, cited as the primary virtue in what is written on the job, the real point is whether the hard-pressed manager in the large corporation wishes to be open and explicit in what he proposes, in what he endorses, in what he requests. The point is not whether he *should* be clear, but whether he feels that he can be and will be. The frequent contrast between his professed aims and his desk-top practice may be comprehensible in the light of the situation (the environmental forces and factors) surrounding his writing. In practical writing, language is as language does.

When the answer to a memo lies in laps of the organizational gods, the writer may not wish to tempt fate by the quick, clean thrust to achieve a purpose. Doubt as to his recipients' reactions may lead to beating around the bush. Whether the ambiguity, circumlocution, and postponement of a point is "right" is another question. The organization man as writer must know corporate tradition and philosophy. He must be sensitive to the "politics" of the company, as one newcomer to a finance staff commented in discussing his writing "hangup." Only in the light of such an awareness can a member of the team judge how frank he can afford to be.

The phenomenon of the already large but still expanding company is placing its special marks upon the accompanying paperwork. And these marks are not always consistent with clarity. The dimensions of an organization inevitably make themselves felt in its communications. The characteristics of the writing done under the rubric of the large company are discernibly different from those of the small one. A certain defensiveness arises from a feeling of necessity to protect, safeguard, even conceal one's ultimate meaning. Even if a writer is merely complying with a request from his superior, his superior's superior may constitute an unknown threat. As the potential for disagreement ("nonconcurrence" it is sometimes called) arises from the factor of multiplicity, so does the reluctance to commit one's self in writing.

Noncommittal writing is engendered in the situation that is fraught with numerous unknowns. In a major business entity, such unknowns range from the expanding number of readers for any one document to diversity of technical matters; from uncertainty as to timing for a touchy message to choice of media whereby to transmit it. It is in the large organization that the mainstream of functional writing is flowing today. Big business depends more and more upon writing as information proliferates. The Chrysler Corporation reported that it handled one million papers on an average day, and that was several years ago.[3] The dimensions of such an organization, extended as they are upward, downward, and across, crisscross a memo writer with uncertainties. The copy machine increases his exposure. Who knows now how many will see, scan, and scrutinize any one document? Each recipient adds to the reading a different set of expectations. The very nature of the managerial matrix causes divergences in need and expectation, all of which jeopardize the writer's hope of concurrence.

The game often is to veil the purport, blur the point, delay the impact. As former Secretary of Labor Willard W. Wirtz commented in his final annual report before leaving office, "The purpose is less to say what is right than to avoid saying anything wrong."[4] Vague writing can become a habit and a technique, conscious or unconscious. Cliches are a royal road to noncommunication, long traveled by political campaigners and public servants. It is a question as to whether big business has to emulate the ambiguities of expression so much criticized in government. Both worlds face the same situational influences; size, turnover, decentralization, diversity. Just as the techniques of being clear (like short sentences, apt wording, and individual adaptation) can be acquired, so too can contrary ways. "He [the writer] says the least that is required, burying it for protection in as much verbiage as the traffic will bear," the Secretary of Labor continued. "Most sentences are long. Three or four ideas are loaded in to increase the odds that one will be impressive and that if another is wrong it will get lost. Paragraphs are built like sandwiches, the meat in the middle."[5]

When the sender does not know the receiver(s), let alone his predispositions, the communicator may resist pinning himself to one and only one clearcut meaning. To give a concrete example in explaining a topic (and Hayakawa says that one way to define is to give an example) is certainly to clarify, but also to open up another possibility: the writer wonders if his example will be construed as unfairly chosen and nonrepresentative.[6] The instinct is to leave a way out, not to define or illustrate, and to stay away from personal involvement. The passive voice, loosely woven sentences, abstract terminology are other means to such an end. For instance: "Requirement computation when engineering estimates are used would be based on the development of demands that have been forecasted." This writer—working within an organizational maze—took refuge behind a semantic barricade, choosing words that were low-key, intangible, conditional, abstract, dehumanized. Why did he not say, instead: "To compute the requirements with engineering estimates involves forecasting demands." Or, the facts permitting, why not: "To compute the requirements with engineering estimates we must forecast demands."

Creeping impersonality leads the writer down the path of stilted, stereotyped wording. Instead of saying, for example, "The production schedule I'm enclosing is to guide you," the statement in question originally read: "Attached is the production schedule for guidance purposes." The tone produced under the circumstances was the tone of anonymity. Hesitancy over use of the first person pronoun is very common, rightly or wrongly. Of course, the corporate authority often does require the third-person approach, but "I" and "we" are not in themselves "bad" words. They are much more communicative (unless over-emphasized) than the formal, old-fashioned reference to "the writer" or "the undersigned."

Besides shying away from the first person, the big-organization man, wisely or unwisely but certainly less communicatively, strips his style of interpretive phrases, denies himself subjective comments, avoids untried expressions in addressing himself to his faceless audience. One analyst in a large firm explained an obscure passage in what he had written on the grounds that he was using "hedging terms" to try to insure accuracy in a nonprecise field. When fishing unknown waters, safety inevitably comes first.

What price brevity?

Sheer length and volume are in themselves devices to enshroud meaning and deflect comprehension, as in this excerpt: "A reduction in uncertainty is conducive to innovation in the event that it gives the businessman an incremental degree of confidence in planning a program for marketing purposes." The sentence might be revised this way to cut the wording in half: "Confidence promotes innovation if it encourages the businessman to plan a marketing program."

Correlated with the businessman's expressed preference for concise presentations (meaning brief yet complete) are his objections to what he has to read as being "too long," "too verbose," and "too numerous." A communication that looks voluminous has an initial disadvantage, time being the coin of management either in public or private enterprise.

When each incoming piece of mail is longer than necessary, the overall volume is all the greater. To quote the Department of Labor report: "Primary reliance on *written* instructions and reports produces a flow of paper which almost defies identification of what is important (encouraging the tendency to disregard all of it). . . ."[7]

Why, when content is capable of reduction and compression, does the manager-writer forego the professed objective of being brief? The man at the top complains that more and more of his working life is spent skimming, reading, and referring. In both business and government some top executives, driven to desperation by "input overload," have set quotas, department by department, on the number of reports. In other offices, including banks, brokerage houses, and the stock market, "business hours" are being curtailed to permit the staff to keep up with the paperwork. Such measures are like trying to hold the lid shut by sitting on it. Real control lies only in the hands of the communicator himself, at the source.

In one of the country's major manufacturing organizations, 127 young management men who had enrolled in training seminars were asked to check in advance whether they thought the amount of writing done in the company was "about right," "too much," "too little." Although 76 said it was about right, the disproportion between the remainder—all who were critical one way or the other—proved striking: whereas only 9 said there was too little, 42 said there was too much.

Notwithstanding the varied facilities now becoming available for other means of communication, the output of paper continues to mount. A conference call by telephone, initiated as a means to quick, conjoint interchange of information or to expeditious arrival at a decision, often results in one or more confirming memos. The oral presentation designed with flip charts and slides is found to require a script or a summary by way of a "handout." The company jet, available for face-to-face visits when a meeting or interview seems indicated, carries its own dictating equipment for preparatory notes or record-making. The communicator seeks to protect himself by building a permanent record. The more alternatives that open up in the communication process, the more writing seems to be required (in another version of Parkinson's Law) for back-up purposes. Again, the point is not what the goal should be but what the actuality is.

To reduce the volume of writing means to reduce the volume of reading—a two-way advantage. As new and varied media develop, writing should be reserved for those situations which it can uniquely serve. No longer is it the quickest medium and it never was the easiest. There begins to be evidence that use of closed-circuit television in industrial processes, as one example, is taking some of the burden off the overworked and costly "procedure" manual. In advocating that the Department of Labor cut its prose in half, the then Secretary had his own suggestion: "With all of their disadvantages, carefully planned meetings (small enough to encourage dialogue) are better."[8]

When the communicator does have to make his message a matter of record, why does he forego the apparent and acknowledged and much sought-after advantage of brevity? He may feel it is impolitic to reveal the gist of his message without enmeshing it in quantities of data, counterarguments, and options. The act of selectivity entails judgmental values that may subject the author to rebuttal. Length in itself not only puts off a reader but slows up his recognition of the real point. If such is the writer's desire, he will be denied its fulfillment if compelled to prepare a synopsis, as is becoming the practice more and more. A one-page summary does much to force a writer's hand. When a message is sophisticated in content and import, one page is more difficult than two or three or four. The long memo or the long letter is often easier to prepare than a short one, hard as it is on the reader. As Mme. de Stael said in a postscript to one of her family letters about French court life: "Pardon, my dear daughter, for such a long letter. I did not have time to write you a short one."

The assumption underlying defensive *driving* is that the other driver is going to do the wrong thing; similarly, the caution-conscious writer assumes that his reader is going to get a wrong idea if given the least chance to do so. When a report conceals rather than reveals by the sheer number of lines or pages, defensive writing is the reason. The fear is that brevity may invite quick, contrary reaction and consequently fail. Whenever it succeeds, it certainly comes about from a writer's confidence in his grasp of the situation as well as from his skill in style and his dexterity in organization.

What price directness?

The goal of manager-writers, as determined from their own statements, is directness, otherwise expressed as "coming to the point." What managers mean by directness they also make evident in the criticisms they cite such as: "rambling," "purpose not apparent," "lack of organization," "failure to focus," "not straightforward," "inconclusiveness."

The deductive method of presentation requires stating at the outset the key point, whether it is the answer to a question, the nub of a proposal, the announcement of a decision, the solution to a problem, or a recommendation itself.

One reason—or rationalization—for indirectness in the way management men organize the sequence may lie in the sensitive nature of what they have to put in writing. The easy, favorable, matter-of-course messages are apt to be transmitted orally—a quick phone call or brief conversation sufficing to give concurrence or to convey good news. The written word often falls heir to more negative subjects. When an announcement impends involving such matters as jurisdiction, funding, or promotions the time comes to go on record. Such a message is committed to paper over the signature of someone high enough on the ladder to make it official. If an assistant is given the task of drafting, the signer himself is sure to go over the page with a fine-tooth comb. Re-writes become numerous, often reducing the immediacy, specificity, and thrust of the communication. Before the reader is allowed to get to the real point, he is slowed up and put through the hoops of exposition.

One still-young but rising member of the marketing staff of a large organization said, in explaining the roundaboutness of a particular memo, "You know, our company is blame prone. We're all busy protecting our backsides. This makes it dangerous to say what you really mean before you've built your case in minute detail." One sentence which he wrote gives the clue: "The purpose of this report is to present the facts which indicate that, from a tax viewpoint, the proposed retirement of Plant A should be given serious consideration and that, in the absence of definite problems in other areas, it be recommended that Plant B increase its capacity in accordance with resultant conditions." If he wished to recommend that Plant B do the work of both A and B, he was not direct in saying so.

Paper communication is customarily called a means of security in managerial operations. A message that is put in writing does become permanent, should become precise, and can be pinpointed for a particular purpose. Writing, theoretically, should be a source of security. Putting one's self on paper is, in reality, regarded as a source of insecurity by many working within large, far-flung, fluid organizations. Robert Graves, the past master of language usage in Britain, explained his criticism on this point: "A fear of feeling definitely committed to any statement that might cause trouble or inconvenience seems to haunt almost everyone."[9]

When forced to resolve a difficult issue on paper, naturally the writer may handle the matter gingerly and transfuse it with a flow of facts, thereby postponing the crucial point. Indirection is sometimes a psychological inevitability; it may even be the better part of valor. When resistance to a message has to be anticipated, induction may be the means to the end in view. But let there be no doubt: the result is a far cry from the highly touted quality of directness. As the late Mike Todd used to say to persons asking him for donations: "How do you want your 'No'? Fast or slow?" There is a time and place for "slowness" in communicating.

What is the reason for this contrariety of the expressed desire for directness and the practice of indirectness? ". . . nobody can be quite sure how things will turn out," said Graves, "and nobody wishes to commit himself."[10] The greater the distance between sender and receiver, whether in point of view, geography, cultural patterns, or level, the greater the hesitancy and holding back. The need for induction springs from a wish to explain at length before getting to the "crunch," to use a favorite word of Sir Winston Churchill's.

Conclusion

What the reader wants and what the writer is willing to deliver may differ. The explanation of the difference lies in the situational relationship of the two parties. Organizational size, sensitivities, distance, the very nature of the message itself, tend to diminish clarity, conciseness, and directness. Defensive writing is a reality in the working world, whether or not it fulfills the generally proclaimed ideals for style and sequence.

Safety first is not a rule easily reconciled with avowed goals of functional English. The symptoms of defensive writing need first to be recognized for what they are and, so far as the situation permits, counteracted. These symptoms look to the reader like vagueness, verbosity, and circumvention. Pressures of time and situation, however, work against fulfillment of the objectives of clarity, brevity, and directness. The reader, bored by repetitive, hackneyed lengthy, circuitous phraseology may let his eye continue to travel across the page long after his mind has, in self-protection, turned off and tuned out. Excessive caution, to say nothing of patent obfuscation, breeds impatience.

The truly communicative writer must be aware of his necessary purposes. He must recognize that writing is the medium now being used for the more difficult messages. To be successful the communicator needs all the technical control of language he can acquire to keep out less conscious motivations and to achieve whatever his purpose in writing may be.

References

1. Robert Graves and Alan Hodge, *The Reader Over Your Shoulder* (London, 1947), p. 38.
2. American Institute of CPA's, *Auditing Standards and Procedures* (New York, 1963), p. 68.
3. *The New York Times* (November 17, 1963).
4. The Secretary of Labor, *Fifty-Sixth Annual Report* (January 16, 1969, Washington, D.C.), p. 15.
5. *Ibid.,* p. 15.
6. S. I. Hayakawa, *Language in Thought and Action* (New York, 1949), p. 173.
7. The Secretary of Labor, p. 13.
8. *Ibid.,* p. 13.
9. Graves and Hodge, p. 29.
10. *Ibid.,* p. 48.

How to write potent copy

DAVID OGILVY

After the founding of Ogilvy, Benson and Mather
in 1948, David Ogilvy went on to become one of
the leading figures in American advertising.

1. Headlines

The headline is the most important element in most advertisements. It is the telegram which decides the reader whether to read the copy.

On the average, five times as many people read the headline as read the body copy. When you have written your headline, you have spent eighty cents out of your dollar.

If you haven't done some selling in your headline, you have wasted 80 per cent of your client's money. The wickedest of all sins is to run an advertisement *without* a headline. Such headless wonders are still to be found; I don't envy the copywriter who submits one to me.

A change of headline can make a difference of ten to one in sales. I never write fewer than sixteen headlines for a single advertisement, and I observe certain guides in writing them:

1. The headline is the "ticket on the meat." Use it to flag down the readers who are prospects for the kind of product you are advertising. If you are selling a remedy for bladder weakness, display the words BLADDER WEAKNESS in your headline; they catch the eye of everyone who suffers from this inconvenience. If you want *mothers* to read your advertisement, display MOTHERS in your headline. And so on.

Conversely, do not say anything in your headline which is likely to *exclude* any readers who might be prospects for your product. Thus, if you are advertising a product which can be used equally well by men and

"How to Write Potent Copy" from *Confessions of an Advertising Man* by David Ogilvy. Copyright © 1963 by David Ogilvy Trustee. Used by permission of Atheneum Publishers.

women, don't slant your headline at women alone; it would frighten men away.

2. Every headline should appeal to the reader's *self-interest.* It should promise her a benefit, as in my headline for Helena Rubinstein's Hormone Cream: HOW WOMEN OVER 35 CAN LOOK YOUNGER.

3. Always try to inject *news* into your headlines, because the consumer is always on the lookout for new products, or new ways to use an old product, or new improvements in an old product.

The two most powerful words you can use in a headline are FREE and NEW. You can seldom use FREE, but you can almost always use NEW—if you try hard enough.

4. Other words and phrases which work wonders are HOW TO, SUDDENLY, NOW, ANNOUNCING, INTRODUCING, IT'S HERE, JUST ARRIVED, IMPORTANT DEVELOPMENT, IMPROVEMENT, AMAZING, SENSATIONAL, REMARKABLE, REVOLUTIONARY, STARTLING, MIRACLE, MAGIC, OFFER, QUICK, EASY, WANTED, CHALLENGE, ADVICE TO, THE TRUTH ABOUT, COMPARE, BARGAIN, HURRY, LAST CHANCE.

Don't turn up your nose at these clichés. They may be shopworn, but they work. That is why you see them turn up so often in the headlines of mail-order advertisers and others who can measure the results of their advertisements.

Headlines can be strengthened by the inclusion of *emotional* words, like DARLING, LOVE, FEAR, PROUD, FRIEND, and BABY. One of the most provocative advertisements which has come out of our agency showed a girl in a bathtub, talking to her lover on the telephone. The headline: *Darling, I'm having the most extraordinary experience . . . I'm head over heels in DOVE.*

5. Five times as many people read the headline as read the body copy, so it is important that these glancers should at least be told what brand is being advertised. That is why you should always include the brand name in your headlines.

6. Include your selling promise in your headline. This requires long headlines. When the New York University School of Retailing ran headline tests with the cooperation of a big department store, they found that headlines of ten words or longer, containing news and information, consistently sold more merchandise than short headlines.

Headlines containing six to twelve words pull more coupon returns than short headlines, and there is no significant difference between the readership of twelve-word headlines and the readership of three-word headlines. The best headline I ever wrote contained *eighteen* words: *At Sixty Miles an Hour the Loudest Noise in the New Rolls-Royce comes from the electric clock.**

---

* When the chief engineer at the Rolls-Royce factory read this, he shook his head sadly and said, "It is time we did something about that damned clock."

7. People are more likely to read your body copy if your headline arouses their curiosity; so you should end your headline with a lure to read on.

8. Some copywriters write *tricky* headlines—puns, literary allusions, and other obscurities. This is a sin.

In the average newspaper your headline has to compete for attention with 350 others. Research has shown that readers travel so fast through this jungle that they don't stop to decipher the meaning of obscure headlines. Your headline must *telegraph* what you want to say, and it must telegraph it in plain language. Don't play games with the reader.

In 1960 the *Times Literary Supplement* attacked the whimsical tradition in British advertising, calling it "self-indulgent—a kind of middle-class private joke, apparently designed to amuse the advertiser and his client." Amen.

9. Research shows that it is dangerous to use *negatives* in headlines. If, for example, you write OUR SALT CONTAINS NO ARSENIC, many readers will miss the negative and go away with the impression that you wrote OUR SALT CONTAINS ARSENIC.

10. Avoid *blind* headlines—the kind which mean nothing unless you read the body copy underneath them; most people *don't.*

2. Body copy

When you sit down to write your body copy, pretend that you are talking to the woman on your right at a dinner party. She has asked you, "I am thinking of buying a new car. Which would you recommend?" Write your copy as if you were answering that question.

1. Don't beat about the bush—go straight to the point. Avoid analogies of the "just as, so too" variety. Dr. Gallup has demonstrated that these two-stage arguments are generally misunderstood.

2. Avoid superlatives, generalizations, and platitudes. Be specific and factual. Be enthusiastic, friendly, and memorable. Don't be a bore. Tell the truth, but make the truth fascinating.

How long should your copy be? It depends on the product. If you are advertising chewing gum, there isn't much to tell, so make your copy short. If, on the other hand, you are advertising a product which has a great many different qualities to recommend it, write long copy: the more you tell, the more you sell.

There is a universal belief in lay circles that people won't read long copy. Nothing could be farther from the truth. Claude Hopkins once wrote five pages of solid text for Schlitz beer. In a few months, Schlitz moved up from fifth place to first. I once wrote a page of solid text for Good Luck Margarine, with most gratifying results.

Research shows that readership falls off rapidly up to fifty words of copy, but drops very little between fifty and 500 words. In my first Rolls-Royce advertisement I used 719 words—piling one fascinating fact on another. In the last paragraph I wrote, "People who feel diffident about driving a Rolls-Royce can buy a Bentley." Judging from the number of motorists who picked up the word "diffident" and bandied it about, I concluded that the advertisement was thoroughly read. In the next one I used 1400 words.

Every advertisement should be a *complete* sales pitch for your product. It is unrealistic to assume that consumers will read a *series* of advertisements for the same product. You should shoot the works in every advertisement, on the assumption that it is the only chance you will ever have to sell your product to the reader—*now or never.*

Says Dr. Charles Edwards of the graduate School of Retailing at New York University, "The more facts you tell, the more you sell. An advertisement's chance for success invariably increases as the number of pertinent merchandise facts included in the advertisement increases."

In my first advertisement for Puerto Rico's Operation Bootstrap, I used 961 words, and persuaded Beardsley Ruml to sign them. Fourteen thousand readers clipped the coupon from this advertisement, and scores of them later established factories in Puerto Rico. The greatest professional satisfaction I have yet had is to see the prosperity in Puerto Rican communities which had lived on the edge of starvation for four hundred years before I wrote my advertisement. If I had confined myself to a few vacuous generalities, nothing would have happened.

We have even been able to get people to read long copy about gasoline. One of our Shell advertisements contained 617 words, and 22 per cent of male readers read more than half of them.

Vic Schwab tells the story of Max Hart (of Hart, Schaffner & Marx) and his advertising manager, George L. Dyer, arguing about long copy. Dyer said, "I'll bet you ten dollars I can write a newspaper page of solid type and you'd read every word of it."

Hart scoffed at the idea. "I don't have to write a line of it to prove my point," Dyer replied. "I'll only tell you the headline: THIS PAGE IS ALL ABOUT MAX HART."

Advertisers who put coupons in their advertisements *know* that short copy doesn't sell. In split-run tests, long copy invariably outsells short copy.

Do I hear someone say that no copywriter can write long advertisements unless his media department gives him big spaces to work with? This question should not arise, because the copywriter should be consulted before planning the media schedule.

3. You should always include testimonials in your copy. The reader finds it easier to believe the endorsement of a fellow consumer than the puffery of an anonymous copywriter. Says Jim Young, one of the best copywriters alive today, "Every type of advertiser has the same problem; namely to be believed. The mail-order man knows nothing so potent for this purpose as the testimonial, yet the general advertiser seldom uses it."

Testimonials from celebrities get remarkably high readership, and if they are honestly written they still do not seem to provoke incredulity. The better known the celebrity, the more readers you will attract. We have featured Queen Elizabeth and Winston Churchill in "Come to Britain" advertisements, and we were able to persuade Mrs. Roosevelt to make television commercials for Good Luck Margarine. When we advertised charge accounts for Sears, Roebuck, we reproduced the credit card of Ted Williams, "recently traded by Boston to Sears."

Sometimes you can cast your entire copy in the form of a testimonial. My first advertisement for Austin cars took the form of a letter from an "anonymous diplomat" who was sending his son to Groton with money he had saved driving an Austin—a well-aimed combination of snobbery and economy. Alas, a perspicacious *Time* editor guessed that I was the anonymous diplomat, and asked the headmaster of Groton to comment. Dr. Crocker was so cross that I decided to send my son to Hotchkiss.

4. Another profitable gambit is to give the reader helpful advice, or service. It hooks about 75 per cent more readers than copy which deals entirely with the product.

One of our Rinso advertisements told housewives how to remove stains. It was better read (Starch) and better remembered (Gallup) than any detergent advertisement in history. Unfortunately, however, it forgot to feature Rinso's main selling promise—that Rinso washes whiter; for this reason it should never have run.*

5. I have never admired the *belles lettres* school of advertising, which reached its pompous peak in Theodore F. MacMann's famous advertisement for Cadillac, "The Penalty of Leadership," and Ned Jordan's classic, "Somewhere West of Laramie." Forty years ago the business community seems to have been impressed by these pieces of purple prose, but I have always thought them absurd; they did not give the reader a single *fact*. I share Claude Hopkins' view that "fine writing is a distinct disadvantage. So is unique literary style. They take attention away from the subject."

6. Avoid bombast. Raymond Rubicam's famous slogan for Squibb, "The priceless ingredient of every product is the honor and integrity of its maker," reminds me of my father's advice: when a company boasts about its integrity, or a woman about her virtue, avoid the former and cultivate the latter.

---

* The photograph showed several different kinds of stain—lipstick, coffee, shoe-polish, blood and so forth. The blood was my own; I am the only copywriter who has ever *bled* for his client.

7. Unless you have some special reason to be solemn and pretentious, write your copy in the colloquial language which your customers use in everyday conversation. I have never acquired a sufficiently good ear for vernacular American to write it, but I admire copywriters who can pull it off, as in this unpublished pearl from a dairy farmer:

> Carnation Milk is the best in the land,
> Here I sit with a can in my hand.
> No tits to pull, no hay to pitch,
> Just punch a hole in the son-of-a-bitch.

It is a mistake to use highfalutin language when you advertise to uneducated people. I once used the word OBSOLETE in a headline, only to discover that 43 per cent of housewives had no idea what it meant. In another headline, I used the word INEFFABLE, only to discover that I didn't know what it meant myself.

However, many copywriters of my vintage err on the side of underestimating the educational level of the population. Philip Hauser, head of the Sociology Department at the University of Chicago, draws attention to the changes which are taking place:

> The increasing exposure of the population to formal schooling . . .
> can be expected to effect important changes in . . . the style of advertising. . . . Messages aimed at the "average" American on the assumption
> that he has had less than a grade school education are likely to find
> themselves with a declining or disappearing clientele.*

Meanwhile, all copywriters should read Dr. Rudolph Flesch's *Art of Plain Talk.* It will persuade them to use short words, short sentences, short paragraphs, and highly *personal* copy.

Aldous Huxley, who once tried his hand at writing advertisements, concluded that "any trace of literariness in an advertisement is fatal to its success. Advertisement writers may not be lyrical, or obscure, or in any way esoteric. They must be universally intelligible. A good advertisement has this in common with drama and oratory, that it must be immediately comprehensible and directly moving."†

8. Resist the temptation to write the kind of copy which wins awards. I am always gratified when I win an award, but most of the campaigns which produce *results* never win awards, because they don't draw attention to themselves.

The juries that bestow awards are never given enough information about the *results* of the advertisements they are called upon to judge. In

* *Scientific American* (October 1962).

† *Essays Old And New* (Harper & Brothers, 1927). Charles Lamb and Byron also wrote advertisements. So did Bernard Shaw, Hemingway, Marquand, Sherwood Anderson, and Faulkner—none of them with any degree of success.

the absence of such information, they rely on their opinions, which are always warped toward the highbrow.

9. Good copywriters have always resisted the temptation to *entertain*. Their achievement lies in the number of new products they get off to a flying start. In a class by himself stands Claude Hopkins, who is to advertising what Escoffier is to cooking. By today's standards, Hopkins was an unscrupulous barbarian, but technically he was the supreme master. Next I would place Raymond Rubicam, George Cecil, and James Webb Young, all of whom lacked Hopkins' ruthless salesmanship, but made up for it by their honesty, by the broader range of their work, and by their ability to write civilized copy when the occasion required it. Next I would place John Caples, the mail-order specialist from whom I have learned much.

These giants wrote their advertisements for newspapers and magazines. It is still too early to identify the best writers for television.

The problem
of jargon

Gobbledygook

STUART CHASE

Stuart Chase worked for many years as a consultant to various government agencies; his other books include *The Tyranny of Words* (1938) and *Democracy Under Pressure* (1945).

Said Franklin Roosevelt, in one of his early presidential speeches: "I see one-third of a nation ill-housed, ill-clad, ill-nourished." Translated into standard bureaucratic prose his statement would read:

> It is evident that a substantial number of persons within the Continental boundaries of the United States have inadequate financial resources with which to purchase the products of agricultural communities and industrial establishments. It would appear that for a considerable segment of the population, possibly as much as 33.3333* of the total, there are inadequate housing facilities, and an equally significant proportion is deprived of the proper types of clothing and nutriment.
>
> * Not carried beyond four places.

This rousing satire on gobbledygook—or talk among the bureaucrats—is adapted from a report[1] prepared by the Federal Security Agency in an attempt to break out of the verbal squirrel cage. "Gobbledygook" was coined by an exasperated Congressman, Maury Maverick of Texas, and means using two, or three, or ten words in the place of one, or using a five-syllable word where a single syllable would suffice. Maverick was censuring the forbidding prose of executive departments in Washington, but the term has now spread to windy and pretentious language in general.

"Gobbledygook" itself is a good example of the way a language grows. There was no word for the event before Maverick's invention; one had to say:

[1] This and succeeding quotations from F.S.A. report by special permission of the author, Milton Hall.

From *Power of Words*, copyright 1953, 1954 by Stuart Chase. Reprinted by permission of Harcourt Brace Jovanovich, Inc.

"You know, that terrible, involved, polysyllabic language those government people use down in Washington." Now one word takes the place of a dozen.

A British member of Parliament, A. P. Herbert, also exasperated with bureaucratic jargon, translated Nelson's immortal phrase, "England expects every man to do his duty":

> England anticipates that, as regards the current emergency, person-nel will face up to the issues, and exercise appropriately the functions allocated to their respective occupational groups.

A New Zealand official made the following report after surveying a plot of ground for an athletic field:[2]

> It is obvious from the difference in elevation with relation to the short depth of the property that the contour is such as to preclude any reasonable developmental potential for active recreation.

Seems the plot was too steep.

An office manager sent this memo to his chief:

> Verbal contact with Mr. Blank regarding the attached notification of promotion has elicited the attached representation intimating that he prefers to decline the assignment.

Seems Mr. Blank didn't want the job.

> A doctor testified at an English trial that one of the parties was suffering from "circumorbital haematoma."

Seems the party had a black eye.

> In August 1952 the U.S. Department of Agriculture put out a pam-phlet entitled: "Cultural and Pathogenic Variability in Single-Condial and Hyphaltip Isolates of Hemlin-Thosporium Turcicum Pass."

Seems it was about corn leaf disease.

On reaching the top of the Finsteraarhorn in 1845, M. Dollfus-Ausset, when he got his breath, exclaimed:

> The soul communes in the infinite with those icy peaks which seem to have their roots in the bowels of eternity.

Seems he enjoyed the view.

A government department announced:

> Voucherable expenditures necessary to provide adequate dental treatment required as adjunct to medical treatment being rendered a pay

---

[2] This item and the next two are from the piece on gobbledygook by W. E. Farbstein, New York *Times*, March 29, 1953.

patient in in-patient status may be incurred as required at the expense of the Public Health Service.

Seems you can charge your dentist bill to the Public Health Service. Or can you?

Legal talk

Gobbledygook not only flourishes in government bureaus but grows wild and lush in the law, the universities, and sometimes among the literati. Mr. Micawber was a master of gobbledygook, which he hoped would improve his fortunes. It is almost always found in offices too big for face-to-face talk. Gobbledygook can be defined as squandering words, packing a message with excess baggage and so introducing semantic "noise." Or it can be scrambling words in a message so that meaning does not come through. The directions on cans, bottles, and packages for putting the contents to use are often a good illustration. Gobbledygook must not be confused with double talk, however, for the intentions of the sender are usually honest.

I offer you a round fruit and say, "Have an orange." Not so an expert in legal phraseology, as parodied by editors of *Labor:*

> I hereby give and convey to you, all and singular, my estate and interests, right, title, claim and advantages of and in said orange, together with all rind, juice, pulp and pits, and all rights and advantages therein . . . anything hereinbefore or hereinafter or in any other deed or deeds, instrument or instruments of whatever nature or kind whatsoever, to the contrary, in any wise, notwithstanding.

The state of Ohio, after five years of work, has redrafted its legal code in modern English, eliminating 4,500 sections and doubtless a blizzard of "whereases" and "hereinafters." Legal terms of necessity must be closely tied to their referents, but the early solons tried to do this the hard way, by adding synonyms. They hoped to trap the physical event in a net of words, but instead they created a mumbo-jumbo beyond the power of the layman, and even many a lawyer, to translate. Legal talk is studded with tautologies, such as "cease and desist," "give and convey," "irrelevant, incompetent, and immaterial." Furthermore, legal jargon is a dead language; it is not spoken and it is not growing. An official of one of the big insurance companies calls their branch of it "bafflegab." Here is a sample from his collection:[3]

> One-half to his mother, if living, if not to his father, and one-half to his mother-in-law, if living, if not to his mother, if living, if not to his father. Thereafter payment is to be made in a single sum to his brothers. On the one-half payable to his mother, if living, if not to his father, he

[3] Interview with Clifford B. Reeves by Sylvia F. Porter, New York *Evening Post,* March 14, 1952.

does not bring in his mother-in-law as the next payee to receive, although on the one-half to his mother-in-law, he does bring in the mother or father.

You apply for an insurance policy, pass the tests, and instead of a straightforward "here is your policy," you receive something like this:

> This policy is issued in consideration of the application therefor, copy of which application is attached hereto and made part hereof, and of the payment for said insurance on the life of the above-named insured.

Academic talk

The pedagogues may be less repetitious than the lawyers, but many use even longer words. It is a symbol of their calling to prefer Greek and Latin derivatives to Anglo-Saxon. Thus instead of saying: "I like short clear words," many a professor would think it more seemly to say: "I prefer an abbreviated phraseology, distinguished for its lucidity." Your professor is sometimes right, the longer word may carry the meaning better—but not because it is long. Allen Upward in his book *The New Word* warmly advocates Anglo-Saxon English as against what he calls "Mediterranean" English, with its polysyllables built up like a skyscraper.

Professional pedagogy, still alternating between the Middle Ages and modern science, can produce what Henshaw Ward once called the most repellent prose known to man. It takes an iron will to read as much as a page of it. Here is a sample of what is known in some quarters as "pedageese":

> Realization has grown that the curriculum or the experiences of learners change and improve only as those who are most directly involved examine their goals, improve their understandings and increase their skill in performing the tasks necessary to reach newly defined goals. This places the focus upon teacher, lay citizen and learner as partners in curricular improvement and as the individuals who must change, if there is to be curriculum change.

I think there is an idea concealed here somewhere. I think it means: "If we are going to change the curriculum, teacher, parent, and student must all help." The reader is invited to get out his semantic decoder and check on my translation. Observe there is no technical language in this gem of pedageese, beyond possibly the word "curriculum." It is just a simple idea heavily oververbalized.

In another kind of academic talk the author may display his learning to conceal a lack of ideas. A bright instructor, for instance, in need of prestige may select a common sense proposition for the subject of a learned monograph—say, "Modern cities are hard to live in" and adorn it with imposing

polysyllables: "Urban existence in the perpendicular declivities of megalopolis
. . ." et cetera. He coins some new terms to transfix the reader—"mega-
decibel" or "strato-cosmopolis"—and works them vigorously. He is careful to
add a page or two of differential equations to show the "scatter." And then he
publishes, with 147 footnotes and a bibliography to knock your eye out. If the
authorities are dozing, it can be worth an associate professorship.

While we are on the campus, however, we must not forget that the technical language of the natural sciences and some terms in the social sciences,
forbidding as they may sound to the layman, are quite necessary. Without
them, specialists could not communicate what they find. Trouble arises when
experts expect the uninitiated to understand the words; when they tell the
jury, for instance, that the defendant is suffering from "circumorbital haema-
toma."

Here are two authentic quotations. Which was written by a distinguished
modern author, and which by a patient in a mental hospital? You will find the
answer at the end of the chapter.

> 1. Have just been to supper. Did not knowing what the woodchuck
> sent me here. How when the blue blue blue on the said anyone can do
> it that tries. Such is the presidential candidate.
> 2. No history of a family to close with those and close. Never shall
> he be alone to be alone to be alone to be alone to be alone to lend a
> hand and leave it left and wasted.

Reducing the gobble

As government and business offices grow larger, the need for doing something
about gobbledygook increases. Fortunately the biggest office in the world is
working hard to reduce it. The Federal Security Agency in Washington,[4] with
nearly 100 million clients on its books, began analyzing its communication
lines some years ago, with gratifying results. Surveys find trouble in three
main areas: correspondence with clients about their social security problems,
office memos, official reports.

Clarity and brevity, as well as common humanity, are urgently needed in
this vast establishment which deals with disability, old age, and unemployment. The surveys found instead many cases of long-windedness, foggy
meanings, clichés, and singsong phrases, and gross neglect of the reader's
point of view. Rather than talking to a real person, the writer was talking to
himself. "We often write like a man walking on stilts."

Here is a typical case of long-windedness:

> *Gobbledygook as found:* "We are wondering if sufficient time has
> passed so that you are in a position to indicate whether favorable action

---

[4] Now the Department of Health, Education, and Welfare.

may now be taken on our recommendation for the reclassification of Mrs. Blank, junior clerk-stenographer, CAF 2, to assistant clerk-stenographer, CAF 3?"

Suggested improvement: "Have you yet been able to act on our recommendation to reclassify Mrs. Blank?"

Another case:

Although the Central Efficiency Rating Committee recognizes that there are many desirable changes that could be made in the present efficiency rating system in order to make it more realistic and more workable than it now is, this committee is of the opinion that no further change should be made in the present system during the current year. Because of conditions prevailing throughout the country and the resultant turnover in personnel, and difficulty in administering the Federal programs, further mechanical improvement in the present rating system would require staff retraining and other administrative expense which would seem best withheld until the official termination of hostilities, and until restoration of regular operations.

The F.S.A. invites us to squeeze the gobbledygook out of this statement. Here is my attempt:

The Central Efficiency Rating Committee recognizes that desirable changes could be made in the present system. We believe, however, that no change should be attempted until the war is over.

This cuts the statement from 111 to 30 words, about one-quarter of the original, but perhaps the reader can do still better. What of importance have I left out?

Sometimes in a book which I am reading for information—not for literary pleasure—I run a pencil through the surplus words. Often I can cut a section to half its length with an improvement in clarity. Magazines like *The Reader's Digest* have reduced this process to an art. Are long-windedness and obscurity a cultural lag from the days when writing was reserved for priests and cloistered scholars? The more words and the deeper the mystery, the greater their prestige and the firmer the hold on their jobs. And the better the candidate's chance today to have his doctoral thesis accepted.

The F.S.A. surveys found that a great deal of writing was obscure although not necessarily prolix. Here is a letter sent to more than 100,000 inquirers, a classic example of murky prose. To clarify it, one needs to *add* words, not cut them:

In order to be fully insured, an individual must have earned $50 or more in covered employment for as many quarters of coverage as half the calendar quarters elapsing between 1936 and the quarter in which he reaches age 65 or dies, whichever first occurs.

Probably no one without the technical jargon of the office could translate this: nevertheless, it was sent out to drive clients mad for seven years. One poor

fellow wrote back: "I am no longer in covered employment. I have an outside
job now."

Many words and phrases in officialese seem to come out automatically, as
if from lower centers of the brain. In this standardized prose people never *get
jobs,* they "secure employment"; *before* and *after* become "prior to" and "subsequent to"; one does not *do,* one "performs"; nobody *knows* a thing, he is
"fully cognizant"; one never *says,* he "indicates." A great favorite at present is
"implement."

Some charming boners occur in this talking-in-one's-sleep. For instance:

> The problem of extending coverage to all employees, regardless of
> size, is not as simple as surface appearances indicate.
> Though the proportions of all males and females in ages 16–45 are
> essentially the same . . .
> Dairy cattle, usually and commonly embraced in dairying . . .

In its manual to employees, the F.S.A. suggests the following:

INSTEAD OF	USE
give consideration to	consider
make inquiry regarding	inquire
is of the opinion	believes
comes into conflict with	conflicts
information which is of a	confidential information
confidential nature	

Professional or office gobbledygook often arises from using the passive
rather than the active voice. Instead of looking you in the eye, as it were, and
writing "This act requires . . ." the office worker looks out of the window and
writes: "It is required by this statute that . . ." When the bureau chief says,
"We expect Congress to cut your budget," the message is only too clear; but
usually he says, "It is expected that the departmental budget estimates will be
reduced by Congress."

GOBBLED: "All letters prepared for the signature of the Administrator will be
single spaced."
UNGOBBLED: "Single space all letters for the Administrator." (Thus cutting 13
words to 7.)

Only people can read

The F.S.A. surveys pick up the point . . . that human communication involves
a listener as well as a speaker. Only people can read, though a lot of writing
seems to be addressed to beings in outer space. To whom are you talking? The
sender of the officialese message often forgets the chap on the other end of the
line.

A woman with two small children wrote the F.S.A. asking what she should do about payments, as her husband had lost his memory. "If he never gets able to work," she said, "and stays in an institution would I be able to draw any benefits? . . . I don't know how I am going to live and raise my children since he is disable to work. Please give me some information. . . ."

To this human appeal, she received a shattering blast of gobbledygook, beginning, "State unemployment compensation laws do not provide any benefits for sick or disabled individuals . . . in order to qualify an individual must have a certain number of quarters of coverage . . ." et cetera, et cetera. Certainly if the writer had been thinking about the poor woman he would not have dragged in unessential material about old-age insurance. If he had pictured a mother without means to care for her children, he would have told her where she might get help—from the local office which handles aid to dependent children, for instance.

Gobbledygook of this kind would largely evaporate if we thought of our messages as two way—in the above case, if we pictured ourselves talking on the doorstep of a shabby house to a woman with two children tugging at her skirts, who in her distress does not know which way to turn.

Results of the survey

The F.S.A. survey showed that office documents could be cut 20 to 50 per cent, with an improvement in clarity and a great saving to taxpayers in paper and payrolls.

A handbook was prepared and distributed to key officials.[5] They read it, thought about it, and presently began calling section meetings to discuss gobbledygook. More booklets were ordered, and the local output of documents began to improve. A Correspondence Review Section was established as a kind of laboratory to test murky messages. A supervisor could send up samples for analysis and suggestions. The handbook is now used for training new members; and many employees keep it on their desks along with the dictionary. Outside the Bureau some 25,000 copies have been sold (at 20 cents each) to individuals, governments, business firms, all over the world. It is now used officially in the Veterans Administration and in the Department of Agriculture.

The handbook makes clear the enormous amount of gobbledygook which automatically spreads in any large office, together with ways and means to keep it under control. I would guess that at least half of all the words circulating around the bureaus of the world are "irrelevant, incompetent, and immaterial"—to use a favorite legalism; or are just plain "unnecessary"—to ungobble it.

My favorite story of removing the gobble from gobbledygook concerns the Bureau of Standards at Washington. I have told it before but perhaps the

[5] By Milton Hall.

reader will forgive the repetition. A New York plumber wrote the Bureau that he had found hydrochloric acid fine for cleaning drains, and was it harmless? Washington replied: "The efficacy of hydrochloric acid is indisputable, but the chlorine residue is incompatible with metallic permanence."

The plumber wrote back that he was mighty glad the Bureau agreed with him. The Bureau replied with a note of alarm: "We cannot assume responsibility for the production of toxic and noxious residues with hydrochloric acid, and suggest that you use an alternate procedure." The plumber was happy to learn that the Bureau still agreed with him.

Whereupon Washington exploded: "Don't use hydrochloric acid; it eats hell out of the pipes!"

Note: The second quotation on page 72 comes from Gertrude Stein's *Lucy Church Amiably.*

The answers to jargon

WILLIAM GILMAN

William Gilman was an editor for *Popular Science* and *Product Engineering*.

We are all guilty, more or less, of writing jargon. We are all guilty, too, of complaining about other people's jargon while we tolerate it in our own writing. Sometimes it sneaks past our guard. Other times we drag it in to brandish our knowledge—or hide what we don't know.

With jargon, as with other types of obscurity, we can blame much but not all of the trouble on "big words." Jargon can be ingratiatingly simple. *Metals Progress* magazine offers these examples of the kinds of statements that occur in research reports, and in parentheses explains what they really mean:

> While it has not been possible to provide definite answers to these questions . . . (The experiment didn't work out, but I figured I could at least get a publication out of it.)
>
> Three of the samples were chosen for detailed study . . . (The results on the others didn't make sense and were ignored.)
>
> It is suggested that . . . (I think.)
>
> It is clear that much additional work will be required before a complete understanding . . . (I don't understand it.)
>
> Correct within an order of magnitude . . . (Wrong.)

These are the tactics of fudging, a euphemistic word for dishonesty. But jargon varies—it can also be quite honest. Perhaps the saddest jargon of tongue or pen, and too common in the sciences, is that of the expositor who has meekly followed instructions.

From *The Language of Science* by William Gilman. Reprinted by permission of Curtis Brown, Ltd. © 1961 by William Gilman.

For example, take a long breath and wade through this offering by a magazine:

> He explained that spatial vector electrocardiograph generalizes transfer impedance into a spatial continuum concept where it becomes representable as a spatial vector point function very useful in determining the sequence of the cardiac cycle temporally and spatially. An extension of this theory, involving a multiple loop feedback dipole synthesizer, makes it possible to compute automatically and instantaneously the optimal vectorial point dipole representation of the heart as a current source.

This is hardly friendly, attractive prose. Even banks have learned that it pays to come out of hiding—that big glass windows and open counters bring in customers.

One thing is clear. The writer shied away from trying to translate. He lifted jargon verbatim from a research report. And the scientist himself probably was not confused. He had substituted a rule for common sense—he was dutifully using "precise" words. Quite likely these words were meaningful to him. But they are also an undiluted outpouring of "big words" that would repel even his fellow specialist. The pity of it is that many others—doctors, instrument makers, computer engineers—would probably find this report valuable if the scientist or writer had only let in some fresh air, some synonyms explaining that we have here a three-dimensional heart-tester that will give instantaneous answers when used with a computer.

Another example has much simpler words, but they are dressed in the garb of false humility:

> In 1941 (Vol. 2, pg. 33) reviewer derived a formula for "Y." In reviewing reviewer's article, author (Vol. 2 pg. 138) criticized reviewer's formula on the grounds that it gave infinite "Z." In a later review of reviewer's article . . .

And so on. This does not even have the doubtful virtue of supplying bizarre words for the crossword puzzler. The writer here was obeying a typical technical journal's warnings against the vulgarity of speaking in the first person. Result: a bewildering company of reviewers and authors that a simple "I" and "my" would have sorted out.

One more example, this time at the other extreme—trying to popularize but, in doing so, forsaking common sense. It's a publicity writer's announcement about some new industrial equipment. Jargon gives him a chance to play cutely with words and you, the reader, abruptly find yourself riddling through a panegyric to "low, low switchgear." What have we here? you ask. Might there be some special meanings for *low*? Or is this a salesman screaming bargains? When "low" and "lowest" become overworked by his competitors, he outpromises them with his "low, low prices." If you care to quarry deeper into the announcement, you discover that the first *low* refers to height of this equipment. It won't bump its head against the ceiling. The second *low* refers to low voltage. The equipment won't shock you.

Here, jargon was also standard ambiguity. Ordinarily, however, jargon is not so much the double meaning of two-faced ambiguity as the frustrating no meaning at all. It is the specialty word that, innocently or serving as intentional fog, floors or vexes the nonspecialist; it is the technical or secret vocabulary that slams the door on everybody who isn't a fellow lodge member.

This concealment, where the mission is "revealment," is a costly kind of writing. Everybody who writes has something he wants to tell or sell, and he wants to be read by more, rather than fewer, readers. Remember that even if you are not selling hardware, you are selling your words—you are persuading the reader to read, and to continue reading. Even the fellow lodge member will flee as quickly as possible from the spatial-vector stuff quoted earlier.

Because it is so universal, like sin, jargon will always be with us, certainly in specialized writing. Much of the "dynamic" language of motivation research is jargon—the up-to-the-minute kind. And the "blameless" science, archaeology, speaks of its peaceful digging in the tongues of yesteryear— again, jargon.

How, then, can we curb this costly nuisance? How can we let most of the wind out of our billowing wordage? How, also, can we avoid being forced into a grim choice between jargon and illiteracy, between a usefully broad vocabulary and a primitively simple one? "Basic English" has been as ineffectual as Esperanto in offering any practical answer.

Any control of jargon must consider these realities:

a. There is no sure cure. Jargon is a universal fault. Merely haranguing against it is too much like the sermons of Calvin Coolidge's preacher, who was merely "agin sin."

b. More than any other writing fault, jargon must first be recognized before we can consider remedies. In this chapter we will see that it is often the mote in the other fellow's eye (and he sees it in your eye too).

c. It speaks in many tongues. Alexander Woollcott, fond of such nostalgic words as *wraprascal* and *tippet,* was as guilty of jargon as the much criticized technician or the semanticist with his "science of non-elementalistic evaluation" that considers the "neuro-linguistic and neuro-semantic environments" of an individual.

d. Don't expect the reader to know what he can't find in his standard dictionary, to recognize *Screwdriver, Countdown* and *Marstini* as vodka drinks of the Space Age. He can't be consulting all the lexicons of slang and jargon, and even they are neither complete nor up-to-date enough.

e. What is jargon to one reader may not be to another. Jargon can be uttered nonsense or precise label-words that science needs. These words have invaded chemistry, for example, in waves: the coal-tar derivatives that came in after Germany's monopoly was ended by World War I; the petrochemicals leading to new polymers and therefore new plastics after World War II. These name-words are needed. The sin of jargon is not so much in using "big words" as in flaunting show-off words, on the one hand, and deliberately esoteric words, on the other.

f. Universal sin is not easily legislated out of existence. Some countries try outlawing prostitution; others prefer licensing as a control. Writing, of course, is traditionally lawless. In a word-game like Scrabble you are restrained from using *syzygy* because there are only two *y*'s in the entire set of players' tiles, but nothing can prevent a typewriter from rattling off many *y*'s and *syzygies*. With jargon, then, the only hope is in moderation. The less jargon, the better; to practice this moderation, the best control is self-control.

g. When in doubt, cling to the reader. He's your salvation as well as your judge. Decide who he is—to what extent he shares your vocabulary—and then use only the technical and jargon words that he can be expected to understand or to decode easily. It's as simple as that.

The company you keep

You cannot swear off jargon effectively until you know just what it is. Otherwise you may think you are being asked to toss out culture and diction and learning. Also, we have seen that science does need its precise name-words. In our specialized age, the evolution from *insecticide* to *pesticide* and then *adulticide* makes some sense, too, even though *bug spray* would satisfy most readers.

An oddity about jargon is that it is so often condemned by practitioners of jargon. When writer A brandishes *existentialism,* writer B calls him *obfuscator.*

This blaming the other chap is common in science, and understandable when we realize that science is not so much a language as a phalanx of dialects. We now have writing by "computer engineers," "gyro engineers," "electronics generalists"; by "behavioral scientists," "human factors scientists" and even "human engineers." This only worsens what is bad enough already. A horticulturist and a physicist, both interested in radiation, complain that they cannot understand each other. And if the physicist happens to be a home gardener, he asks why the horticulturist gets lost in jargon instead of explaining why squash and pumpkin do not crossbreed. Moreover, if they are music-lovers, they share Debussy's disgust with the "fog of verbiage" under which music critics have buried Beethoven's Ninth Symphony.

Then, too, all the old-line sciences snicker at the tall talk that befogs writing in the "pseudo" and social sciences. Yet we know that both psychiatry and surgery, for example, have had to contend with impostors who learned the jargon and went ahead successfully to practice the profession.

Nevertheless, jeering at the other fellow has its value. When you learn to spot the other chap's jargon, you have taken the first step toward recognizing your own "parrot talk" and "baffle gab."

Jargon, of course, has many relatives. It stands midway between cant, which is first-degree murder of the language because it is deliberate, and the cliché, which is more often empty-headed meaninglessness. It was cant that made the author of *Tristram Shandy* choleric:

> Grant me patience, just Heaven!—Of all the cants which are canted in this canting world—though the cant of hypocrites may be the worst— the cant of criticism is the most tormenting!

Before science grew so big and voluble, philology and its subdivisions did most of the fretting about jargon and how to define it. On their tongues the word experts rolled the differences and similarities—jargon, lingo, argot, gibberish, and then the gobbledygook of bureaucracy and the weirdies of the rock-'n'-roll and beatnik clans. The experts generally saw close kinship between jargon and cant. This was unfair, because cant is often defined as the secret language of thieves and vagabonds. The jargonist is a thief only in the sense that he steals a reader's time. Nevertheless, it is manifest that jargon keeps rather bad company.

Sir Arthur Quiller-Couch derided "the Vanity Fair of jargon" and called it the doorstep to ambiguity. As another outspoken English scholar, Fowler, did later, he was flailing jargon in general rather than the technician's variety, and had fun linking it to prim prose—the elegance that substitutes "domicile" for "home," "perspiration" for "sweat," and "lady dog" for "bitch."

This, then, is the pretentious type of jargon. It betrays innocents into saying "between you and I" when "between you and me," though less ornate, happens to be correct.

But jargon is also the blah-blah of a politician who says he doesn't want higher taxes or a cabinet office when he actually does. Shortly after taking up his duties in Washington, a Secretary of Defense complained, "The language of legislation is spooky. I keep asking myself, 'What is it really saying?'"

Jargon is the bucolic affectation of the truck driver who says "tarpolean" when he knows it's "tarpaulin"; the member-of-the-club badge worn by cavalrymen, including educated West Pointers, who disdained the rest of the world by calling themselves the "calvary"; the speech of the baggy-pants burlesque comedian who gets a laugh from the yokels by pronouncing "connoisseur" as "conna-sewer."

But jargon is also the language of the science student who outgrows pig Latin and plausisounding nonsitalk—in favor of a spanking new amusement that will set him and his classmates apart from the rest. After making you guess, in vain, he explains that

$$\ln\left[\lim_{z \to \infty}\left(1 + \frac{1}{z}\right)^{z} + (\sin^2 x + \cos^2 x)\right] = \sum_{n=0}^{\infty} \frac{\cosh y \sqrt{1 - \tanh^2 y}}{2^n}$$

is the scientific way to say: One plus one equals two. Contrast that contrived equation with the simplicity of Einstein's literally earthshaking $e = mc^2$, which explains the power of a nuclear explosion.

Jargon can be the exhilarating slang of the barkers and midgets who work at carnivals. It can be the delightful nonsense (with pinpricks of meaning) of Lewis Carroll writing about Alice in Wonderland and of baseball's Casey Stengel testifying before a congressional committee.

But jargon can also be serious stuff—pomposity of the cultist and passwords of the secret-society member. The jingoist is usually a jargonist outfitted with a flag-waving set of catchwords; and Communist jargon has irritants of its own. Where is the difference when you weigh: deviationism, dogmatism, fractionalism, reformism, sectarianism, revisionism? All these, C. L. Sulzberger wrote in the New York *Times*, were Moscow synonyms condemning Marshal Tito's independent-mindedness.

Capitalism has its jargon, too, and critics such as Thorstein Veblen have had a merry time at the expense of soothsaying economists by mimicking their language with deadpan derision.

Education, of course, has its own jargon. An example is from a teacher's report on her youthful pilgrim's progress:

> He is adjusting well to his peer group and achieving to expectancy in
> skill subjects. But I'm afraid his growth in content subjects is blocked by
> his reluctance to get on with his developmental tasks.

(In other words, this lad is a good mixer, okay in the three R's but not much imagination.)

And the best jargon of all is the kind that can jeer at itself. Listen to this draftsman. He is explaining in doggerel that, to show how much he knows, "I have marked all my lines/ With mysterious signs/ That Einstein could never decode," and he goes on:

> Now my drawing is finished and printed,
> And I'm proud of its hazy design,
> For I know there'll be chaos and ulcers
> When it finally comes out on the line.
> And a feeling of pride starts a stirring inside,
> As my tracing is filed on the shelf,
> For my quest has been solved with a print so involved
> That I can't even read it myself.

Now let us dig a little deeper, more clinically, into this matter of detecting other people's jargon so that we can better recognize our own. Here's a glimpse at the language of two quite different technical fields.

Example 1—architecture. Paintings, clothes and buildings have this in common: They sell themselves to us through our eyes—they are designed. The fashion designers and painters have their jargons, of course, but neither of these fields is closely related to science. Their jargons are not deadly, but merely those of aesthetics.

Architecture, on the other hand, does incorporate much applied science, such as the physics of load-bearing structures and the chemistry of materials. And in architecture the floodgates of jargon open wide.

One illustration . . . [can be seen in] the three decades that R. Buckminster Fuller had to wait before the world understood and paid tribute to his "Dymaxion Principle" and the "tensegrity" (tension plus integrity) incorporated into his fantastically strong geodesic domes. He had evangelized for "energetic-synergetic" geometry and the distribution of forces in lattices made up of tetrahedrons. He had not explained that the dome is an exquisite balancing of the forces that try to make it collapse and the forces that try to tear it asunder; that this is the trick with which you could build a sort of thick-skinned tent in which the tautness is built right into the latticework of the skin—so that there is no need for a centerpole.

Another example shows how easy it is to note only the mote in the other fellow's eye. In a discussion of architectural jargon, a professor of architecture writes:

> The aspects of architecture embody so many factors that its definition has become almost unintelligible. It encompasses sociology, biology, physiology, aesthetics, engineering, space, decoration, etc., to the extent that architects attempting to write about it invariably engage in such mixed jargons that it results in an incomprehensible babel.

He then goes on to explain himself in such terms as "emanation" of a drawing, "disbalance," "cumulative field of reference," "dynamic equilibrium" and "prosaic agglomeration."

Certainly even rhapsodizing by John Ruskin tells us much more:

> For indeed, the greatest glory of a building is not in its stone, not in its gold. Its glory is in its age, and in that deep sense of voicefulness, of stern watching, of mysterious sympathy . . . which we feel in walls that have long been washed by the passing waves of humanity.

Example 2—medicine. This field, of course, is rife with jargon, partly because its roots are in the witch-doctor mumbo-jumbo that considers *toxicosis* always better than *poisoning*. Partly, too, because of the morale-building approach that gives the patient some pink pills for imagined ills and holds back the crisp truth about serious ones. As long as the prescription is written correctly, the patient is probably as proud of long-word ills as of plebeian ones; the misunderstandings are no more fatal than that between the young husband and wife who slept separately one summer because polio experts had

been warning that the disease is spread by "intimate contact between people."
The young couple understood "intimate" only in the prim-prose sense.

It is likely that medicine's jargon is most harmful to the doctors themselves. A specialist said as he came away from a research symposium: "I had to
listen so hard to the words that I didn't have a chance to grasp the idea." And
colleagues admitted nodding off during the blessed dark moments when slides
were shown.

Yet medical matters can be described clearly—as a medical researcher
like Hans Zinsser, and other writers such as Sinclair Lewis and Arnold Zweig
have so brilliantly demonstrated.

The following passage is from Aldous Huxley's *After Many a Summer
Dies the Swan.* This is a novel, but Huxley is a walking encyclopedia of
science as well as an extremely competent writer, and his science fiction is as
disciplined as any research report. In this passage, disregard his "style"; instead, note the expositional clarity—how words that might be jargon are
quickly unfolded for you. At the beginning you know little about carp and
probably less about the sterols; at the end you are ready to live as long as
Methuselah:

> Those sterols! (Dr. Obispo frowned and shook his head over them.)
> Always linked up with senility. The most obvious case, of course, was
> cholesterol. A senile animal might be defined as one with an accumula-
> tion of cholesterol in the walls of the arteries. . . . But then cholesterol
> was only one of the sterols. They were a closely related group, those
> fatty alcohols. . . . In other words, cancer might be regarded, in a final
> analysis, as a symptom of sterol-poisoning. He himself would go even
> further and say that such sterol-poisoning was responsible for the entire
> degenerative process of senescence in man and the other animals. What
> nobody had done hitherto was to look into the part played by fatty
> alcohols in the life of such animals as carp. That was the work he had
> been doing for the last year. His researches had convinced him of three
> things: first, that the fatty alcohols in carp did not accumulate in exces-
> sive quantity; second, that they did not undergo transformation into the
> more poisonous sterols; and third, that both of these immunities were
> due to the peculiar nature of the carp's intestinal flora. What a flora! . . .
> In one way or another, in combination or in isolation, these organisms
> contrived to keep the fish's sterols from turning into poisons. That was
> why a carp could live a couple of hundred years and show no signs of
> senility.

Less jargon—your guide

Now let's focus on your own writing. You think you can recognize jargon. You
want to cut it out of your sentences and paragraphs, or at least cut it down.
But how?

    1. *Preventives come first.* Beware of infection by the other person's

jargon and you will save time on cures. Here are some ways to avoid infection.

a. Don't parrot the instructor's bigger words. They may get you a college degree, but professional life requires writing that is more than regurgitation. Jargon, for example, doesn't impress a capable boss. He's too busy, and wants to pick your brains in a hurry. He doesn't equate complex writing with complex thoughts and, in fact, is suspicious of thoughts that cannot be simplified to the length of, say, Lincoln's Gettysburg Address.

b. Spurn the words that bother you in your reading—they may bother your own readers. For example, just as too many isms, each requiring its own political party, can paralyze the functioning of a government, so can the spinning off of too many -ologies throw our language into bedlam. Let metaphysics insist on its ontology, but need our writing stagger under all these: behavioristic psychology, Gestalt psychology, normic psychology, structural psychology, functional psychology, act psychology, dynamic psychology, reflexological psychology?

c. If you are editing or rewriting the work of others, translate the jargon when you can; when you can't, call for something simpler from the author. Otherwise, you are an accessory after the fact. As editors know, this can lead to troublesome bickering. The best cure is to let the author take his jargon elsewhere. Of course, before you challenge fact or jargon, be sure of your ground. A garbage grinder, for example, may prefer the sweet smell of another name. A magazine editor learned this from a plaintive letter sent in by a manufacturer:

We prefer that you call it correctly as "Industrial Disposal Unit." Garbage grinder connotes shoddy appearance, etc. Certainly, any machine capable of disposing of "Top Secret" documents should not be called a garbage grinder.

2. *Who's your reader?* Delay writing until you have decided who the reader, or class of readers, will be. If you don't know, you are still too hazy about the subject itself.

Is it to be a proposal to the boss? That isn't identification enough. Is he strictly a management man, does he have a smattering of science, is he a fellow technician? Or is it to be a pass-along proposal that will be read by all three types of person?

If your paper is for fellow specialists, the jargon content can go up. But again, remember that people in promotion and advertising may have to read it, too, and they cannot translate what they cannot understand.

If you are writing for a magazine, who are its readers? If for students, are they at graduate or freshman level? And what of the so-called general public? It turns thumbs down quickly even on a literate writer if he strays too far from words like *home* and *income*.

When picturing the audience, remember: (a) Clarity brings its own reward—the less jargon, the wider the potential readership; (b) if you really prefer a narrower audience, don't be misled by specialization. Writing for "farmers" isn't narrow enough—the applegrower has one lingo, the poultryman another. Similarly, your comrade technician isn't your twin in training and interests.

3. *Simplification isn't that simple.* Don't let the preaching against jargon panic you into such lisping simplicity as "A river pump house pumps water to the water treatment plant" and "He was a self-educated man educated by himself."

And by all means don't be panicked into popularization that falls on its face. When the United States Weather Bureau introduced its Discomfort Index, that term was simplicity itself compared with the attempt by a newspaper to explain it:

. . . The relationship between such variables is found by computing a third measure. This is a magnitude so related to the magnitudes of temperature and humidity that to values of these measures there correspond values of the third measure. This third measure is called a function, a measure of relationship. . . .

4. *If you don't know, say so.* Is your chain of facts secure? If links are missing, you have this choice: (a) Ignore the gaps—but this leaves you open to being called slipshod, or worse; (b) delay the final draft until you can supply the missing facts, or bypass the trouble area and limit your writing to what you do know about; (c) come right out and say "I don't know." Truly great scientists frequently exhibit such humility. It can also be very refreshing. Thus, in a nonpompous article in *Scientific American,* Robert T. Wilson, the physicist, discusses Soviet particle-accelerators:

Veksler . . . envisages a small bunch of ions in a plasma. . . . These waves are to act together coherently to give an enormous push to the ions being accelerated. If this is not clear to the reader, it is because it is not clear to me. The details have managed to escape most of us because of a linguistic ferrous curtain, but Veksler speaks of the theoretical possibility of attaining energies up to 1,000 bev. . . .

5. *Ordinary words are respectable.* Don't let very simple words cause you shame. Note that Wilson, above, used *bunch.* Other topnotch technicians are similarly unafraid of writing like human beings. If nuclear writing can be handled this way, why not that of the applied sciences? For example, medicine—which concerns everybody—might well emulate agricultural science, which also deals with quite ordinary people. Agronomy, horticulture, animal genetics—these have ponderous jargons of their own. But listen to the homely language of a typical county agent talking to his farm flock over the radio, or read the yearbooks issued by the United States Department of Agriculture. Some of the most capable writing by experts and editing by experts can be found in these technical annuals. The researchers in agriculture, fighting the gloomy predictions of Malthus, learned long ago to clarify their writing or let others do it for them; that a discovery is incomplete until fellow technicians, and eventually the farmers, can apply it.

6. *Common cure—a synonym.* Whenever you suspect jargon is creeping in, call on substitute words that are easier. . . . In general, simplicity of the word should depend on simplicity of the reader. New York's radio station WNYC, addressing all kinds of people, was smart enough to use "the coming bookkeeping year" instead of "fiscal year"; this avoided confusion in listeners' minds between fiscal and calendar years. Experts, too, are grateful for simpler words, for each time the chemist says "nylon" instead of giving the full molecular name of the polyamide.

7. *But some jargon is necessary?* If so, rush in to explain it to the reader. This can be done in several ways. A shortcut method is the parenthetical one. Be quite formal, use jargon if you must, but immediately define the word. The New York *Times* does this frequently and nicely, with the synonymous material flanked by parentheses or dashes. Thus:

The volume, amounting to 417 lots (50,000 pounds to a lot) was the second highest this year.

The metal is as light as magnesium alloys, yet its modulus of elasticity— or stiffness—is about three and one-half times that of steel.

The same method works handily when writing for a more technical audience. Thus, from the Beckman Instrument Company, an announcement about its D2 Oxygen Analyzer says:

. . . Oxygen is unique among gases in being strongly paramagnetic (attracted into a magnetic field). Other gases are, with few exceptions, slightly diamagnetic (repelled out of a magnetic field). . . .

Obviously, to be effective, the explanation must explain. In the following, from *Scientific American,* the reader either understands or doesn't understand precisely what is meant—the explanation (which I italicize) merely adds bothersome words:

The rate of change of the orbital period of a satellite, *that is, the rate of change in the time it takes to fly its orbit,* is directly proportional to the density of the atmosphere through which it passes.

8. *Comparisons are practical.* Another effective way to make jargon more palatable is to put similarity to work. An example is the "For example . . ." method so useful in all expositional writing.

For example, the atom was formerly likened to an infinitesimally tiny billiard ball—a hard little atom. But later, when the concept was revised to include spinning electrons, the student was asked to think of a tiny planetary system.

Or take mathematics—almost as much of a terror to most technicians as it is to laymen. A mathematician with a new concept about finite groups was asked by a newspaper reporter to explain it. His first answer was that this could not be done simply enough for the layman. But he then did it very effectively in terms of wallpaper patterns.

This method, however, requires considerable caution and common sense. The horrors of a mixed metaphor must be avoided. The analogy must be sharply to the point—or the reader's mind is sent wandering off the subject. And it's hardly helpful to have the mitosis of a human's cells likened to the mitosis of a guinea pig's cells—if the reader doesn't know what mitosis means.

Allow the example to be lengthy only if it is itself an integral part of the exposition. And don't reduce the reader's mental stature to that of a child. A New York *Times* story, in the course of reporting a speech by a university president, quoted this sentence, "Today, our specialists, as they study man and his behavior, are all too frequently like the blind men studying the elephant." At this point the reporter, evidently disbelieving that *Times* readers are fairly literate, launched into a parenthetical paragraph of 85 words that retold the familiar blind-men-and-elephant story.

9. *This is the smoothest way.* The good craftsman, like Aldous Huxley, quoted earlier, can have his cake and eat it too. He throws in troublesome words when necessary but quickly explains them with what might be called built-in paraphrasing, which advances the exposition while explaining the jargon. Difficult word and explanation come so closely together that the reader feels no pain, hardly realizes what has been done for him.

Let us work through a step-by-step example. The problem I am about to describe actually exists. Someday it may be solved. I am imagining that day has arrived and I want to announce the triumph. If I were writing a typical research paper, I would begin something like this:

The literature contains many references to a problem that has been important in silviculture for the last fifty years. . . .

And so on, until I come in pages later with what it is I want to announce.

An unappetizing beginning? Yes. But clarity is our main concern here. Focus on the word *silviculture*. How many readers can I assume would have a roughish idea of its meaning? Worse, how many would know its precise meaning? Very well then, I can conquer jargon this way:

The literature contains references to a problem that has been important in silviculture for the last fifty years. Silviculture is defined as the art of producing and caring for a forest. . . .

With this interruption for definition I have obeyed the injunction to explain any jargon. But at considerable expense. The unappetizing beginning has become even more deadly, and I have wasted space just to give a definition.

Yet this *silviculture* is a word I really want to use throughout the article; I also believe sincerely that if the reader doesn't know the word, it's high time he learn it.

Now let's try the technique by paraphrasing. If I insist on beginning with a review of the literature, this will at least purge the jargon (the difficult word and the explaining words are in italics):

The literature contains many references to a *forest-growing* problem that has been important in *silviculture* for the last fifty years. . . .

Or, the same, but with dullness thrown away:

Science is now certain that the American chestnut *tree* can be brought back into our *forests.* Government *silviculturists* are successfully *growing thousands* of chestnut *seedlings.* These are identical in species with the towering trees that perished when a mysterious blight began attacking them fifty years ago. . . .

Or, the same, extremely popularized:

The deadliest killer of America's *trees* has now been licked. Fifty years ago, *silviculturists* watched helplessly as a mysterious blight swept across the country, turning *forests* of lordly chestnut trees into companies of gray ghosts. Five years ago, science found in coal tar a chemical that was just as deadly against the blight. A month ago, *silviculturists* of another generation jubilantly began *planting new forests* of chestnuts. . . .

Or, very simply, merely telling somebody about something I do on my farm:

I like *silviculture. Growing forest trees* is more than a hobby with me.

Here, I have had different audiences in mind but the method is always the same. I define the word as I move along.

Another example. I cannot assume that all readers of this book are steeped in the jargons of grammar and semantics. But I do assume that most of you have had a college education or will have. Therefore I feel no need to define such words as *antecedent* and *adjective.* But in the chapter on new words I was much more doubtful about *neologism*. Yet I felt you should know this word. So I hastily defined it, not by pedantically saying, "A neologism is . . ." but by letting the act of definition do some other work for me. I had been discussing new words. Then I went on, "Even if the neologism has been broken in a little, enough to be found in some dictionary . . ."

All of the preceding how-to's can be lumped together as follows: Don't expect the reader to supply the explanation. He's too busy or doesn't know how. If you cannot explain, change the subject, or aim for another kind of reader.

While I was at lunch one day with some visiting engineers from the USSR, the conversation turned to translations. I asked if these foreigners had read Vance Packard's *The Status Seekers*. They said they expected to—the book was being translated into Russian. And what about *The Hucksters*? I asked. They nodded with comprehension—yes, they had heard about it. But, they added, it wouldn't be translated into Russian. Why? Their answer was convincing. The USSR had status-seekers too—so the Packard book would make sense. But the concept of free-enterprise advertising, of huckstering, defied translation into terms that Russians could understand. So Frederic Wakeman's book on hucksters would be jargon—to Russian readers.

A rationale for the use of common business-letter expressions

J. HAROLD JANIS

J. Harold Janis is Professor Emeritus of Business
Communication at New York University; a third
edition of his textbook *Writing and Communication in Business* was published by Macmillan in
1978.

The aim of this paper is to provide a rational basis for the use of stock words and phrases in business letters. This aim follows the hypothesis that such expressions can, under controlled conditions, serve the needs of business and at the same time avoid criticism on stylistic grounds. Resolving the question of usage is important in order to stop the great waste of time in promoting language values that are often at odds with the business culture. It is also important if the constantly increasing volume of routine correspondence is to be handled in an effective and acceptable way by computer or other systematic means.

The number of pejorative terms used to describe common business-letter expressions suggests the difficulty of treating (and viewing) the subject dispassionately. Adjectives like *stereotyped, stilted, hackneyed,* and *trite,* and nouns like *clichés, jargon, bromides, businessese,* and *gobbledygook* have so colored out attitudes toward certain types of words and phrases that any attempt to treat the offending usages on a reasonable basis risks skepticism and antagonism. To eliminate, or at least reduce, the affective connotation, we shall hereafter use the abbreviation CBE to signify a common business-letter expression.

J. Harold Janis, "A Rationale for the Use of Common Business-Letter Expressions," reprinted from
the *Journal of Business Communication,* 4 (October 1966), pp. 3–11, by permission of the American Business Communication Association.

Factors favoring CBE's

This author has previously shown that the use of certain common business expressions is grounded in the demands of the business situation.[1] The organizational factors favoring the use of CBE's may be summarized as follows:

    1. Letter writing in business is highly repetitive. The same kinds of situations occur again and again, providing the writers with ample precedent for both the substance and phrasing of the letters. If this were not so—if each situation were unique or had to be treated as if it were—business correspondence on a large scale would take a disproportionate amount of the organization's energies.

    2. CBE's increase efficiency by providing ready clues to rhetorical patterns and consequently reducing the uncertainties of expression. For example, given the initial phrase *with reference to your letter of,* the writer is easily able to begin not just one letter, but a great many. When the writer is required to begin the letter in less redundant (less predictable) fashion, e.g., *We don't know how we mislaid your order,* he is left completely to his own devices and, furthermore, cannot rely on such phrasing to provide any assistance in composing other letters.

    3. CBE's help to reduce the uncertainties of response. From the point of view of the writer's superior, any new language treatment increases the risk of message failure, including misunderstanding and legal liability. He is therefore inclined to reject originality in favor of phrasing proved by experience. Conformity is thus enforced by the threat of non-acceptance.

    4. CBE's permit the correspondent to be impersonal in the many instances when he does not have any personal involvement in his subject or considers it desirable to avoid personal responsibility. In many instances the correspondent has had only a small part in the transaction about which he is writing, or he may be writing for some other person's signature. The tradition of the particular company or department for which the writer works may also encourage his self-effacement. The use of CBE's like *receipt is acknowledged, the undersigned,* and *our records indicate* becomes more understandable in the light of this explanation.

Reconciling conformance with effectiveness

If, as it is indicated, the business environment nurtures conformance in language rather than freshness and originality, how is the use of CBE's reconciled with the need for effectiveness? Several explanations may be offered. First, despite the emphasis on the human relations function—and the need for individuality that goes with it—the task function is paramount in a huge volume

[1] J. Harold Janis, "The Writing Behavior of Businessmen," *Journal of Communication,* 15 (June, 1965), pp. 81–88.

of business correspondence, certainly in the routine situations most likely to be handled by subordinates. And whatever the prevalence of CBE's, the routine business-letter tasks apparently do get done.

Second, the factors that make CBE's desirable for the writer also make them desirable for the reader. When similar situations keep arising between the two parties, the reader's response to the language is conditioned by his experience with it. Changing the language then becomes analogous to changing the color or design on a can of beans. Whatever the improvement, there is at least temporary disorientation.

Third, the value the reader places on the distinctiveness of a business letter can easily be overestimated. Apart from the substance, which is of the most immediate concern to the reader, a number of other factors contribute to the total impression the letter makes. These include its physical make-up, its timeliness, the rapport with the signer, and the reputation of the source.

Finally, the balance between an efficient style and effectiveness is preserved by what we shall call the fraction of composition. Following Schramm's concept of the fraction of selection (the attention paid to a communication)[2] the fraction of composition may be represented as follows:

$$\text{Fraction of Composition} = \frac{\text{Expected Reward}}{\text{Expected Energy Required}}$$

As the formula signifies, the more meaningful the anticipated response to the letter, the more available energy the writer or organization expends. Thus routine letter situations which have been adequately (if not triumphantly) handled in the past by CBE's, provide little incentive for change. On the other hand, unique situations that promise greater rewards (or greater penalties) provide greater incentive for individual treatment. In the simplest terms, the language of a letter gets all the emphasis it warrants, consistent with the proficiency of the writer and the competition for his time and energy.

Stylistic considerations

We have yet to deal with the stylistic or esthetic objection to CBE's. This objection appears to be based on the loss of individuality that occurs whenever clichés are used. Thus *cliché* becomes the operative word. According to Beckson and Ganz, a cliché is "a timeworn expression which has lost its vitality and to some extent its original meaning."[3] Margaret Nicholson defines clichés as hackneyed phrases that "have acquired an unfortunate popularity and come into general use even when they are not more but less suitable to the context than plain speech."[4] Fowler says that "cliché means a stereotype;

[2] Wilbur Schramm, "How Communication Works," in *The Process and Effects of Mass Communication,* ed. by Wilbur Schramm (Urbana, Ill.: University of Illinois Press, 1960), pp. 19-20.

[3] Karl Beckson and Arthur Ganz, *A Reader's Guide to Literary Terms* (New York: Noonday Press, 1960), p. 29.

[4] Margaret Nicholson, *A Dictionary of American-English Usage* (New York: Oxford University Press, 1957), p. 88.

in its literary sense it is a word or phrase whose felicity in a particular context when it was first employed has won it such popularity that it is apt to be used unsuitably and indiscriminately."[5]

The test of a cliché, then, is not that it is common, but that it is both common and unsuitable for its context. On this point Fowler offers some elaboration:

> The word is always used in a pejorative sense, and this obscures the truth that words and phrases falling within the definition are not all of a kind. There are some that deserve the stigma. . . . There are others that may or may not deserve to be classed with them; that depends on whether they are chosen mechanically . . . or are chosen deliberately as the fittest way of saying what needs to be said.[6]

Adding that "the enthusiasm of the cliché hunter is apt to run away with him," Fowler quotes from J. A. Spencer that "the hardest working cliché is better than the phrase that fails" and "journalese is best avoided by the frank acceptance of even a hard-worn phrase when it expresses what you want to say."[7]

What has been said of clichés can be said of CBE's. The words and phrases falling within the definition are not all of a kind. What matters is their appropriateness in the context in which they are used. To give an example from commercial writing, *we wish to advise you* would be stereotyped in a letter acknowledging an order, but not necessarily inappropriate in a legal notification. As the example suggests, an important clue to the aptness of CBE's can be found in the stratification of style, which is characteristic of organizational correspondence. In this respect, four levels of usage may be noted (Fig. 1):

Official. This style is used in correspondence of a legal or quasi-legal kind, including claims, requests, notifications and acknowledgments. In addition to its immediate utility, the correspondence also serves as a formal record of a transaction. The style is highly impersonal and characterized by stilted expressions that would be considered out of place in other kinds of writing. Such expressions arise out of either the desire to preserve the legal tone (and force) of the message or the need for exact reference. They include *pursuant to, advise* (in the sense of "inform"), *above-captioned, therein, thereto, thereof, therefor, due to* (as a preposition), *subsequent to, held in abeyance, duly,* and *pending receipt of.*

Formal. The formal style serves many purposes calling for an impersonal but not legalistic treatment. The communications may include letters of introduction and recommendation, credit references, early collection letters, and correspondence on routine matters with agents who are not emotionally involved in the situations. In addition to the use of the impersonal *we* (for *I*), *the writer,* and *the undersigned,* the style is also characterized by polite expres-

[5] H. W. Fowler, *Modern English Usage* (New York: Oxford Unversity Press, 1927), p. 90.
[6] *Ibid.,* pp. 90-91.
[7] *Ibid.,* p. 91.

Fig. 1. Levels of Business-Letter Usage

OFFICIAL

As requested in your letter to us of November 28, 19___, all of the $200,000 principal amount of your Corporation's 5% Registered Debenture Bonds due 1970 called for redemption on December 1, 1965 at the principal amount thereof and three months' accrued interest have been presented to us and paid. After such redemption, there remains outstanding $850,000 principal amount.

With further regard to your claim covered by our File No. 1467B, we regret to advise that after due consideration of the circumstances surrounding the accident, the Claim Board has reached the conclusion that we are not justified in making payment in this instance.

FORMAL

This will serve to introduce Miss_____, who has been in our employ since July 2, 1964 as a typist in our Credit Department. Miss_____, an excellent worker, is leaving our Company on March 22, 1966 to reside in Puerto Rico. Mr. William_____ of the New York Hilton Hotel, one of our valued customers, said you might know of some job opportunities for Miss_____.

With regard to your recent inquiry, Mr. John_____ has been numbered among our depositors since this office opened ten years ago. Mr._____ maintains a satisfactory personal account on which balances average consistently in four figures, and he is also known to us in connection with several substantial business accounts. On the basis of our experience we have no hesitancy in recommending Mr._____ as deserving of the usual courtesies.

INFORMAL

We have your letter of September 25 requesting information concerning 300 shares of Blanko Corporation that you sent us for transfer.

In order to help us identify the item, will you please note on the carbon copy of this letter the name of the person to whom the stock was to be transferred and also the certificate numbers of the shares you sent us. We would appreciate your writing on the enclosed carbon of this letter and returning it to us in the envelope we have provided.

I am sorry about the lost check. If you will complete the enclosed Affidavit, I will be happy to send you our official check for $256.70.

COLLOQUIAL

My face is red over the delay in sending you and Ed the tax information I promised. Life has been hectic but not that hectic.

Lunch Friday will be just fine. See you at the Lawyers Club at 12:30.

sions like *kindly* (for *please*) and *at your earliest convenience,* and such formal but wordy expressions as *in the amount of, with reference to, in connection with, in the event that,* and *our records indicate.*

Informal. The informal style is suitable for most business letters. It is characterized by a personal interest in the reader and contains a considerable amount of affective language, including such expressions as *glad, pleased, sorry,* and *appreciate.* Thus the human relations function, while not necessarily absent in the official and formal styles, is more prominent—sometimes predominant—here. Informality is enhanced by the personal pronouns *I, we,* and *you,* active verbs, and natural (unstilted) phrasing.

Familiar. When writer and reader know each other quite well, and especially when they meet socially or address each other by their first names, the familiar style may be appropriate. It is marked by colloquial expressions, clipped sentences, and an occasional touch of humor. Although any form of stiltedness is incongruous in this style, such CBE's as *with all good wishes,* and *kindest regards* are quite common.

Guidelines for the use of CBE's

Given these classifications of usage, we are in a better position to determine the rightness of CBE's in particular situations. We are also better able to form judgments about the use of CBE's generally:

    1. The chief objection to CBE's in business letters is that they are "not natural." Obviously, such a criticism cannot apply to the official and formal styles, which imply a degree of stiltedness. When the criticism is applied to letters for which the informal style would be best suited, the substitutes usually recommended are not original modes of expression but other CBE's that will pass as natural. The contrasting phrases that follow, for example, have been compiled from several well-known texts on letter writing:

STILTED CBE's	NATURAL CBE's
at your earliest convenience	as soon as you can[8]
attached herewith	attached is[8]
This is to acknowledge	thank you for[8]
awaiting your further orders	we shall expect to hear from you[9]
under separate cover	separately[9]
as per instructions	following your instructions[10]
pursuant to your request	as you requested[10]
we thank you kindly for your letter	thank you for your letter[10]

[8] Charles C. Parkhurst, *Business Communication for Better Human Relations,* 7th ed. (Englewood Cliffs, N. J.: Prentice-Hall, 1966), pp. 19–20.

[9] Mona Sheppard, *Plain Letters* (New York: Simon & Schuster, 1960), p. 99.

[10] Walter K. Smart, Louis W. McKelvey, and Richard C. Gerfen, *Business Letters,* 4th ed. (New York: Harper & Row, 1957), pp. 36–37.

2. Much of the prejudice against CBE's is really a prejudice against the use of official or formal language in situations that would be more appropriately handled by informal language. This is legitimate criticism. The following letter, for example, is needlessly stilted, as the writer himself seems to sense in the postscript:

Gentlemen:

We are carrying you on our mailing list as follows: . . . Will you please return this notice with any corrections shown thereon which should be made. If the above information is correct, we would appreciate advice from you to that effect so that our records will be complete.

Your truly,

P. S. In other words, we would appreciate having your correct mailing address.

3. Any excesses in the use of CBE's are bad style. Thus while *thank you for* is suitable in informal usage, it palls when it is used without discrimination to acknowledge incoming letters. Similarly, the stiltedness characteristic of formal or official usage becomes a travesty in a passage like the following:

In response to your letter of March 26 which was in reply to our letter of March 24, which was in reply to yours of March 16, we are enclosing herewith the photostatic copy of our check No. 60432 dated February 26, 19—, payable to (Name) in the amount of $6,455.54.

4. Some CBE's are hard to justify in any circumstances. This judgment would apply to trade jargon which is not adapted to the reader and for which there are reasonably adequate substitutes. It would also apply to archaic or stilted or pretentious expressions which have no redeeming advantage. Illustratively, such expressions might include *and oblige, we remain, as per, your goodselves,* the *instant matter, favor* (for letter), and *summarization* (for *summary*).

5. Regardless of the level of usage, expressions that are stylistically undesirable in some instances are defensible and even appropriate in others. For example, a certain credit department recommends to its correspondents a guide letter in which the following form appears: ". . . (company) is engaged in the (manufacture) of. . . ." One might contend that "the company manufactures" is simpler and therefore better. From the credit department's point of view, however, the phrase *engaged in* is a clear reminder of the kind of information that is to be given at that point. The word *manufactures* following the word *company* would not suggest as well to the correspondent the possibility of such substitutions as *imports, retails,* or *jobs.* It is also evident that the noun construction, which gives the common name of the company's activity, is less awkward than the verb construction in some instances (as "the company jobs") and is better suited to the purpose of the letter.

In summary, (1) use of the common business expressions (CBE's) most often associated with routine business letters is a normal consequence of the business culture, (2) such use is not inconsistent with the need for effectiveness, (3) CBE's are not necessarily clichés and may therefore be exempt from criticism on esthetic grounds, and (4) the criterion of good usage in a CBE is its appropriateness to the business situation and to the formality of the context.

3

Resumes
   and letters
about
employment

Writing an advertisement for yourself

CAROLINE DONNELLY

Caroline Donnelly is a staff writer for *Money*.

Because finding a good job often hangs on luck, an earnest job hunter takes pains with the details he can control. He may get a shoeshine or a haircut before a crucial interview, and he probably picks the best grade of bond paper for the letters and résumés he sends out. More important, he carefully weighs the words he puts on that paper. A stand-out letter or résumé, he knows, improves the odds that he will be in the right place at the right time.

Everyone who sets out to find a job that requires professional skill or training needs a résumé. It's wise to have an up-to-date résumé at your fingertips, even if you aren't actively looking for a job. Letters may play an important role in a job search, and résumés customarily are accompanied by introductory notes, but the résumé is the essential sales tool of the job seeker. Says John Sibbald, a vice president of the management consulting firm of Booz, Allen & Hamilton: "Drawing up a résumé is the single most important thing a person does to make a job change." A good résumé is the thin edge of the wedge that opens the door to a face-to-face meeting. It makes a job candidate out of a job applicant.

To their readers, résumés are people-screening devices. Personnel professionals tend to read résumés with a negative bias, skimming each for an excuse to throw it away. "I don't spend more than 15 seconds on a résumé," admits executive recruiter Peter Lauer of Lauer & Holbrook, in Chicago. The obvious—but often overlooked—solution: leave out any information that would disqualify you.

Caroline Donnelly, "Writing an Advertisement for Yourself." Reprinted from the January 1974 issue of *Money* Magazine by special permission; © 1974, Time Inc.

100

There are as many opinions on what makes a good résumé as there are people reading résumés. Still, professionals and recent job seekers in various parts of the country generally agree that what you should know about résumés falls into six categories: what you should put in, what you should leave out, what form you should use, what tone you should take, what the résumé should look like and what kind of letter you should send with it. The following is a discussion of each of those points—with some specific advice.

What to put in

The main ingredients of a good résumé are a comprehensive work history, a short outline of educational background and a smattering of personal data. Educational background should include degrees earned, scholarships, honors or participation in special programs. Personal data—hobbies and club memberships, for example—can add character, and some prospective employers look here for signs of leadership and community service. A résumé also ought to mention memberships in professional organizations, published books or articles, inventions or patents and fluency in foreign languages.

Some other particulars:

• Keep it short. A mid-career executive should aim for two pages. Three pages is the limit.

• Don't shorten your résumé by lopping off chunks of your career. Your work history should concentrate on your most recent jobs, but you should also describe the first six months in the mailroom—though not in detail.

What to leave out

Too much information wastes space and risks exasperating the reader. For example, unless the writer never attended college, a résumé need not mention where or when he went to high school. Summer or part-time jobs should be included only if the applicant is a recent graduate, or if the jobs were unusual and showed gumption or ingenuity. Windy statements of career objectives waste precious space. Alan Neely, a personnel officer at the First National Bank in Atlanta, recalls that one applicant described his goal as "a challenging position leading to increased responsibility and self-actualization within a dynamic company." Says Neely: "That doesn't mean anything. The objective should be specific, like 'management trainee in the financial community.'"

Many other personnel professionals advise against including any statement of objectives, no matter how terse, in a résumé since it can only limit the applicant's opportunities. Mention of religion, race or politics looks unprofessional.

While a good résumé omits or glosses over unfavorable information, the consequences of any serious distortion of facts can be dire. "There isn't one single company I know of that would not discharge someone on the spot if they learned of a lie," says Sheldon Hirsch, who heads his own executive search firm in Los Angeles. "And those things have a way of surfacing." Many companies check the facts in résumés; large companies with formalized hiring procedures and firms with government contracts are almost certain to do so. A fib that occasionally appears on résumés is a false claim to a college degree— a risky business, since such credentials are fairly easy to verify. Peter Lauer estimates that the applicant's educational background is misrepresented in 5% of the résumés he attempts to check.

What does a résumé writer do with potentially damaging information—a long period of unemployment owing to mental illness, for example? One New York personnel executive has some extreme advice: "I'd say lie about it. Say 'self-employed as a consultant.' But at the interview you've got to tell them, because they'll find out." A man applying for a job as an auditor sent the First National Bank in Atlanta a résumé that said: "During the past seven years I have been involved with top secret government work." A check revealed that he had done a stretch in prison for armed robbery and other crimes; that put him out of the running.

Another personnel man suggests covering an embarrassing interlude by specifying only the years, not the exact dates of employment. An alternate solution might be to send out a form letter focusing on career highlights instead of a conventional résumé. Letters offer a way to omit embarrassing facts.

Other guidelines:

• Play the coquette. Be comprehensive, but don't give every detail. That should stimulate the reader's appetite and prompt an invitation to an interview. There are exceptions, though. If you usually perform badly in interviews, a résumé packed with favorable information can take up the slack.

• Don't mention salary. Include anticipated salary in the covering letter only if you know the job and the company well enough to be sure you aren't overpricing or undervaluing yourself. Otherwise, save such delicate negotiations for the interview.

• Keep your references for the interview. Consideration for their privacy suggests that you leave their names and addresses out of your résumé and supply them only on request.

What form to use

Most employers feel the same way about the information in a résumé as Constance Klages of Battalia, Lotz, a New York executive recruiting firm. She says bluntly: "I want it fast, and I want it easy." Those who do the hiring prefer résumés that outline the applicant's work history in reverse chronological order and that stick to a Western Union literary style. Since a job applicant wants to put his best foot forward, his résumé should state his strongest points first and save less important matters for later. Usually his last job is of greatest significance, but if he has, say, a graduate degree in business from a well-regarded school, he may want to give it top billing.

Form letters used instead of résumés, containing only selected details from the applicant's work record, may be helpful as a last resort. But they are unpopular with employers. Such letters tend to be aggressively self-promoting and incomplete. First cousin to the form letter is the résumé that touts the accomplishments of an individual without anchoring them to dates, places and job titles. Résumés and letters that intermingle pertinent information with puffery get low marks from most readers. Even if they work, there is a risk, says William Billington, partner in the Chicago recruiting firm of Billington, Fox & Ellis. "They appeal to impulsive individuals, small businessmen," he says. "People who impulsively hire, unfortunately, also impulsively terminate."

All the same, using résumés that are narratives of experience rather than simple listings of job descriptions may help job hunters with special problems. Besides people who want to hide a dark past, those with a history of job hopping find them useful. They are well suited to people whose careers consist of a series of projects—consultants, for example, or engineers, whose responsibilities grow over the years while their job titles remain the same. Women who reenter the job market after years of community service or charity work may find this type of résumé the most flattering way to present their unpaid work experience; those whose careers have been sidetracked can use narrative résumés to draw attention away from their most recent jobs.

What tone to take

Some personnel consultants find an inventory of job titles sterile and uninformative, and so favor résumés that tick off accomplishments—growth in company earnings, say, or savings traceable to job performance. Others are irritated by a hard-sell approach, which they feel rings false. "A résumé might say, 'During my eight years there, the company's profits grew from $2 million to $4 million.' That's great, I say, but maybe if you weren't there, they would have grown from $2 million to $6 million," says Peter Lauer. The director of materials management at a Midwest firm agrees: "Anybody who puts down great glowing sales and cost savings, I figure he is kind of conning me a bit." Other advice:

- Assume your résumé is not going to please everyone. Suit yourself. Adopt a style and tone that you are comfortable with.

- Take into the account the conventions of your profession. If you are a banker or accountant, you would probably do well to compose a conservative, bare-bones kind of résumé. For an advertising man, a touch of salesmanship might be appropriate.

What it should look like

Résumés should be attractive to the eye, but some job seekers go overboard, turning out résumés as elaborate as wedding cakes. Because dignity and good taste are valued in people in responsible jobs, attention-getting devices—photos or brightly colored binders, for example—can backfire. John Sibbald of Booz, Allen & Hamilton once received a job application from a product manager who attached a sample of his product—an aluminum bolt—to his letter. The gimmick caused a mild sensation among Sibbald's colleagues, but, he recalls, "None of us could remember the man's name."

A further tip:

- Stay away from the cluttered look. An inviting résumé, like many classy advertisements, includes a lot of white space.

The covering letter

Even a first-class résumé is wasted if it is sent out without a covering note. Thomas Freyberg, who is in charge of hiring at the Cleveland headquarters of Eaton Corp., a manufacturer of car and truck parts, says his office often does not answer job applicants who send résumés without letters. The average job seeker can make do with one version of his résumé if he writes covering notes tailored to the job opportunity. They should be brief—not more than three or four short paragraphs. Covering notes give the job seeker a chance to use his charm. He can emphasize a salient virtue only touched upon in his résumé. He can indicate whether his job search is confidential, why he is looking and whether he is willing to relocate. If the writer was referred by a mutual acquaintance, the note should say so.

Most important, the note should make it clear that the applicant knows something about the company he is asking for a job. Unless he is mailing out hundreds of résumés in a blanket job search or answering a blind ad, a job seeker should do some homework on his prospective employer. Covering letters should be addressed to the individual most likely to make the hiring decision. For executive-level jobs, that decision is usually made not by the personnel department, but by supervisors or even by the head of the firm. An urgent job search may necessitate a scatter-shot approach. If a job seeker is mailing his résumé to many companies, he will probably not be able to research each one. But a covering letter should go with each résumé, and even a form letter should be addressed to a particular person. The names of company executives can be found in business directories.

Avoiding the canned look

A follow-up letter after an interview reminds the interviewer of the writer's qualifications, confirms his interest in the job and gently presses for further action, perhaps a second meeting. The interview gives the applicant a chance to learn what his prospective employer's needs are. The follow-up letter gives the applicant a chance to show the employer that he meets those needs. A letter showing interest in the employer's problems—volunteering solutions, even—should go over well. "Give free advice," suggests Peter Lauer. "It's the greatest thing you can do to get a job."

It's probably a good idea to have the résumé typed and printed professionally, which generally costs about $10 for 100 copies of a one-page résumé. For the job hunter who doesn't feel up to mounting a mass mailing, the Yellow Pages list letter shops, printers and résumé services that will engineer such campaigns—typing and reproducing résumés, attaching form letters, addressing and mailing envelopes. That complete service typically costs between 40¢ and 60¢ a letter. A job hunter who uses mass mailing techniques should not expect a reply rate of more than 5%.

While help with the mechanics can be worth paying for, personnel men frown on professionally written résumés, which can cost from $20 to $150. "They always seem to be a poor substitute for a person telling about himself," says John Coats, a recruiter at Raymond International, a Houston engineering and construction company. "They tend to look canned." Do it yourself, urge experienced résumé readers—and don't wait until you need it. John Sibbald recommends revising your résumé every three years as a way of taking stock. "Update your résumé as soon as you take a new job," suggests San Francisco marketing manager Thomas Parker. "That's when you feel up about yourself. If you wait until you are out looking for a job, you'll be writing while you are depressed."

November 19, 1973

Mr. Ralph A. Pomeroy
Vice President-Marketing
Regal Foods & Sundries Inc.
Canton, Ohio

Dear Mr. Pomeroy:

   I am the founder and Marketing Vice President of Frigifoods,
a new venture in frozen convenience foods. We have just completed the sale of this business and, as a consequence, I am
now seeking a new job.

   The attached resume shows that I have focused my career
on corporate growth through new products, ventures and strategies. My experience lies mostly in consumer products and
services. While I would prefer a general management opportunity
in a small to medium-sized company, I would also consider senior
marketing management opportunities. My salary expectations
would be in the $25,000-$30,000 range, with an incentive or equity
possibility on top of that.

   I do not know if you are the most appropriate individual in
your company for me to write to, but I am interested in what
Regal is doing, particularly in the convenience pet food area.
Your response to my inquiry will be greatly appreciated.

   I look forward to hearing from you.

                              Sincerely,

                              Thomas A. Barcklay

Home Address:

   256 Eastwood Avenue
   Barrington, Illinois 60010

Fig. 1. Toward a more perfect résumé

Money asked a senior personnel executive at a major management consulting firm to
prepare what he would consider the perfect résumé and covering letter. The samples
he drew up are entirely hypothetical. Neither Frigifoods, Inc. nor Thomas A. Barcklay
of Barrington, Illinois, exists. Barcklay, says the personnel man, is an entrepreneurial
sort; after the sale of the small company he helped found, he would insist on equity
in any firm he joins, as his covering letter points out. Of course, Barcklay's résumé

RESUME

THOMAS A. BARCKLAY   Born: June 20, 1935
256 Eastwood Avenue
Barrington, Illinois 60010   Telephone: (312) 852-9466

Married, 2 children   6 feet 1   180 pounds Good health

business   FRIGIFOODS, INC.   Skokie, Illinois
experience · Vice President, Marketing. Assisted in formation of
            company in 1970 to manufacture and market frozen convenience
            foods. Initial product line was a range of German and
            Italian hors d'oeuvres and sidewalk specialties.
1970 to   Major responsibilities included management of all marketing
present   and sales operations, with a total work force of 55 people;
            development of marketable product lines; and establishment
            of goals and strategies for staffing and personnel, adver-
            tising and promotion and business development.

            Key accomplishments:

                 Took company from no sales in 1970 to revenues
            ·   of $4 million in 1973 and pretax profits of 16%.

                 · Hired all marketing and sales employees.

                 Developed and introduced three complete frozen
            ·   food product lines - one was retail, the other
                 two institutional.

                 · Established internal cost and financial control
                 system.

                 Was instrumental in sale of the company at con-
            ·   siderable profit to one of America's largest
                 food processors.

1962-1970   GENERAL MILLS, INC.   Minneapolis, Minnesota
1965-1970   · Marketing Manager. Big G division is the company's
            largest profit contributor and competes in the highly
            advertised and promoted cereal category. Brand names
            include Cheerios, Total and Wheaties. Had responsi-
            bility for product management, market research, adver-
            tising and sales promotion.

was easier than most to write, since his work history shows a high level of accomplishment and consistently good judgment in moving to better jobs. But his résumé
also goes beyond a routine presentation of credentials to give a glimpse of his
personality—it records the fact that his father was a sheepherder, for example, and
that Barcklay paid his way through the University of Nevada by working as a black-
jack dealer.

Page Two   Continued

Resume of T. A. Barcklay

Key accomplishments:

· Using media and consumption analysis, developed plan that resulted in 8% gain in market share for old, established brand.

· Directed product and marketing development for two nationally successful new products.

· Successfully managed an outside R&D project on the first successful noncereal breakfast product.

1963-1965   · <u>Manager, New Breakfast Products</u>. In Big G division, successfully launched six new cereal products including one that is now the market share leader. Supervised three product managers.

1962-1963   · <u>Product Manager</u>. Created a rapid-feedback product testing system that reduced introduction lead time by one-half and increased sales and market share on all assigned products.

1959-1962   <u>PFIZER, INC.</u>   New York, New York
· <u>Market Research Manager</u>. Leeming/Pacquin, Pfizer's health proprietaries division. Brand names include Visine, Pacquins, Hai Karate. Instrumental in market testing of Visine.

1960-1961   · <u>District Sales Manager</u>. Lower Westchester district won eastern award two years in a row for highest gains in sales. Supervised five sales representatives.

1959-1960   · <u>Sales Representative</u>. Joined Leeming/Pacquin division in testing program and moved into sales force. Promoted to sales manager one year later.

education   <u>HARVARD GRADUATE SCHOOL OF BUSINESS ADMINISTRATION</u>
1957-1959   · <u>Degree of Master in Business Administration in June 1959</u>. Baker Scholar.

Page Three   Continued

Resume of T. A. Barcklay

1953-1957   UNIVERSITY OF NEVADA
            · Degree of Bachelor of Arts in June 1957. Varsity
            basketball, track and football. ROTC regimental
            commander. Earned way through college as "21" dealer
            in local casinos.

1957-1964   UNITED STATES ARMY
            · Platoon leader, executive officer and company commander,
            infantry, in reserves and National Guard. Resigned
            commission as captain in 1964.

early   · Grew up in small town, Winnemucca, Nevada. Graduated
backround   second in high school class of 14. Active in sports
            and school activities. Father a sheepherder.

community   · Five years as board member and vice president of Tower
activities Lakes Improvement Association. Vestryman of church.
            President of Barrington Paddle Tennis Association.

interests   · Duffer tennis, basketball, creative writing, pen and
            ink drawing, antique automobiles and country music.

references · References will be provided upon request.

Letters about employment

J. H. MENNING,
C. W. WILKINSON, and
PETER B. CLARKE

The late J. H. Menning was Professor of Marketing at the University of Alabama. C. W. Wilkinson is Professor of Behavioral Studies at the University of Alabama. Peter B. Clarke is President of the Arcus Company.

Writing the prospecting application

A salesman, like a fisherman, almost has to have a feeling of success consciousness and optimism so that he can think positively. You can hardly force yourself to really try to catch fish or make sales unless you feel that you have an attractive bait or an appealing product or service. Other people (and seemingly even fish) sense quickly how you feel about yourself, and respond accordingly. And since application letters are sales letters in every way—sales letters selling your services—you have to have self-confidence and positive thinking. . . .

With a well-prepared data sheet you will have done a good job of lining up your qualifications, of realizing what you can do, and of deciding on those qualifications which most nearly equip you for efficient performance. You are then in much better shape to write an application letter—a sales letter selling your services.

At times you may want to send a prospecting letter without a data sheet. That's your decision. We don't think it's the better decision; most personnel people prefer to receive a data sheet. Even if you elect not to use one, you'll write a better letter for having prepared one. Having prepared it, you're throwing good money away if you don't let it work for you.

You're also being very foolish if you fail to capitalize on your investment of time and effort (and maybe even cash) by slavishly following the points and aping the style of another person's application letter. The good "model" appli-

J. H. Menning, C. W. Wilkinson, and Peter Clarke, *Communicating Through Letters and Reports,* 6th ed. (Homewood, Ill.: Richard D. Irwin, 1976), pp. 350–74. © 1976 by Richard D. Irwin, Inc.

cation letter doesn't exist—and never will for applicants of average intelligence and above. They realize that *the application letter must be an accurate reflection of the writer's personality as well as aptitudes.* And so they will write their own.

Securing favorable attention

As in sales letters, the infallible way to secure interest in your application letter is to stress your central selling point in writing about serving the reader. Your central selling point may be an ability based on education, experience, or personal qualities or a combination of them. . . . [This young man has] successfully combined all three:

With my college background of undergraduate and graduate work, my teaching experience, and a temperament which helps me to adapt easily to college people and circumstances, I believe I could do a good job as a field representative for your firm.

And after talking with several field representatives about the nature of the work, I know I'd have the added factor in my favor of being very enthusiastic about it.

While I certainly don't know all the reasons why college teachers choose certain textbooks, I have taught enough while completing a master's degree at Alabama to realize that format and price are only minor factors affecting a teacher's decision.

Possibly the most significant realization from my year as a graduate student and instructor is that there is no true "academic" personality — that a successful representative has to be prepared to meet and talk freely and convincingly with a wide range of personalities.

Teaching classes in Economic Problems and Policies, discussing my thesis with committee members both collectively and individually, and talking with staff members about teaching problems (in staff meetings and in bull sessions) have helped me to think on my feet, to have self-assurance when speaking to groups and to individuals, and to adapt myself to varying situations. I've learned to feel at home with all types of college teachers.

The fact that I have studied business at Alabama rather than liberal arts at an Ivy League school may actually make me a better representative, Mr. Dayton — especially if I'm assigned to the South, where I already know the territory. I could serve happily as your representative in any district, however; I've traveled over most of the U.S. (and to Europe and the Far East while in the Navy)

and can adapt readily to the fine people and country one finds
everywhere.

I believe you'd find me quick to learn; the men I've listed as
references on the enclosed data sheet will probably tell you so if
you'll write them.

After you've had a chance to verify some of the things I've said
about myself in this letter and on the data sheet, will you write me
frankly about the possibilities of my working for you?

Possibly I could talk with one of your regional representatives in
this area as a preliminary step. And I can plan to go to New York
sometime this summer to talk with you further about my successfully
representing your firm.

(You may be interested to know that the 22 copies of this letter brought
22 replies within a couple of weeks. Half a dozen of the firms wanted to
interview the applicant right away, another half dozen, within a month afterward. The writer had four job offers.)

To get started rapidly and pertinently, one applicant began her letter to
the American Red Cross this way:

I can be the versatile type of club director the American Red
Cross seeks.

As a result of five years' specialized training in dietetics and
institutional management and 10 years' practical experience in
meeting and serving people as a volunteer worker in service clubs
from New York to Trinidad, from France through Germany, I know the
kind of program which will best meet the needs and interests of
service men and their families everywhere.

A young man just graduating from college got favorable attention with
this:

Because I have had an unusual five—year educational opportunity
combining the study of engineering and management, I feel sure of
my ability to do efficient work in your industrial engineering
department and to steadily increase in usefulness.

I could conduct a time study with a technical knowledge of the
machines concerned or work on the problems of piece wage rates
without losing sight of the highly explosive personnel situation
involved.

A 19-year-old-girl with two years of college summarized her outstanding
qualifications in the following well-chosen lead:

As a secretary in your export division I could take your dictation
at a rapid 120 words per minute and transcribe it accurately in
attractive letters and memos at 40 words per minute — whether it is
in English or Spanish.

There's nothing tricky about these openings. They just talk work.

You may be able to capitalize on a trick in some situations—provided it
shows knowledge of job requirements. The young advertising candidate who
mailed a walnut to agencies with the lead "They say advertising is a hard nut
to crack" got results from the message he had enclosed in the walnut. The
young man who, in seeking radio work, wrote his message in the form of a
radio script marked "Approved for Broadcast" and stamped with a facsimile of
the usual log certification indicated above-average knowledge of working conditions. The secretary who started her letter with a line of shorthand characters indicated qualifications from the start. The statistical worker who drew at
the top of his letter a line graph showing the Federal Reserve Board Index of
Industrial Production and in the opening lines of his letter commented on the
significance of its recent movements certainly had a head start on other candidates for the job. If you can think of one which is pertinent, in good taste, and
not stereotyped (such as the balance sheet from an accounting candidate), it
may help you. But it is by no means a must and can do you more harm than
good unless you handle it carefully and thoughtfully.

You do need to concentrate on rapidly and naturally establishing your
qualifications with the attitude that you want to put them to work for the
reader in some specific job. Having held out such a promise, you need to back
it up.

Supplying evidence of performance ability

Your evidence in an application is simply an interpretation of the highlights of
your data sheet. For persuasiveness, you phrase it in terms of "doing something for you." If you didn't notice how each of the paragraphs two through
seven in the letter beginning on p. 111 gives evidence in support of the opening promise, go back and read the letter again.

The applicant to the Red Cross whose opening you read in a preceding
passage continued her letter this way:

With the full realization that the Red Cross necessarily operates
on an economical basis, I can use my thorough college training
in institutional organization as a sound basis for financial
management, cost control, personnel management, employee training,
and job specification, all of which I know are vital in a well-run
Red Cross club.

When it comes to food service, I feel at home in the planning,
selection, buying, preparation, and serving of party food for a
group of 500 or 1,000 or behind the snack bar of a canteen or in
planning the well-balanced meals for the hardworking Red Cross
girls who live in the barracks. During my year as assistant
dietician at Ward Memorial Hospital in Nashville, I successfully
supervised the preparation and serving of from 3,000 to 20,000
meals a day.

Having been an Army wife and lived in many places under varying
circumstances, I have learned to use my own initiative in developing
the facilities at hand. I've learned to be adaptable, patient,
resourceful, and — through grim necessity as a widow — cheerful!
I believe in punctuality but am not a clock watcher. And I know from
experience that I can direct people without incurring resentment.

I've always enjoyed and participated in the many sports and social
activities that are listed on the enclosed data sheet. As a Red
Cross director I could help others to share their pleasures too.

> The industrial-management applicant followed up his opening like this:

The program I followed at Northwestern University required five
years of study because I felt that qualification for work in
industrial management should include basic engineering
information. The scope of such courses as Business Organization and
Cost Accounting were therefore enhanced and expanded by related
work in Machine Design and Properties of Engineering Materials.

Three years in the Corps of Engineers of the U.S. Army form the main
basis of my experience. A large part of this time I spent as a
section officer in a large engineer depot. The knowledge, skills,
and experience I gained concerning layout, storage, freight
handling, and heavy packaging relate very closely to the problems of
factory management in the production of heavy machinery. While
working with the problems of shipping bulldozer blades, I was
gaining experience that will aid me in understanding the special
techniques required in handling cotton pickers and tractors.

I've learned how to get my ideas across in business-writing courses
here at Northwestern as well as through being a reporter for the
Daily Northwestern. As a member of the student governing board and
the senior council, I've had good lessons in cooperation and
patience. And despite a pretty rugged schedule of classes and
extracurricular activities, I've kept myself in good physical
condition by participating on my fraternity's intramural
basketball and football teams.

The enclosed data sheet and inquiries to the men I've listed will
probably give you all the information you want about me before
seeing me, but I shall be glad to furnish any further particulars
you may wish.

And the secretarial applicant to the exporting firm continued (after her
opening) in the following vein, drawing exclusively on her schooling:

In secretarial courses during my two years of study at Temple
College, I've consistently demonstrated my ability to handle
material at these speeds. And as a matter of practice in my course in
conversational Spanish I take down what my teacher and my classmates
say. I have no difficulty transcribing these notes later.

I learned a good deal about your markets and your clientele while
doing research for a report I submitted this semester in marketing,
"Some Recent Developments in Latin—American Markets." In the
process I became familiar with such publications as The American
Importer, Exporting, and The Foreign Commerce Yearbook.

I'm neat and conservative in appearance. Early in my life mother
impressed upon me the desirability of a low—pitched voice and
distinct enunciation; probably for that reason my college speech
teacher has been especially interested in helping me to achieve
poise and dignity before a group of people. On the telephone or in
person I could greet your clients pleasantly and put them at ease.

After I start working, I hope to further my knowledge of the people
and language of Latin America by using my vacation time for trips to
Mexico, Central America, and South America.

Overcoming deficiencies is a function of the letter, not the data sheet. In
almost any application situation you'll have one or more. In many cases the
wiser course of action is simply not to talk about it! In other cases, if you feel
that it is such an important consideration as to merit identification and possibly discussion, embed it in your letter, and endow it with as much positive-
ness as possible.

The young man wanting to be a publisher's representative had two
strikes against him and knew it: he had gone through a commerce school and
he was a product of a state university in the South rather than an Ivy League
school. Turn back and note how in the fifth paragraph of his letter he met the
issue head on and capitalized on it.

The industrial-management applicant had no experience. But did he
apologize for it? Not at all! He held out his service experience confidently and
showed its relation to the job sought. "Three years in the . . . U.S. Army form
the basis of my experience," he wrote—instead of the weak-kneed statement,

"The only experience I've had was in the Army," or even worse, "I've had no experience. But I did serve with the Corps of Engineers in the Army."

Probably one of the finest examples we've ever seen of turning an apparent handicap into a virtue is that of a young woman who at first didn't know where to turn when confronted with the necessity for getting a job. After thoughtful analysis of what she had done in college and how it could be used in business, she sent the following letter to a large Chicago mail-order firm. The third paragraph is the epitome of positive thinking.

Isn't one of the significant qualifications of a correspondent in your company the ability to interpret a letter situation in terms of the reader?

Because I believe that I could express an understanding of a situation clearly and imaginatively to your customers (a degree in English from the University of Illinois, an <u>A</u> in Business Communication, and the editorship of my sorority paper suggest that I can), will you allow me to become a trial employee in your correspondence division?

Learning your particular business policies and procedures in writing letters would come quickly, I believe; I am used to following assignments exactly, and I have no previous working experience to unlearn.

I have a good background in writing. I can type 60 words a minute. And the varied extracurricular activities listed on the enclosed data sheet are my best evidence for telling you that I've successfully passed a four-year test of getting along with people.

Will you call me at 876–2401 and name a time when I may come in and talk with you?

It worked! And the same kind of positive approach to any handicap you may have—physical or otherwise—is probably your best way to treat it.

Talking the special language of your reader's business also convinces your reader of your performance ability and helps to overcome any deficiency. In all the examples you've been reading in this analysis, you've probably noticed that each incorporated specific and special references to conditions or products or activities peculiar to the given job. Such references certainly further the impression that you are aware of job requirements and conditions. The would-be publisher's representative referred to books, teachers, college circumstances, and adoptions (the end and aim of that particular job). The industrial management applicant referred easily and sensibly to two products of the company, tractors and cotton pickers. The applicant to the Red Cross referred to service clubs, canteens, and the hardworking Red Cross girls who live in the barracks.

From your research you can readily establish such references. If significant enough information, they may be good choices of talking points for your beginning, as in the following three instances:

With the recent improvements on the foot—control hydraulic—power lift on Farmall tractors and the construction of a new implement plant at Poplar Bluff, Missouri, the International Harvester Company of Memphis will no doubt be selling more farm machinery than ever before. As a salesman of Farmall tractors and equipment, I am sure I could help to continue your record of improving sales.

—

The marked increase in General Motors sales for the first two quarters undoubtedly reflects the favorable public reception of the new passenger car models and the new Frigidaire appliances.

These increased sales plus the increased production as announced in your annual report also mean more work for your accounting staff. I can take care of a man—sized share of this extra work, I believe — and with a minimum of training.

—

The regular Saturday night reports your retail dealers submit show consumer trends which I want to help you translate into continued Whirlpool leadership — as an analyst in your sales department.

Each of these candidates continued to talk the terminology peculiar to the job. For example, the sales applicant referred knowingly to farmers and farming activities and to the selling activities of making calls, demonstrating, closing, and—probably most important in selling farm machinery—servicing. Such informed references are highly persuasive in any application letter because they establish in a desirable way the impression that the writer is well aware of the work conditions and requirements.

You want to show such knowledge, of course. But if you state it in independent clauses (flat facts which the reader probably already knows) you'll sound wooden and dull.

The desirability of *emphasizing qualifications instead of analysis* will be clearer to you through comparing the following original letter and the revision. The original is almost painful in its flat, obvious statements. It also uses so much space stating requirements of the job that it fails to establish qualities of the applicant. The revision eliminates the flatness and preachiness through implication or incidental reference.

Original	Revised
It takes a secretary who is versatile, accurate, reliable and dependable for a firm like the Brown Insurance Company. I	My year's work as a secretary, four years' thorough college training in commercial studies, and lifetime residence in

<table>
<tr><th>Original</th><th>Revised</th></tr>
</table>

Original	Revised
realize the importance of your having such a secretary, and I believe I have the necessary qualifications.	Tuscumbia should enable me to serve you well as a secretary and further the friendly relations between you and your clients.
Having graduated from the University of Alabama with commercial studies as my major, I am familiar with such machines as the adding machine, Mimeograph, and Comptometer. Since my graduation I have been employed as a secretary with the Reynolds Metal Company. This has given me an opportunity to combine my knowledge with experience.	Whether you want to send a memo to a salesman, a note to a client, or a letter to the home office, I could have it on your desk for signing within a short time. While earning my degree at Alabama, I developed a dictation rate of 100 words per minute and a transcription rate of 45, which I demonstrated daily during my year's work as secretary with the Reynolds Metal Company.
Insurance takes a lot of time and patience. A large amount of bookkeeping is required because every penny has to be accounted for. My one year of accounting at the University will enable me to keep your books neatly and correctly; and if it is necessary for me to work overtime, I am in good physical health to do so.	To help with the varied kinds of record keeping in a large insurance agency, I can use the knowledge and skills from a year's course in accounting and my study of filing systems, office practices, and office machines — all applied during my year of work. You can trust me to compute premiums accurately, send notices on schedule, and devise and turn out special forms when necessary.
Since the Brown Insurance Company has many customers in different parts of the country, a large amount of business letters and transactions are carried on. As your secretary, I could take dictation at 100 words a minute and transcribe your letters accurately and neatly at 45 words a minute.	I realize that in an insurance agency everyone from the janitor to the bookkeeper affects the feeling of the public and that all must exercise friendliness and tact in any contact with a client. I anticipate the unexpected, and I meet it calmly; so I am prepared to handle a number of duties and to adjust to the demands of a busy, varied work schedule (including overtime work when it's

| Original | Revised |

Even though accuracy and speed are important, personality is an important characteristic too. Because of the many kinds of people who are connected with this type of business, it is important to have a secretary who not only can file, take dictation, and type, but who can be a receptionist as well. Since I have lived in Tuscumbia all my life, I will know most of your clients as individuals and can serve them in a friendly manner.

I have enclosed a data sheet for your convenience.

Will you please call me at 374–4726 and tell me when I can talk to you?

necessary). I would expect to maintain cordial relations with all your customers quite naturally and easily because most of them are the neighbors and friends I've lived around all my life.

Mr. Bills and the other references I've listed on the enclosed data sheet will be glad to confirm my statements that I can work efficiently and cheerfully for you as a secretary who is able and willing to do more than turn out letters. After you've heard from them, please call me at 374–4726 and name a time that I may come in and talk with you.

Although the revision is a little longer, it accomplishes a good deal more: It establishes qualifications in a good lead; it talks the special language of the reader; it establishes more qualifications. It also has a much better work-for-you interpretation. But the major improvement of the revision over the original is that it eliminates the preachy, flat statements (particularly at the beginnings of paragraphs) that made a smart girl sound dull.

Asking for appropriate action

Whatever action you want your reader to take, identify it as specifically as possible, and ask confidently for it. Ordinarily it is to invite you in for an interview. As a self-respecting human being who has something to offer, you do not need to beg or grovel; but you do need to remember—and to show your realization of the fact—that the reader is under no obligation to see you, that giving you time is doing you a favor, that the time and place of the interview are to be at the reader's convenience, and that you should be grateful for the interview.

The action ending of the sales letter needs to be slightly modified in the application letter, however. You cannot with good grace exert as much pressure. For this reason most employment counselors and employers do not advocate using any reply device (an employer is happy to pay the postage to send a message to a potentially good employee, and writing and mailing a letter are routine actions). But your application action ending still suggests a specific action, tries to minimize the burdensome aspects of that action through careful phrasing, establishes gratitude, and supplies a stimulus to action with a reminder of the contribution the applicant can make to the firm.

You've already seen several action endings in this chapter. But to drive home the point, let's look at the action endings of the four letters with which we started this analysis.

The Red Cross applicant definitely planned a trip to Washington for job-hunting purposes; so she concluded her letter logically and naturally with

When I'm in Washington during the first two weeks in August, I should be grateful for the opportunity to come to your office and discuss further how I may serve in filling your present need for Red Cross club directors. Will you name a convenient time in a letter to me at my Birmingham address?

The industrial-management applicant phrased his ending in this simple fashion:

Please suggest a time when you can conveniently allow me to discuss my qualifications for work in your industrial engineering department.

And the secretarial applicant confidently asked her exporter-reader:

Won't you please call me at 615–5946 and tell me a time when I may come to your office and show you how well my preparation will fit into your firm?

The publisher's-representative applicant was in a slightly atypical situation. He couldn't afford to ask directly for an interview in New York because he had neither the money nor the time right then. So he wrote:

After you've had a chance to verify some of the things I've said about myself in this letter and on the data sheet, will you write me frankly about the possibilities of my working for you?

Possibly I could talk with one of your regional representatives in this area as a preliminary step. And I can plan to come to New York sometime this summer to talk with you further about my successfully representing your firm.

(As it turned out, he flew to New York at the expense of the firms on two occasions within two weeks after sending the letters, but that was the result of further correspondence—and it's certainly not anything to count on!)

Such letters as suggested in the preceding pages and in the checklist for applications won't work miracles. They won't make a poor applicant a good one. They won't ordinarily secure a job; usually they can only open the door for an interview and further negotiations, but that is their purpose. To make yours do all it can, you may want to review the list of suggestions on pp. 126–27.

Writing the invited application

Often a firm makes its personnel needs known (especially for middle- and upper-management positions) by running an ad, by listing with an agency (commercial, where they'll charge you a fee, or governmental like the U.S. Employment service offices and state-government equivalents), or simply by word of mouth. As you probably know, most large companies also list their needs for college-graduate personnel with college placement bureaus and have recruiting personnel who regularly visit campuses scouting for talented young men and women.

These situations (where the prospective employer actually goes out searching for new employees) give you one drawback (you'll have more competition because more people will know about the job) and two advantages in writing a letter: (1) you don't need to generate interest at the beginning (you already have it!); and (2) the ad, agency, or talent scout will give you the job requirements or as a bare minimum identify the job category and principal duties.

Even when you hear of the job through other people, they will usually tell you what you'll be expected to do. So matching up your qualifications with the job requirements is easier in the invited situation than in the prospecting because your source will usually identify requirements in some order indicating their relative importance to the employer.

If you are equally strong on all points of preparation, you have no problem. You simply take up the points in the order listed. But such a happy condition you'll rarely find. Most often your best talking point is not the most significant requirement, and usually you'll be deficient in some way. The solution is to employ the same strategy you did in writing the invited sales letter: Tie in your strongest point of preparation with something the reader wants done; take up those points wherein you are weakest in the middle position of the letter and attempt to correlate them with some positive point.

Your analysis of job requirements and compilation of a data sheet are exactly the same procedures as in a prospecting situation. Adaptation is simply easier. And once past the opening, supplying evidence and asking for appropriate action are the same. Since the beginnings in the prospecting and the invited applications do differ somewhat, we need to consider why and to make some suggestions that will help you write good ones.

Whether you learn of the job through an ad, through an agency, or via a third person, your beginning is pretty much the same. The first requirement is that it mention your main qualifications; the second, that it identify the job; the third, that it show a service attitude; and the fourth that it refer to the source of the information (*subordinately* unless it is significant). The reason for naming this fourth function is simply that the reference to the ad, or the bureau, or the person who told you about the job is an automatic attention getter which favorably reinforces the reader's willingness or even eagerness to read your letter. One good sentence can accomplish all four functions and point the trend of the letter.

The opening of the following letter puts emphasis on service through work, clearly identifies the specific kind of work sought, and desirably subordinates the reference to the source. Note that after the opening the letter reads much the same as a prospecting application (indeed, if you omit the lead in the faked address block and the first two lines, it could be a prospecting letter). Note also the adaptation of talking points—the stress on experience rather than on formal training.

I'm "sold
on insurance"

and I believe I can be the aggressive salesman for whom you
advertised in Thursday's Express.

Five years of experience in dealing with people very similar to
your prospects -- in addition to technical training in insurance
and salesmanship -- would aid me in selling your low-premium
accident policy.

As a pipeliner in Louisiana in 1971 I made friends with the kind of
men to whom I'd be selling your policies. I had a chance to study
people, their hopes and fears and desires for protection and
security, while doing casework for the Welfare Society in San
Antonio in the summer of 1972. And while working as a waiter both
in high school and in college I learned how to work for and with
the public.

The most significant thing I learned was to keep right on smiling
even though dog-tired at the end of my 6-12 p.m. shift after having
been to school most of the day. And I certainly learned the meaning
of perseverance when I had to go home after midnight and get on the
books for the next day's assignments.

The same perseverance that earned me B's in Insurance and Income
Protection, Liability Insurance, and Personal Salesmanship will
help me find leads, follow them up, persuade, and close a sale. I
know an insurance man makes money for himself and his company only

when he sticks to a schedule of calls. But I'm equally aware of the value of patience and the necessity for repeat calls.

Because I'm friendly and apparently easygoing, your prospects would like to see me coming. I was elected a Favorite at Schreiner Institute, and at the University of Texas I was tapped for Silver Spurs, a service-honorary organization. Making these many friends has resulted in my knowing people from all sections of the state.

My build and obvious good health inspire confidence. And since I'm 24 and single, I am free to travel anywhere at any time, as well as to work nights.

Dr. Fitzgerald and the other men I've listed on the enclosed information sheet can help you evaluate me professionally and personally if you'll write or call them.

I should be grateful for your telling me a convenient time and place when I may talk with you further about my qualifications for being the hardworking salesman you want.

Frequently your source—especially an ad—gives you an effective entering cue and provides you with useful reference phrases throughout the letter. From the key phrases you can almost reconstruct the ad the young man answered in the following letter:

Because of my college training in accounting and my work experience, I believe I can be the quick-to-learn junior accountant for whom you advertised in the May Journal of Accountancy.

Having successfully completed down-to-earth studies in tax accounting and auditing while earning my degree in accounting at Alabama, I should be able to catch on to your treatment of these problems quickly.

And while working as assistant ledger clerk for the Grantland Davis firm in Atlanta one semester, I developed a great respect for accuracy as well as an appreciation of the necessity for the conscientious, painstaking labor so essential in public accounting. There, too, I also saw clearly the necessity for absorbing confidential information without divulging it in any manner to others.

My natural aptitude for synthesis and analysis, strengthened by special study of the analysis of financial statements and reinforced with a broad background of economics, law, and statistics, should enable me to handle the recurring tasks of compiling comparative statements of earnings and net worth. And my training in writing reports will help me to tell the story to my seniors as well as to clients.

Realizing that the public accountant must gain the confidence of his clients through long periods of accurate, trustworthy service, I welcome the offer of a long-range advancement program mentioned in your ad. I'm not afraid of hard work. And I enjoy the good health essential in the long, irregular working hours of rush business seasons.

Will you study the diversified list of courses and the description of my internship listed on the attached data sheet? Note also, please, the wide range of activities I took part in while maintaining an A average. Then will you write the references I've listed as a basis for letting me talk with you further about my qualifications for beginning a career of immediate usefulness to you?

I can start to work any time after graduation on June 4.

A variation of source doesn't affect your procedure—except that you *emphasize a source that would be influential in your getting the job; otherwise, subordinate the source.* If you learn of the work through an agency or a third person, the procedure is still the same. Here are some openings bearing out our statement:

Since I have the qualifications necessary for successful selling that you listed in your recent letter to the dean of students here at the University of Illinois, I believe I could serve you well as a salesman.

When I talked with Mr. Hugh Lomer this morning, he assured me that I am qualified by experience and professional training for the duties of a field auditor with your firm.

During the four years I worked as a branch-house auditor for the L. B. Price Mercantile Company to put myself through school, I became thoroughly familiar with every phase of accounting work necessary for a branch office of a large installment concern and with the reports required by the home office.

I'd certainly like the chance to prove that my education and personal characteristics parallel the description of the desirable management trainee that you gave to Dr. Morley, head of our placement bureau, when you visited the campus last week.

Two warnings need sounding, however. *The first* is to guard carefully against the stupid question, the one with the obvious answer. It is usually the result of asking a question which is made perfectly clear from the ad or the situation. When a young lady began her application to a legal firm with—

```
Are you looking for a college-trained secretary who can do the work
in your law office efficiently and accurately and who is eager to
learn law work? If so, I think I can meet your exacting requirements
for a legal secretary.
```

—she was earnestly trying to highlight the employer's needs. But the reader had made the answer to her question perfectly clear in the ad! And an efficient candidate only looked silly in the eyes of this reader.

You don't need to worry about setting out requirements; they are already clearly established. Even this opening is questionable because the answer is so obvious:

```
Wouldn't that junior accountant you advertised for in the Tribune
be more valuable to your firm if she had a sound understanding of
accounting theory and principles and basic training in industrial
accounting?
```

The reader would probably snort, "More? She wouldn't be valuable if she didn't!"

The second warning is against showing signs of selfish glee over having discovered a job possibility of your choice. When you read or hear about the job, you may rightly think, "That's just what I want!"—but don't write this or any variation of it. Resist the impulse and start writing in terms of doing something for the reader: what you can give instead of what you hope to get.

Perhaps a third warning should be sounded against assuming that you don't have much of a selling job to do because the reader is on the asking end. Nothing could be further from the truth. The competition you're up against for an advertised job is keen even in the heyday of prosperity. And because many others will apply, you'll have to write a superior letter to be chosen as one of the final few for interviewing.

In fact, the reader may face such a heap of letters that yours may not even get read. For that reason you may want to do one of several things so that your letter will command attention and thus be selected for reading. Most of these have to do with the physical impression or the mechanics of sending.

A favorite device is sending the letter by special delivery. Few personnel people ever object. If you are in the same town, you can deliver the letter yourself, with the request that it be turned over to the appropriate person.

If you insert the letter in an envelope large enough to accommodate an 8½- by 11-inch page without folding and put a piece of cardboard under it to keep it smooth, the contrast between your letter and all the others that have been folded will call attention to yours.

Prospecting Application Checklist

---

1. The prospecting application must generate interest from the start.
    a. Establish early your central selling point of education or experience or both, in terms of doing something for the reader. You may also cite your research on the company or the field, or tell a human-interest story; but they postpone the real message.
    b. Avoid the preaching or didactic, flat statement.
    c. Avoid implying that your up-to-date techniques are better, or telling the reader how to run the business.
    d. Make clear early that you are seeking work of a specialized nature, not just any job.
    e. Be realistic; talk work and doing, not "forming an association with." Avoid *position, application, vacancy,* and *opportunity.*
    f. You need verve and vigor, not stereotypes like "Please consider my application . . . ," "I should like to apply for . . . ."
    g. Don't let your biography drown out what you can do now.
    h. Don't give the reader an opportunity to shut you off with a negative response.
    i. Mere graduation (rather than the preparation back of it) is a poor lead anywhere, especially at first.
    j. Eliminate selfish-sounding statements or overtones of them.

2. Interpretation and tone are important from the start.
    a. Maintain a consistent, acceptable tone, neither apologizing for what you don't have nor bragging about what you do.
    b. For conviction, back up your assertions of ability with specific points of education or experience as evidence.
    c. Generalizing and editorializing are out of place: "invaluable," "more than qualified," even "excellent."
    d. Avoid needlessly deprecating your good qualifications.
    e. Project your education or experience right to the job.
    f. Use enough "I's" for naturalness, but avoid monotony.
    g. Show the research and thought which have gone into the project. Address the letter to the appropriate individual if at all possible; talk about company operations and trends in the industry; even a deft, tactful reference to a competitor can be a point in your favor.

3. Your education and experience are your conviction elements.
    a. Talk about your experience, schooling, or personal characteristics in terms of accomplishing something. For example, you may register for, take, attend, study, receive credit for, pass, learn, or master a course.
    b. The emphasis should go on a phase of work connected with the job you're applying for.
    c. Refer to education as work preparation (in lowercase letters) rather than exact course titles (in capitals and lowercase).
    d. You need highlights rather than details in the letter.
    e. But even highlights need to be specific for conviction.

Prospecting Application Checklist

---

    f. Your data sheet supplies thorough, detailed coverage. Refer to it incidentally, in a sentence establishing some other significant idea, just before asking the reader to take action.

    g. A one-page letter may be desirable, but it's more important that you tell all of your story in the most effective way for you.

4. Reflect your personality in both content and style.

    a. Refer to the more significant personal characteristics affecting job performance, preferably with evidence that you have them.

    b. Incorporate phrases which reveal your attitude toward work and your understanding of working conditions.

5. Ask for appropriate action in the close.

    a. Name the action you want; make it specific and plausible.

    b. Don't beg and don't command; just ask. And avoid the aloof, condescending implications of "You may call me at . . . ." Usually you ask for an appointment to talk about the job.

    c. Eliminate references to application, interview, position. Use action references to work and the steps in job getting.

    d. Clearly imply or state that you will be grateful. But "Thank you for . . ." in present tense sounds presumptuous.

    e. Show success consciousness without presumptuousness.

    f. A little sales whip-back at the end will help strengthen the impression of what you can contribute.

FOR WRITING INVITED APPLICATIONS

6. When writing an application in response to an ad or at the suggestion of an agency or friend:

    a. Primary emphasis should be on putting your preparation to work for the reader. But since your reference to the source is an automatic way of securing attention, you should identify it early and emphasize it if it carries an implied recommendation.

    b. Avoid stating what the reader would infer ("I read your ad").

    c. Don't ask questions or phrase assumptions which are clear pushovers: "If you are seeking X, Y, and Z, then I'm your man." "Are you looking for an employee with X, Y, and Z? I have X, Y, and Z."

    d. Postpone salary talk until the interview if you can. If the phrase "State salary required" is included in the description, your reply of "your going rate" or "your usual wage scale" is acceptable to any firm you'd want to work for.

Cutting out the ad and pasting it neatly at the top of the page may single out your letter for attention. Beginning your message with a faked address block which quotes from the ad is another device. Hanging indention may help to make a rushed reader reach for your letter instead of another. Even appropriate color may cause the employer to read yours rather than another in the stack.

When competition is keen, you'll need to take the time and exert the effort to be sure that your letter is one of the earliest arrivals. This may mean getting up early to get the first edition of the newspaper and having your material in such shape that you can have a complete, well-written letter and data sheet in the hands of the employer hours or even days before less alert candidates get theirs there. Even though you may not get the immediate response you want, your letter (if it is good) becomes better in the eyes of the employer as poorer ones come in through the mail. Remember, too, that people are relieved by the first application that comes in and feel kindly toward it. It relieves the fear of every such advertiser, that maybe no one will answer the ad.

But none of these devices will make much difference if your letter is not written from the viewpoint of contributing to the firm through effective, efficient work.

As you already realize, the items we suggested to you in the prospecting application checklist (p. 126) apply equally when you write an invited letter. Study them again, and review the additional items at the end of that checklist which are peculiar to the invited situation.

Continuing the campaign

Regardless of the results from your application, you have some follow-up work to do.

If you get an invitation to an interview, you know how to handle it. Accept promptly, pleasantly, and directly (if that's your decision). . . . Just remember to continue your job campaign by indicating continuing interest in serving. If you decide to turn down the invitation, . . . remember, also, the adage about never burning your bridges behind you.

If within a reasonable time you do not hear from the person or firm you've applied to, you'd probably better send a follow-up letter indicating continuing interest.

Follow-up letters

A good salesperson doesn't make one call and drop the matter if that doesn't close the sale. Neither does a sales-minded job applicant. Even if you receive the usual noncommittal letter saying that the firm is glad to have your application and is filing it in case any opening occurs, you need not hesitate to send another letter two, three, or six months after the first one. It should not be another complete application (yours will still be on file); it is just a reminder that you are still interested.

To have a reason for sending a follow-up letter two or three weeks after the original application, some applicants intentionally omit some pertinent but relatively insignificant piece of information in the original.

I noticed in rereading my copy of the application I sent you three weeks ago that I did not list Mr. Frank Regan, manager, Bell's Supermarket, Anniston, Alabama.

Since I have worked under Mr. Regan's direct supervision for three summers, he is a particularly good man to tell you about my work habits and personality. I hope you will write to him.

Such a subterfuge we cannot commend, if for no other reason than that so many other approaches are available to you. One acceptable one is this:

I know that many organizations throw away applications over six months old.

Because that much time has elapsed since I sent you mine (dated April 15), I want to assure you that I'm still interested in working for you, in having you keep my record in your active file, and in hearing from you when you need someone with my qualifications.

Only a lackadaisical applicant would end the letter there, however. Just a few more words could bring the information up to date and perhaps stimulate more interest in the application, like this:

Since graduation I have been doing statistical correlations at the Bureau of Business Research here at the University. I've picked up a few techniques I didn't learn in class, and I've certainly increased my speed on the computer keyboard and calculator.

I still want that job as sales analyst with your firm, however.

Election to an office or an honorary society, an extensive trip that has opened your eyes to bigger and better possibilities of the job, a research paper that has taught you something significant to the job, and certainly another job offer are all avenues of approach for reselling yourself and indicating continuing interest.

Thank-you letters

Following an interview, whether the results seem favorable or unfavorable, your note of appreciation is not only a business courtesy; it helps to single you out from other applicants and to show your reader that you have a good sense of human relations.

Even when you and the interviewer have agreed that the job is not for you, you can profitably invest about two minutes writing something like this:

I surely appreciate the time you spent with me last Friday
discussing employment opportunities at Monitor and Wagner.

The suggestions you made will help me find my right place in the
business world now.

After I get that experience you suggested, I may be knocking at your
door again.

When you are interested in the job discussed and feel that you have a
good chance, you're plain foolish not to write a letter expressing appreciation
and showing that you learned something from the interview.

Your description of the community relations program of Livania has
opened new vistas to me, Mr. Lee.

The functions of the public relations department in your company as
you described them made me much more aware of the significance and
appeal of this work.

As soon as I returned to the campus, I read Mr. Fields's book that
you suggested and the pamphlets describing U.S. Steel's program.

Many thanks for your suggestions and for the time you took with me.

I shall be looking forward to hearing the decision about my
application as soon as you can make it.

Job-acceptance letters

When an employer offers you a job and you decide it's the one for you, say so
enthusiastically and happily in a direct . . . letter that keeps you in a favorable
light.

I certainly do want to work with Franklin & Franklin — and I didn't
need a week to think it over, Mr. Bell, although I appreciate your
giving me that much time to come to a decision.

I've filled out the forms you gave me and enclosed them with this
letter.

Anything else?

Unless you tell me differently, I'll take off two weeks after
graduation. But I'll call you on Friday, June 11, to get
report-to-work instructions for Monday, June 14.

Job-refusal letters

Sometime in your life you'll have to tell somebody that you don't want what
has been offered. You may feel that it's routine, that it doesn't mean anything
one way or the other to a busy person who interviews many applicants and
has many other people available. Remember, though, that a human being
with pride and ego is going to read the letter. And make yourself think, "I
don't want that job *now*," for you may want to reopen negotiations at some
future point.

To wind up negotiations pleasantly and leave the way open for you, write
a . . . letter with a pleasant buffer of some favorable comment about the
company or the work, some plausible and inoffensive reason, the presentation
of the refusal as positively as you can phrase it (possibly with the statement of
where you are going to work), and an ending expressing good feeling and
appreciation or both. The following letter is a good example:

Meeting you and talking with you about working for Bowen's was one
of the more interesting job contacts I have had.

The opportunity to learn the business from the ground up and to grow
with an expanding company is a challenging one, one for which I am
grateful.

As I told you, however, I am primarily interested in product
research. Since I feel that my abilities will best be utilized in
that way, I am going to work for (a company) that has offered me such
employment.

I shall certainly continue to watch your company's progress with
interest, and I shall look forward to reading or hearing about the
results of your prepackaging program.

Letters of resignation

When you have worked for a firm, you have benefited in some way (in addition to the regular pay you have drawn). Regardless of how you may feel at
the time, remember that you can say something complimentary about how
things are run, about what you have learned as a result of your experience, or
about the people with whom you have associated. By all means, say it! Then
announce your plan to leave, giving consideration to the necessity for ample
time in which to find a replacement. In some cases no more than two weeks is
enough advance notification; sometimes it should be long enough for you to
help train the person who will take your place.

Remember, however, that you want to stay in the good graces of the individuals who have assisted you in your career. You will be wise to give ample notification, to give credit where credit is due. The suggestion to "Be kind, courteous, and considerate to the people you pass on the way up the ladder of success; you will likely meet them on your way back down" is good advice to keep in mind when you leave a job.

In many circumstances your resignation can be oral. And in many circumstances it may be better that way. But when you need to write a letter, consider adaptations of the following:

I've certainly learned a great deal about the clothing market from my work as sales analyst at Foley's the past 18 months.

I shall always be grateful to you and the other personnel who have helped me to do the job and to prepare for a more challenging one.

You will perhaps recall that when I had my interviews with you before starting to work, I stressed my interest in working toward a job as a sales coordinator.

Since I now have such an opportunity at Sakowitz, Inc., I am submitting my resignation. Apparently it will be some time before such an opening is available for me in this organization.

I should like to terminate employment in two weeks. But I can make arrangements to work a little longer if this will help to train the person who takes my place.

My thanks and good wishes.

Often when another offer comes your way, you'll feel free to discuss the opportunity with your current employer before making a final decision. Such a conference has many advantages for both employee and employer. Often a counteroffer results, to the mutual satisfaction of both, and the job change doesn't take place. If, despite a counteroffer, you still decide to make the change, you can resign in good grace with a letter somewhat like this:

Your recent offer is one I appreciate very much, and it made me give serious thought to continuing at Bowen's.

Let me say again how much I have appreciated the cooperation, the friendliness, and helpfulness of everyone with whom I've been associated here.

After considerably more evaluation, however, I believe I can make a greater contribution and be a more successful business manager by accepting the position offered me by Lowen's.

I hope that I can leave with your approval by (specific date); I feel sure that all my current projects will be completed by that time.

You'll hear from me from time to time —— if for no other reason than
that I'll be interested in how the new credit union works out.

But I'll always want to know how things are going for Bowen's and the
many friends I've made here.

When appropriate, a possible talking point is the suggestion of a succes-
sor to you; often this is a big help. A constructive suggestion, phrased positively, implies your continuing interest in the organization.

Letters of resignation written by college students who resign after having
agreed to work for someone but before actually reporting for work are something we take up with reluctance. Many personnel people regard them as
breaches of contract. Certainly a practice of sliding out from under such agreements will soon give you a black eye employmentwise.

We would urge you to give serious thought before definitely accepting a
job offer. Don't make the mistake of grabbing the first job offered you, only to
have something infinitely more to your liking come along later. We'd further
urge you never to let yourself get caught in the position of being committed to
two employers at the same time. If you have agreed to go to work for a firm
and then you have a later offer which you want to accept, do not accept it until
you are released from the first contract. To the second potential employer,
reply in some vein like this:

I certainly would like to accept your offer to come with your firm.
As attractive as your proposal is, however, I must delay accepting
it until I can secure a release from the Jenkins firm in Blankville.
After my interview with you, I accepted this position, which at the
time appeared to be the most promising available.

Can you allow me enough time to write the Jenkins personnel manager,
explaining my reasons and requesting a release? (I can give him the
names of two friends who might be suitable replacements.)

This shouldn't take longer than a week to settle. I appreciate your
offer, regardless of how things work out.

If necessary, phone the second potential employer, explain frankly, and
get approval to wait. But for your own protection, do it *before* writing a letter
like the following:

As you know, I am now planning to report to work as an executive
trainee shortly after the first of June.

Before I made this agreement with you, I had talked with a
representative of the Larkin organization in Sometown concerning
possibilities of my working there as an analyst in the quality
control division, which is the kind of work I have specifically
trained for and know I want to do.

I believe I'd be a better adjusted and qualified employee in the
Larkin job. That is the main reason I ask that you release me from my
commitment with you. The fact that Sometown is a considerably larger
city and that the starting salary is somewhat larger are only
secondary considerations.

No doubt you have other people you can call on to take my place, but
you may be interested to know that Don M. Jones and Peter Lawson are
interested in the Jenkins program. You can get portfolios on both of
them through the placement bureau here at school.

Since the Larkin people have agreed to postpone a decision until I
have heard from you, I should appreciate a quick reply.

You can rest assured that I shall keep my word with you and that if
your answer is no, I shall report to work as promised and do all I can
to be an efficient, cooperative, and cheerful employee.

Only a Simon Legree would say no to the foregoing letter. If the company
releases you, you'd then write the appropriate acceptance letter to the second
firm; but you should, as a matter of business courtesy, write a short thank-you
letter to the first company.

Two useful modifications of applications

The following two letter possibilities for helping you get the job of your choice
are *not printed here with the implication that they will take the place of the
complete sales presentation* we have suggested to you. Because they may help
you sometimes, we simply remind you of them.

The job-anticipating letter

Most personnel people are willing to give advice. And most of them are
pleased with a show of interest in their companies and evidence of long-range
planning on the part of a student. Several of our students have had successful
results from letters like the following, sent in the junior year of college:

A course in the operation of business machines under Mrs. Lora Osmus
in the Statistics Department at Alabama gave me skill in their
operation and showed me the tremendous possibilities of Burrows
equipment for business use.

After comparing Burrows and ABL equipment that was on exhibit on
Commerce Day and talking with the Burrows representative in
charge of your display, I am coming to you directly and frankly for
some help.

Since I have completed practically all of the courses required for the B.S. in commerce, I am free to elect practically all courses I shall study next year before June graduation. On the attached sheet I've listed the courses I've completed and those I'm contemplating. Will you please rank the ones you consider most beneficial for a prospective Burrows representative?

Naturally, I will regard your suggestions as off—the—cuff assistance that implies no commitment. I'm just trying to equip myself as well as I can to meet the competition for the first available job with your company after I graduate.

I shall be most grateful for your comments.

The telescoped application inquiry

We realize that good applications take time. They're worth the time, however.

But we also know that sometime, somewhere, you may need to send some inquiries in a hurry and simply cannot write a complete one. You may be able to make profitable use of the services of your college placement bureau in a letter, as one young man did. He was too busy writing a thesis and sitting for graduate examinations to prepare a thorough application. He sent the following request and a reply card to six firms:

With completion of an M.S. degree in accounting at the University of Alabama and two years of retail merchandise accounting experience, I believe I could make you a good accountant with a minimum of training — and be able to advance more rapidly than the majority of accountants you could hire.

I am not just an accountant: A well—rounded background of finance, transportation, economics, and other related subjects will enable me, in time, to do managerial work as well.

May I have the Placement Bureau here at the University send you a transcript of my college record together with a detailed record of my experience, faculty rating statements, and names and addresses of former employers?

I shall be happy to furnish any additional information you may want and to be available for an interview at your convenience later if you will check and return the enclosed card.

He received replies from all six firms, it's true. But only one resulted in an interview.

This may be a stopgap measure sometime. But this young man's experience simply reconfirms the fact that an applicant must tell a complete story if he expects to get a show of effective interest. . . .

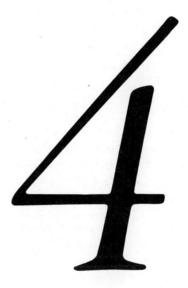

Letters
and
memoranda

Effective letters

JAMES M. REID, JR., and
ROBERT M. WENDLINGER

James M. Reid, Jr., of the James M. Reid Company and Robert M. Wendlinger of the Bank of America, San Francisco, prepared the book from which this selection is excerpted in collaboration with the New York Life Insurance Company.

Effective letters are important to you, too, as a writer. If you spend a large part of your working day writing letters, you're a professional writer. Many business writers turn out more copy in a day than a working journalist, and as a business writer, you should want to do your job as professionally as you can. This means you should want to write effective letters.

Professionals know how to use the basic tools of their trade. If you are to become professional at writing business letters, you must take the time to learn and practice the basic techniques and principles of effective letter writing. If you do, something like the following may happen to you.

Mr. Johnson, an insurance company employee, wrote the letter on page 140 to Mr. Green. A few days later Mr. Johnson received his own letter back, along with Mr. Green's check—with a note hastily scribbled on the bottom.

Mr. Johnson showed this letter to his boss, who was impressed.

But who would care to have the boss receive the letter on page 141 from an important customer?

Let's summarize, then, with four reasons why effective letters are important.

1. They carry on the business of the organization by getting the reader to do what is necessary.

2. Letters are a major expense, and this investment should not be wasted. A good letter costs no more than a poor one and usually costs less.

From *Effective Letters, A Program for Self-Instruction,* 3rd ed., by James M. Reid, Jr., and Robert M. Wendlinger (New York: McGraw-Hill Book Company, 1978), reprinted by permission of the McGraw-Hill Book Company.

3. When a letter makes a good impression on the reader, it can help to influence public opinion and create a favorable sales climate.

4. You can help yourself professionally by writing effective letters.

The eight qualities of an effective letter

All right, we've now covered why effective business letters are important. Now let's talk about the qualities of an effective letter. If your letters are to be effective, they should be—

Clear
     Concise
          Forceful
               Well organized
                    Natural
                         Friendly
                             Courteous
                                   Personal

We feel that business letters having the first four of the above qualities are *easy to understand* and those containing the second four have *proper tone.*

Clarity

Let's talk briefly about each of these eight qualities, starting with *clarity.* In order to have such a quality, a letter must be understandable without requiring several readings. Consider the following letter from an insurance company to a farmer:

Mr. Henry Blane
RFD 1
Brandywine, West Virginia 26802

Dear Mr. Blane:

Surrender of the policy is permissible only within the days attendant the grace period on compliance with the citation relevant options accruing to the policy so we estopped from acquiescing to a surrender prior to the policy's anniversary date.

                                    Yours truly,

Presumably the writer of the above letter had ideas to get across, but this letter was nonsense to the farmer, as it would be to most people who are not

NEW YORK LIFE INSURANCE COMPANY   51 MADISON AVENUE. NEW YORK. NEW YORK 10010. TELEPHONE : (212) 576-7000

September 2,

Mr. John R. Green
404 Main Street
Belleville, New York 13611

Dear Mr. Green:

    This is a friendly reminder that your payment which was due on
July 26 has not yet reached us. The August 26 payment is also due.

    Everyone is apt to overlook things now and then, and if it has
slipped your mind, please let us have your payment by return mail.

    If payment has been mailed, please accept our thanks and disregard
this notice.

               Sincerely,

               George W. Johnson
               George W. Johnson

Gentlemen: I am embarassed — I did overlook payment. I was once a financial officer of a large corporation where I had to write collection letters. I struggled in trying to be friendly and effective at the same time. Your letter is the best I have ever seen.

               Sincerely,
               J. R. Green

MERRYMOUNT TOYS, INC.

The Merrymount Building, Los Altos, California 94022

May 11,

Mr. Farley Auchincloss
President
Uniflex Steel Corporation
511 Daly Street
Scranton, Pennsylvania 18504

Dear Mr. Auchincloss:

I believe you will be interested in knowing the impression made upon me by the enclosed letter of reprimand from one of your company correspondents, James Mulreedy.

This condescending letter extremely annoyed me for many reasons. I am an adult and expect to be so treated by responsible companies with whom I do business.

I have been a customer of your company for a number of years, and it seems to me that your people could have treated the first oversight in this period in the payment of a bill in a more personal way. A well-worded letter, calling the fact to my attention, would have been understood. I believe our relationship should be a mutual one, with definite obligations, including courtesy, on each side. I do not believe that either you or I would be interested in buying something from a company which dealt with its good customers in the fashion represented by the enclosed letter.

I am not presuming to tell you how to run your business, but I do know from my own personal experience that courteous service goes a long way toward getting customers and keeping their business and goodwill. May I have your opinion on this?

Very truly yours,

H T Feeley

Harold T. Feeley
President

in the insurance business. To be effective, it most be understood by the person for whom it is intended—whether a carpenter, accountant, atomic physicist, or farmer. You must choose your words so that the reader will be sure to understand them without waste of time and effort.

Here is a classic example of another communication breakdown of this kind:

> A plumber found hydrochloric acid excellent for cleaning drains. He wrote a Washington bureau to find out if it was harmless. Washington replied as follows:
>
> > The efficacy of hydrochloric acid is indisputable, but the chlorine residue is incompatible with metallic permanence.
>
> The plumber wrote back, thanked the bureau, and said he was very glad they *agreed* that it was effective. Back came:
>
> > We cannot assume responsibility for the production of toxic and noxious residues from hydrochloric acid, and we suggest, therefore, that some alternative procedure be instituted.
>
> The plumber answered that he was getting fine results thus far. Would the bureau like to suggest the use of hydrochloric acid to other people? Finally, someone in Washington wrote:
>
> > Don't use hydrochloric acid. It eats hell out of the pipes.

Although the third message is blunt, it is far superior to the others because the reader can understand it. Clarity, then, is the first requirement of an effective letter.

1. Which of the two sentences below is *clearer?* _____

    A. He did not refuse to send the proper amount because he was not informed of the requirements.

    B. Because he was not informed of the requirements, he refused to send the proper amount.

       B

Conciseness

2. *Conciseness* is saying everything you have to say in the fewest possible words. This means be brief but *complete*. Dickens' *David Copperfield* contains many thousands of words, yet for a hundred years, few readers have thought it was not concise. Nor have they thought that the *Gettysburg Address* (268 words) was too brief. Both works are concise because their writers said everything that had to be said in the fewest possible words.

This holds true in business writing as well, since there are times when a ten-page letter may be too brief and a one-page letter with a single paragraph may be wordy.

If you cut words from a sentence and it loses either clarity or courtesy, then it is not concise but merely brief. However, you will *always* make a sentence more effective if you cut words and the sentence *doesn't* lose clarity and courtesy.

In the following three sentences, the writer wanted to say something and also make a good impression. Which sentence is concise? _____

> **A.** During the past two weeks, we have been wondering if you have as yet found yourself in a position to give an indication of whether you have been able to come to a decision on our offer. (thirty-seven words)
>
> **B.** What about our offer? (four words)
>
> **C.** Could you tell us if you have decided on our offer? (eleven words)

C (Sentence A is much too wordy. "During the past two weeks, we have been wondering" is unnecessary. The rest of the sentence is loaded with other unnecessary or wordy phrases. Sentence B is too abrupt, too brief. Some readers might very well react to this sentence with, "Well, what *about* your offer?" Sentence C is courteous and clear without being wordy.)

3. Someone has said,

> The writer does most who gives his reader the most knowledge and takes from him the least time.

However, many business writers believe that concise letters are abrupt or discourteous. But concise letters *include* courteous words, and conciseness itself is a form of courtesy. By packing more meaning into fewer words, you are clearer and more forceful. And you show courtesy by saving your reader's time.

With competition for the reader's attention becoming keener every day, business writers must write concise letters. Your reader wants to know as quickly as possible what you have to say. The reader needs quickly understood, easily absorbed sentences.

Which sentence below is more *concise*? _____

> **A.** Today, business needs qualified correspondents.
>
> **B.** There is a need in today's business world for properly qualified correspondents.

A

4a. Which of these two sentences is *clearer?* _____

    A. It is the understanding of those at this office that the ship-
    ment in the amount of four hundred steel girders has no
    situs in any of the states on the Eastern seaboard.
    B. We believe that the missing shipment of four hundred steel
    girders is not located in any of the East Coast states.

    B

4b. Which sentence is more *concise?* _____

    B

4c. The concise sentence is shorter by how many words? _____

    Eleven

Force

    5. Easily understandable writing is not only clear and concise but
also *forceful.* Force is a general term we use to sum up more concrete
qualities. For the moment, think of forceful writing as being *specific* and
containing *action.*

WEAK: We seemed to be beset by a period of inclement weather.
FORCEFUL: It rained every day for a week.

Notice that the first sentence contains many more general words than the
second. Also compare the action verb "rained" with the vague and limp
"seemed."
    No doubt you have read a letter which you knew had something very
interesting to say. Yet despite the inherent value of its ideas, it bored you to
death. The writer talked all around the subject, never coming to the point.
    On the other hand, some letters capture and hold your interest even
though the subject matter is rather ordinary. Your eyes jump from one sentence to the next, the writer's ideas developing clearly in your mind. This kind
of writing interests you partly because it contains plenty of action verbs and
specific words. It has *force.*
    Read the following two paragraphs. Which is more forceful? _____

    A. Minton engineers found that the redesigned Suprex Auto-
    matic Envelope Folder produces four hundred envelopes per

minute. The machine's efficient cutter arm, which slices over an arc of only ¼ inch, increases its production by one hundred envelopes per minute. After thirty Folders were installed on the production line, total output shot up by 40 percent.

B. It has been concluded upon investigation by the Minton engineers that the redesigned Suprex Automatic Envelope Folder has a production rate of four hundred envelopes per minute. This represents an increased production capacity for the machine of one hundred envelopes per minute. The reason for this increase is due to a more efficient cutter arm which has a slicing arc of only ¼ inch. Installation of thirty of these devices on the production line has accomplished an increase of production of 40 percent.

A (The first paragraph is not only more concise than the second but more forceful and therefore more interesting to read. Perhaps you noticed that strong verbs such as "increases," "slices," and "shot up" are primarily responsible for making this paragraph forceful, while word groups such as "It has been concluded upon," and "the reason . . . is . . ." make the second roundabout and weak. The difference between these two paragraphs may not seem impressive to you at first glance, but, as you will see later, it is the difference between fair writing and effective writing.)

6a. Which of the following two sentences is more *forceful*? _____

A. Interviewing a carefully selected population has been the traditional method of doing market research by the Greg & MacDonald advertising agency.

B. The Greg & MacDonald advertising agency traditionally does its market research by interviewing a carefully selected population.

B

6b. Which sentence has the more specific, more active predicate? _____

B (The predicate of sentence A is the *being verb* "has been," while the predicate of sentence B is the *action verb* "does.")

Good organization

7. Writing that is easily understood is not only clear, concise, and forceful—it is also *well organized*. Sometimes, the difference between good and bad organization lies in putting ideas in their proper order. Examine the two sentences below. Which is better organized? _____

A. To mix, place beaters in the revolving head of the electric mixer. Turn switch to "on."

B. To mix, turn switch to "on." But be sure to place beaters in the revolving head of the electric mixer beforehand.

A (In A, the writer has properly instructed the reader to insert the beaters before turning on the mixer. In B, the instruction comes as an afterthought.)

8. When your letter contains relevant ideas only, when the major and minor ideas are clearly indicated, when these ideas are presented in the proper order, your letter is well organized. Examine the following. Which is well organized? _____

A. A charge account is a convenience. For instance, if you want a book from our book department, simply call the store, ask for our book department, tell them what book you want, and say "charge it." Just sign and mail the enclosed card. Also, this privilege is available in all fifty-one departments of the store.

B. A charge account is a convenience. For instance, if you want a book, simply call our book department and say "charge it." This privilege is available throughout our fifty-one departments. If you want to open an account with us, just sign and mail the enclosed card.

B (The first sentence of the sloppy presentation has so many ideas that the process of acquiring a book does not seem "simple" at all. The third sentence is out of place. It should have some sort of transitional phrase in front of it and should conclude the paragraph. In the well-organized presentation, only relevant ideas are included; they are given their proper importance and are presented in a clear, meaningful order.)

9. Which of the following two letters is better organized? _____

A. Dear Ms. Danvers:

I recently purchased some used office furniture and equipment at a bankruptcy auction held last Wednesday at a warehouse on Tremont Avenue. In the lot I purchased was an old Underwood typewriter. As you probably know, these machines are pretty good if they are fixed up, and it appears that this one needs some work. It looks as if it has been stored in someone's attic and probably needs a good cleaning. By the way, my secretary took a look at it this morning and says the ribbon does not wind properly. How long do you think it would take to fix it? I am writing to several repair shops to get estimates for this job. So I'd appreciate a prompt reply.

B. Dear Ms. Danvers:

Please give me your estimate for cleaning an old Underwood typewriter and for repairing the ribbon rewind mechanism. May I have your estimate as soon as possible for the cost of the work and for the time it will take to complete the job? Thank you.

B (Letter A is very badly organized because it has a whole flock of ideas which are of no interest to the reader. Letter B gets to the point right away. It is well organized.)

Proper tone

10a. Now look at this letter:

Mr. Sam T. Muldoon
Langtry, Texas 78871

Dear Mr. Muldoon:

Your application for employment finally arrived last Wednesday. After carefully examining it, I find that you are over sixty years old. This is *much* too old! So I am obliged to inform you that we cannot hire you at this time.
Sincerely yours,

This letter is easily understandable in that it is clear, concise, forceful, and well organized. But apart from its illegality, it is far from effective. It lacks the four qualities that are necessary to proper tone. In fact, it is downright insulting.
Which of the two letters below has proper tone? _____

A. I'm sorry that we no longer manufacture the Variflex model S-2 camera. Last June, we replaced the S-2 with our S-3 model, which has several new features. I am enclosing a pamphlet describing the new model. If you'd like to order one, we'll be most happy to hear from you. On the other hand, if you want an S-2, you might write to Sam's Used Camera Exchange, 802 Main Street, Flushing, New York. He ordinarily has a good supply of used models.

    B. We no longer find it worthwhile to manufacture the Vari-flex model S-2, as there is no demand for it. You may not be aware that as of June, 1977, the S-2 was replaced by the S-3, which is a far superior instrument. Enclosed herewith is a pamphlet describing the S-3 and an order blank. However, if you still want the old model, write to Sam's Used Camera Exchange, 802 Main Street, Flushing, New York.

    A

10b. What sort of person wrote letter A? _____ (Answer in your own words.)

    Your opinion, of course. But most people would think of the writer as courteous, friendly, and natural—in short, an intelligent, helpful person.

Naturalness

    11. Many words can be used to describe a letter with proper tone, but we will stick to the four we listed earlier. Let's first talk about being *natural.* Effective letters are natural in that their wording is familiar to and comfortable for the reader.

If your words and phrases are pompous, unnecessarily technical, or old-fashioned, your readers will be distracted from your message. They will have to struggle with your phrasing before they can approach your ideas. They may think you are showing off your vocabulary rather than telling them what they need to know. Or, they may even think you have no ideas at all.

    Generally, the language of conversation is the best language for effective letters. It is not distracting to your readers and encourages them to concentrate on what you have to say. It is *natural.* Which of the following is more natural? _____

    A. Its operational deficiencies were attributed by the agency to a lack of personnel resulting from budget limitations.

    B. The agency said that it could not do a good job because it did not have enough money to hire enough people.

    B (Notice how the long, overly complicated wording of sentence A calls attention to itself. As a reader, you must fight through this fog of big words to find the writer's meaning. Sentence B is easy to read because it is written in simple, conversational language that does not stand between the reader and the idea expressed.)

12. Which of the following sentences is more *natural?* _____

    A. In the event that this does not meet with your approval, please notify this writer as to your wishes.

    B. If you do not approve of this, please let me know what you want.

    B

Friendliness

13. Proper tone also means that your letters should be *friendly.* These days, many readers are particularly sensitive to any suggestion that an organization, particularly a large one, does not care about individuals or is using its power unfairly. That is why it is important that your letters be as sympathetic, helpful, and concerned with the reader's problems as you can make them. Note the difference in the following two sentences. Which one is friendly? _____

    A. We are obliged to inform you that the completion of processing of your application has been delayed until the end of next week.

    B. I'm sorry that we've had to keep you waiting, but it's taken us a little more time than we expected to process your application. We'll have it completed by next Friday.

    B

14. Which of the following sentences are *friendly?* _____ (More than one choice may be correct.)

    A. Because you forgot to sign your employment application, I am returning it so that this oversight may be corrected.

    B. If you will send us a check for $159.61, we will be happy to ship your recent order for automotive parts right away.

    C. You must realize that we are doing everything in our power to investigate your claim that you did not receive our check for $1,000.

    D. As you asked, I am enclosing our annual report for the fiscal year ending December 31. Good luck with your report on the paper industry.

    B and D

Courtesy

15. If you use polite words like "please" and "thank you," and if you take your readers' point of view by recognizing their needs, your letters will be *courteous*. Which of the following is more courteous? _____

    A. May we please have your check for $23.97 by December 1?
    B. Submit your check for $23.97 not later than December 1.

    A

16. Which of the sentences below are courteous? _____

    A. May I visit you sometime during the week of April 28?
    B. Please accept my apologies for not answering your letter sooner.
    C. A prompt reply would be very convenient for me.
    D. If you had read the directions on the box carefully, you would not have broken the antenna while unpacking your radio.

    A and B

Personal

17. Finally, an effective letter will show that you think of the reader not as a statistic but as a person. And it will prove that you are a person too, and not a mere cog in the organizational machinery. You can do both these things by getting *people* into your letters, by making your letters *personal*. Which of the following is more personal? _____

    A. It is hoped that the difficulties of the past two weeks have been overcome.
    B. I hope that you have overcome your difficulties of the past two weeks.

    B (Notice that in sentence A all mention of the reader—or the writer—has been carefully avoided. In sentence B, the writer has not hesitated to insert "I," "you," and "your.")

18. Which of the following sentences are *personal*? _____

    A. This letter is to acknowledge receipt of the letter of July 8 and to inform those concerned that proper action has been taken.

    B. I'm sorry to tell you that we have decided to award the contract to Mr. Halloway.

    C. I'm happy to tell you that we have credited your account with $189.17.

    D. A decision to use the heat-sealing packaging process has been reached, and orders for the necessary equipment will be forthcoming.

    B and C

These, we feel, are the eight qualities of an effective business letter. It must be easy to understand; that is, it must be *clear, concise, forceful,* and *well organized.* And it must have proper tone, by being *natural, friendly, courteous,* and *personal.* . . .

Letters
that
sell

THE ROYAL BANK OF CANADA

Everyone writes letters that sell, and every letter has as its purpose the selling of something: goods, services, ideas or thoughts.

Someone may say that a family letter has no such purpose, but consider this: a letter telling about the children seeks to promote a favourable impression of their welfare and happiness; a letter telling about illness is designed to gain sympathy; the letter that says nothing but "I hope you are well" is selling the idea "I am thinking of you".

Family letters are usually rambling letters. They would be improved both in their readability and their informativeness if they adopted some of the principles that are used to sell goods and services. Business building letters, on the other hand, could with advantage incorporate some of the friendly informality of family letters.

Salesmanship of any kind is basically a person moving goods by persuading another person that he needs them, or winning that person's support or approval of an idea or a plan.

Some non-commercial type sales letters are those that champion good causes, such as community welfare or health standards or national unity. They seek to influence the thinking of individuals or groups.

It is not a simple task to compose a letter designed to sell. Like any other product of value, it calls for craftsmanship. There are techniques to be learned, techniques of conveying ideas, propositions, conclusions or advice appealingly and purposefully.

"Letters That Sell," reprinted from *The Royal Bank of Canada Monthly Letter*, 55 (May 1974), with permission of the Royal Bank of Canada.

In the beginning

In creating a letter to sell something we need to begin by thinking about the person to whom we are writing. A lawyer studies his opponent's case just as sharply as his client's; the manager of a baseball or hockey team analyses the qualities, good and bad, of members of the opposing team.

The writer must anticipate and answer in his letter questions that will occur to the reader: What is this about? How does it concern me? How can you prove it? What do you want me to do? Should I do it?

People buy goods or services because these will give them a new benefit or will extend or protect a benefit they already have, so the writer needs to translate what he offers into owner benefits.

The proffered benefits must be accessible and adapted to the reader's position, environment and needs. No letter is likely to sell sun-bonnets to people who live beyond the Arctic Circle or baby carriages to bachelors. We may classify a potential customer as a man, woman, company or institution that will have use for a product or service, has sufficient money to pay for it, and in whom a desire for possession may be created.

The reader's interest: that is the guiding star in sales letter writing. See his interests, his angle, and accommodate your stance to them. A simple precaution against sending a letter to the wrong person is to ask yourself what use you would have for the commodity if you were in the reader's place.

It is a good rule to spend more time thinking about the reader than about what you have to say. Otherwise you may become wrapped up in the virtues of your product so that you forget that the decision to buy rests with your prospect.

The self-interest of the person to whom you write is a major factor to consider in successful sales communication. When you remember it you give the impression that you have singled out this reader as being an important individual, and that is an excellent introduction.

It is not to be expected that the writer of letters that sell will know every person to whom he writes, but he must know certain facts: approximate income and age, occupational level, his business, and things like that. Then he is able to slant his sales points accurately toward the reader's needs, interests and purchasing power.

Know your product

The reader's attention should be attracted to the product or service, not to the grand style or picturesque phraseology of your letter. When you catch a person's attention you are focusing his consciousness on something. Concentrate on your commodity. The best magnet to draw and hold attention is what you say about the product, showing it to be useful and the means of fulfilling a desire.

It is no small accomplishment to analyse and marshal into order the facts about a product so as to win the thoughtful consideration of a person who has plenty of other things on his mind.

In purchasing almost any sort of commodity the buyer has a choice between what you are offering and what others are selling. Your sales job is to show the superiority of your product. Tell why what you offer is necessary or desirable, what it will accomplish in your reader's business, and how it can be fitted into his present layout and his plans. Do not content yourself with telling about the article as it sits on display: picture it in use in the reader's home or factory.

Your letter needs to convey the assurance that you are telling the truth about your goods. It is not a sensational offer that makes a letter convincing, but the feeling that the reader can depend upon what is said. He should feel assured that he will be buying what he thinks he is buying. Customer dissatisfaction caused by misleading sales talk can cause shock waves that affect the whole selling organization.

Let your personality show

Make your letter sound friendly and human: put your personality on paper. Your letter is you speaking. Some of the features in your personality that you can display are: friendliness, knowledge, keen-mindedness, trustworthiness and interest in the prospect's welfare.

What you have in your mind about the good quality, appearance and usefulness of your product has to be communicated to your reader so as to arouse his interest, create a desire to possess, and induce him to buy.

Communication is not the easiest thing in the world to attain in writing, in art, or in music. Dr. Rollo May wrote in *Man's Search for Himself:* "We find in modern art and modern music a language which does not communicate. If most people, even intelligent ones, look at modern art without knowing the esoteric key, they can understand practically nothing."

It is not enough to write something so that it can be read. The degree to which communication occurs depends upon the degree to which the words represent the same thing for the reader as they do for the writer.

The recipient of a letter that is not clear is likely to blame its opacity on the lack of intelligence of the writer.

The art of composing sales letters is not one to be mastered by minds in which there is only a meagre store of knowledge and memories.

The art consists in having many mental references and associating them with new thoughts. Consider a poem. Its theme will likely have arisen from a single event, but the images used in its construction will have been drawn from the total life experience of the poet.

Put some flavour into your letters so that they taste good. Your letter will not be like anyone else's. That is a virtue, just as being an individual is a virtue in conversation. Who wishes to be a carbon copy of a textbook letter or to parrot phrases that other people use?

Practise talking on paper as if you were on the telephone. First write down the imagined questions asked by the person on the other end of the line and then your answers, given in simple, direct and pleasing words. To humanize your letters in this way with the natural idiom of conversation does not mean that you use cheap slang or clever verbal stunting.

Show some style

The style in which you write is not a casual feature of your letter. It is vital to your reader's understanding of what you are saying to him. It is not your job to please the reader's sense of the aesthetic, but to tell and explain plainly what is necessary to introduce your goods or your idea to his favourable attention. This may be done in a way that has grace and comeliness.

Never "talk down" to a reader. Make him feel that he knows a great deal, but here is something he may have missed. There is a big difference, when trying to build business, between making a suggestion and preaching a sermon.

It is highly important in writing a letter to sell something that it should be appropriate. Whatever your writing style may be, it will fit the occasion if it gives this particular correspondent information that will be useful to him, conveys to him a feeling of your interest in him and his business, and assures him of your goodwill.

Besides being grammatically correct, language should be suitable. At one extreme of unsuitability is the language that is too pompous for its load, and at the other is the language of the street which belittles the receiver's intellectual level.

Your words should be the most expressive for their purpose that the language affords, unobstructed by specialty jargon, and your sentences should be shaken free of adjectives—the most tempting of forbidden fruit to a person describing something.

Properly chosen words will convey your appreciation of the addressee as a person, and such friendliness is contagious. Some people are afraid to be friendly in their letters. They fear they will be thought of as "phonies" who have disguised themselves as Santa Claus for the occasion. Being friendly and showing it should not raise this scarecrow. It would be a grave mistake, indeed, for any of us to indulge in flowery language foreign to our natural talk;

but it is no mistake at all to incorporate in our letters the warm, personal language that comes naturally to us in person-to-person social contacts.

Letter writing invites us to use the same etiquette as we use in courteous conversation. We look at the person with whom we are talking, converse on his level of understanding, speak gently, and discuss matters he considers important or interesting.

What the reader of your letter will notice is not its normal courtesy, but the extra touch that demonstrates care and understanding, a genuine interest in the reader's wants, a wish to do what is best for him, and the knowledge you show of how it can be done.

Everyone who writes a letter has a moral as well as a business reason to be intelligible. He is placing his reader under an obligation to spend time reading the letter, and to waste that time is to intrude upon his life plan.

There is an eloquence of the written as well as of the spoken word. It consists in adapting a statement to the receptive system of the reader so that he will have maximum help against confusion, against mistaking what is incidental from what is fundamental. A familiar device to use in this effort is to relate the new commodity you are offering to something that is familiar.

Use suitable formulas

There are formulas you may wish to make use of. Your letter must conform in some respects to what letters are expected to be. This does not mean pouring all letters into the same mould. Within the accepted pattern you are free to develop your talent for expression.

Skill is needed in the use of formulas. A form letter reveals itself to the reader and gets short shrift. It is possible to make use of the form as a guide to what points to cover, and then speak your piece on paper in a natural way.

Here are three formulas for letters. The first may be called the sales formula, the second the logical formula, and the third the rhetorical formula.

1. Get attention, provoke interest, rouse desire, obtain decision. Attention is curiosity fixed on something; interest is understanding of the nature and extent of what is new and its relationship to what is old; desire is the wish to take advantage of the proffered benefits; decision is based on confidence in what the writer says about his goods.

2. This is summarized: general, specific, conclusion. You start with a statement so broad and authoritative that it will not be disputed; you show that the general idea includes a specific idea; the conclusion is that what has been said about the general idea is also true of the specific.

3. This is very simple: picture, promise, prove, push. You write an attractive description of what you are selling; you promise that it will serve the reader well in such-and-such a way; you give examples of the commodity in use, proving that it has utility and worth; you urge the reader to take advantage of the promised values.

Selling needs ideas

Selling is done with ideas, so never throw away an idea even if it is of no use at the moment. Put it into your idea file where it will rub against other ideas and perhaps produce something new. The file is like an incubator. Thoughts and fancies you put into it will hatch out projects and plans.

Imagination helps in this operation. A correspondent of ordinary ability may never write anything that is not absolutely accurate and yet fail to interest his readers. This is a real weakness: to be perfect as to form but lacking in imagination and ideas.

Imagination should be given priority over judgment in preparing your first draft of a letter designed to sell. Then put reason to work: delete what is unnecessary, marshal your sentences into logical form so that your ideas advance in an orderly way; revise your words so that your thought is conveyed exactly as you wish it to be.

When you tell the advantages of your product or service or idea, and show how it will fill a need in the reader's life or job, in clear, truthful words placed in easily understood sentences brightened by ideas and imagination, you have done a good job of writing a sales letter.

Desire of the reader to do what you want done is created, just as in conversation, by both rational and emotional means, by proof and by persuasion, by giving reasons. Some goods and some buyers need nothing more than facts. An office manager buying pencils or pens for his staff will respond to an informative, factual, statistical sales letter. He is already sold on the idea of using pencils and pens, so you do not have to coach him about their usefulness; in fact, you may lose a sale if you give the impression of "teaching grandmother to suck eggs". What is needed is to catch his attention, give pertinent information about your product, and show him why buying from you will be profitable to him.

Try to make the information you give really enlightening. Comparing something unknown with something already known makes it possible to talk about the unknown. The analogy (like that between the heart and a pump) can be used as an aid in reasoning and in explaining or demonstrating.

The soft sell

The tone of a letter designed to sell something should be persuasive rather than insistent. It should seek to create a feeling of wanting, or at least an urge to "let's see".

People do not want to be told how to run their affairs, but anyone who shows them how to do things more economically or faster or better will find keen listeners. Soft sell gives the prospect credit for knowing a good thing when it is shown him, and acknowledges his right to make up his own mind.

The soft sell is recognition of the Missouri mule in human nature. Try to push a mule and he lashes out with his heels. Try to pull him by the halter rope and he braces his legs and defies you to budge him. "In the old cavalry," says A. C. Kemble in *Building Horsepower into Sales Letters,* "they said all it took to get a mule working for you was to recognize that he was an individualist who hated nagging and needed a chance to make up his own mind about things."

One hears a lot in advertising circles about "appeal". It is, according to the dictionary, "the power to attract, interest, amuse, or stimulate the mind or emotions."

Obviously, when you wish to influence someone you must take into account the kind of person you are addressing and what you want him to do. Your appeal must touch his feelings, needs and emotions. It strengthens your position if you can relate your own experience to that of the person you are addressing and write your message around the overlap of that experience.

The sort of mistake to be avoided with great care is slanting your appeal in a way that runs counter to the feelings of those whom you wish to influence.

It has been found in recent years that the advertising messages addressed to older people *as* older people did not win the desired response. In travel, for example, only a very small minority who want or need a sheltered situation are attracted by the semicustodial "trips for the elderly".

The Swiss Society for Market Research decided that "to sell anything to the over-65 age group it is important to keep one concept in mind: most senior citizens are vigorous and independent. Don't try to reach them with a head-on approach to the senior market. It probably won't work."

Writing a letter that pleases the recipient is not enough: it must be designed to lead to action. Do not fear to be explicit about what you want. Coyness in a letter is not attractive, and it exasperates the reader. Answer the reader's questions: "What has this to do with me?" and "Why should I do what this person is asking me to do?"

You may answer these questions and encourage a purchase by appealing to emotional motives like pride, innovation, emulation, or social prestige; or to rational motives like money gain, economy, security, time-saving or safety.

Read your letter critically

Imagine your letter to be your garden upon your return from vacation. You have to get into it and prune, clean up, tie up, and trim the edges.

Read the letter as if you were the recipient. How does it strike you? What can be added to attract attention? Is there anything irrelevant in it? Read the letter aloud to capture the conversational rhythm.

If you are not satisfied, do not crumple up the paper on which your draft is written. Try rearranging the paragraphs, the sentences, the words. Give the letter a new twist. Change the shape of your appeal. Delete anything that is distracting.

Be careful when trying to shorten a letter that seems to be too long. While a letter should be as short as possible, consistent with clearness and completeness, it is not the length that counts, but the depth. Since clearness and brevity sometimes get in the way of each other, remember that the right of way belongs to clearness. It will make a good impression if you find occasion to write: "I can be quite brief because this letter deals with a topic already well known to you."

The end of your letter, like the end of your pencil, should have a point. It should answer the reader's natural question: "So what?"

Follow through

Do not let your customer forget you. When you produce a piece of copy that hits the bull's-eye, that is not the time to sit back and take things easy. It is a time to imagine what you would do if you were in your competitor's chair . . . and then do it first.

Competition is a fact of life. Wherever there are two wild animals trying to live on the same piece of land or two persons depending upon the same source of sustenance, there is competition. The customer who was a prospect to you before he bought your goods is now a prospect to your competitor. With the proper follow-through attention he will turn to you when he needs up-dating of equipment or new goods.

Writing a letter that sells goods or ideas, and following through so as to retain the customer, requires just as much specialized talent and mental ability as any other kind of advertising, if not more.

When you run into difficulties, composition of the sales or follow-up letter may give you a feeling of confusion. You may feel like throwing up your hands in despair of finding the exactly right slant or the perfect array of words. That is not unnatural. Nietzsche, the German philosopher, said in *Thus Spake Zarathustra:* "I tell you, one must still have chaos in one, to give birth to a dancing star."

The effort is worthwhile. When you set yourself to snap out of the depressing pedestrian type of letter that is so commonplace, you are raising yourself and your firm to a place where people will sit up and pay attention. As a student of sales letter writing you will generate ideas, as a philosopher you will assess the letters as to their purpose and usefulness, and as a writer you will energize them.

To summarize: the backbone of the principles of writing letters that sell is made up of these vertebrae—know why you are writing and what about; believe in what you are writing; be tactful and friendly and truthful; base your appeal on the prospect's interests . . . and check your letter and revise it.

Letters can say <u>no</u> but keep or make friends

KERMIT ROLLAND

When he wrote this article, Mr. Rolland was a member of the Public Relations Department of the New York Life Insurance Company. He subsequently became a consultant specializing in better letter-writing programs.

An executive of a large New York business house has a unique collection of fan letters, each carefully mounted in a large leather album which he keeps close at hand as he runs through his mail each morning. Each letter in the growing collection is a testimonial to the man's talent for saying *No* and making a friend while doing so.

The letters were written to him in reply to *turn-down* letters he wrote for his company: refusals to extend credit, grant discounts, make adjustments, contribute to causes, or lengthen terms. Each of his original letters denied a request. Yet somehow each captured the good-will of a reader! Here are a few typical replies:

> "My first reaction when I read your letter (refusing a discount) was to take my business elsewhere. But since thinking it over, I have decided to place my order anyway. You can credit for this the staff of psychologists you employ to write your letters for you."

> "No one has ever said *No* to me before and made me like it."

> "You made your reasons for refusal very clear and understandable. Thank you for having taken the trouble to do so. Another business house would just have said *No* and let it go at that."

> "If more people would write as you did, there would be less suspicion on the part of the public toward the large corporations."

The man whose letters prompted this mail would hasten to explain that for every reader who will swallow a *No* and like it, there are two who will

Kermit Rolland, "Letters Can Say *No* but Keep or Make Friends," reprinted from *Printers' Ink,* 229 (October 7, 1949), pp. 46–53, by permission of the Hartford National Bank and Trust Company.

refuse to be moved by any appeal, no matter how effectively it may be presented. They will remain disappointed and disgruntled, though even one of these will occasionally accept a *No* albeit with bad grace.

> "I think of my turn-down letters as a salvage operation," the writer explains. "I have found that an effective turn-down will often keep a friend who might otherwise have been lost through a stupid letter—and, surprisingly, a turn-down will sometimes create a new friendship."

Turn-down letters form a part of everyone's mail. In a large organization the bulk of the turn-down mail is handled by correspondents who often fail to realize the damaging chain reaction they may be setting off each time they send a flat *No* to a reader. The reader will rarely complain, it is true. But he will often chalk up an unfavorable impression of the company—and take his business elsewhere.

Long experience has shown one large company that the majority of its correspondents either lack the ability or are too pressed for time to take the trouble to compose an effective turn-down. It meets the problem by sending such letters on to its public relations department. The company feels that answering such correspondence is too important to be entrusted to anyone who has not had special experience in that field. For the bulk of the turn-downs, the PR people write guide letters to be used as patterns by the regular correspondents. But PR continues to handle all turn-downs that do not fit into the several categories of the guide letters. That its program is effective is attested by the fact that customers and others often write notes of appreciation for the thoughtful letters they have received.

Possibly no large corporation handled as many turn-downs during recent years as did the New York Telephone Company. Because of a shortage of equipment the company was unable to fill more than a fraction of its requests for new installations. People had to be put off, and they're still being put off. But so adroit are the turn-down letters the company sends out that most of the disappointed subscribers entertain no ill-will toward the company. Instead, they blame the war* for their disappointment, or material shortages, or a perverse fate—but rarely the company.

The secret of the telephone letters is that they *explain* to the reader why he can't have a telephone, and they explain so convincingly that the company retains the priceless good-will of the reader, even as he trudges to the neighbors to make a phone call.

In contrast to the successful technique used by the telephone people is the thoughtless approach of a utilities company whose turn-downs are so abrupt and so inconsiderate that more than one customer has thought wishfully of the day when bankruptcy could be visited upon it for its sins.

It is a maxim of modern correspondence practice that every letter should be a sales letter. It is relatively simple to accomplish this objective in routine

---

* Ed.'s note: World War II.

letters of a positive nature. A turn-down letter is another matter. To be effective it does not seek to sell: it tries to buy. The commodity it bids for is the good-will of the reader.

The technique of an effective *No* letter is built upon an appeal to the reader. An effective turn-down is slanted to the reader's point of view; it emphasizes the fact that the reader is very important to the company. Here are a half-dozen tested methods for creating successful *No* letters:

1. Explain to your reader, if you can, the reason for the rejection

Nothing antagonizes a reader more than to be told that the granting of his request is not in line with company practice. This is a favorite evasion of many writers. It's easier to say "I regret to tell you that it is not the policy of the Company to . . ." or "The Company, has never . . . ." The company, not the writer, is to blame for the turn-down; or so many writers imply.

But these writers fail to realize that to the reader the writer is the company. So passing the buck will not work. It puts the writer and the company in the same hole as far as the reader is concerned. The reader's knowledge of a company is very often limited to the correspondence he exchanges with the individual or individuals who write the company's letters. The personality of the writer as it is reflected in a letter is the personality of the company on whose letterhead he is writing. Is it a friendly letter? Then it is a friendly company. Is it a cold letter? Then it is a cold company. Is it a stuffy letter? Then it is a plug-hat company.

Most readers are satisfied with a convincing explanation for a rejection. If the writer will ask himself, "Why can't we grant this request?" and then set down his answer is simple, direct, prose he will have solved half of his onerous problem.

Occasionally, it is true, it is difficult or awkward to tell the reader the precise reason for a refusal. If the reason is confidential, it requires a master touch to say *No* convincingly enough to leave the reader unruffled. A successful method in such situations is to assure the reader, and then reassure him, that his request has been thoroughly considered—and then screen the reason for the turn-down behind a generalization.

Here is a generalization which has proved effective in some instances: "We wish it were possible for us to grant every request for ————. Your request, I wish to assure you, was very carefully considered. But you will understand, I know, that it is not possible for us to say *Yes* in every instance. I regret that I must tell you that . . . ."

Another device which has been used with considerable success in handling a turn-down where it is not possible to give the reason is to hold the turn-down reply for a few days before mailing it. *It should be mentioned here that promptness is ordinarily a virtue in answering letters.* The delayed return letter opens with an explanation, not for the turn-down, *but for the delay in replying,* the implication being that the request was debated in the company for a number of days. Some magazine editors have used this device in rejecting manuscripts without being noticeably conscience-stricken.

2. Be sparing with apologies

An overly apologetic letter bears the stamp of insincerity. Few readers are so naïve as to believe that a company is really very upset about rejecting a request. It is very well to be "disturbed" or "distressed" when a *complaint* letter is being answered. But for an ordinary turn-down "I am sorry to tell you" or "I regret that we cannot" is usually sufficient. An explanation is more acceptable to a reader than profuse apologies. The reader is no dope. He knows the sound of wind when he hears it.

3. Try the *you* approach

The one person in the world who is important to the reader is himself. His interest in anything is directly linked to self-interest. He is really not very interested in the problems of the company, except so far as the problems affect him personally. This being the nature of the reader, it is wise to direct an appeal to him on his own terms. Convince the reader you have his interest at heart, and he will give you his good-will.

A reader who will stiffen at the sentence, "We give every request fair consideration," will relax when he meets the sentence rewritten, "*You* may be sure that we have given *your* request every consideration." Talk about the reader, not about the company.

4. But don't be afraid of *I*

While it is important to emphasize the *you* in a letter, it is not desirable to rule out every *we*. The company, although subordinate, is important, too. But let's examine this *we* for a moment.

For many years writers have been lurking behind the *we* of the company. Occasionally a very bold one would venture to call himself *the writer* or *the below signed writer*. It is difficult to understand this excessive timidity. If a letter is written by anyone with any kind of authority at all, why should he not make use of *I* instead of cloaking himself in the phony anonymity of *we*?

The use of the first person singular can be very effective in a turn-down letter. It establishes the important man-to-man atmosphere. "Take my word for it," the writer says in effect. "I am looking after your interests here."

I wish to assure you that we . . . I know you will understand that . . . I hope you will . . . I want you to know . . . I regret that I must tell you that we . . . You will appreciate, I know . . . Let me say that . . . etc., are phrases that have proved their effectiveness time and again.

5. Accentuate the positive

Occasionally it is possible to offer an alternative when denying a specific request. In this situation it is effective to offer the alternative goods or service at the beginning of the letter. Give the reader something positive at once if it is at all possible. Let the turn-down wait until the end of the letter when he has been cushioned for the shock.

6. If you can say *Yes,* say it at once. If you must say *No,* take a little longer

This rule-of-thumb is used successfully by one of the large philanthropic foundations. For each grant the foundation makes, it turns down a hundred appeals. So the bulk of the mail is made up of *No* letters.

The reason for the effectiveness of the "take a little longer" approach is explained by the underlying psychology of the third suggestion in this list: *the reader wants to feel important.* When he receives a *long* letter from an organization as well-known as the foundation, it puffs him up. It is apparent to him that some very busy and highly paid executive was sufficiently impressed by him and by his request to take the time to answer in full. And even though his request was denied, the stinger has been pulled.

A truly effective correspondence technique cannot, of course, be reduced to a half-dozen suggestions, and these suggestions are not offered as the basis for building a technique from scratch. But they have proved to be a useful supplement to an established correspondence method. They have salvaged good-will and good business that might otherwise have been lost.

How
to
write
better
memos

HAROLD K. MINTZ

Harold K. Mintz was Senior Technical Editor for
the RCA Corporation when he wrote this article.

Memos—interoffice, intershop, in-
terdepartmental—are the most important medium of in-house communication. This article suggests ways to help you sharpen your memos so that they
will more effectively inform, instruct, and sometimes persuade your cowork-
ers.

Memos are informal, versatile, free-wheeling. In-house they go up, down
or sideways.* They can even go to customers, suppliers, and other interested
outsiders. They can run to ten pages or more, but are mostly one to three
pages. (Short memos are preferable. Typed single-space and with double-
space between paragraphs, Lincoln's Gettysburg Address easily fits on one
page, and the Declaration of Independence on two pages.) They can be issued
on a one-shot basis or in a series, on a schedule or anytime at all. They can
cover major or minor subjects.

Primary functions of memos encompass, but are not limited to:

- Informing people of a problem or situation.
- Nailing down responsibility for action, and a deadline for it.
- Establishing a file record of decisions, agreements and policies.

Secondary functions include:

- Serving as a basis for formal reports.
- Helping to bring new personnel up-to-date.

* We will return to this sentence later.

Harold K. Mintz, "How to Write Better Memos," reprinted by special permission from *Chemical
Engineering,* January 26, 1970. Copyright © 1970 by McGraw-Hill, Inc., New York, N.Y. 10020.

- Replacing personal contact with people you cannot get along with. For example, the Shubert brothers, tyrannical titans of the American theatre for 40 years, often refused to talk to each other. They communicated by memo.

- Handling people who ignore your oral directions. Concerning the State Dept., historian Arthur Schlesinger quoted JFK as follows: "I have discovered finally that the best way to deal with State is to send over memos. They can forget phone conversations, but a memorandum is something which, by their system, has to be answered."

Memos can be used to squelch unjustified time-consuming requests. When someone makes what you consider to be an unwarranted demand or request, tell him to put it in a memo—just for the record. This tactic can save you much time.

Organization of the memo

Memos and letters are almost identical twins. They differ in the following ways: Memos normally remain in-house, memos don't usually need to "hook" the reader's interest, and memos covering a current situation can skip a background treatment.

Overall organization of a memo should ensure that it answer three basic questions concerning its subject:

1. What are the facts?
2. What do they mean?
3. What do we do now?

To supply the answers, a memo needs some or all of the following elements: summary, conclusions and recommendations, introduction, statement of problem, proposed solution, and discussion. Incidentally, these elements make excellent headings to break up the text and guide the readers.

In my opinion, every memo longer than a page should open with a summary, preferably a short paragraph. Thus, recipients can decide in seconds whether they want to read the entire memo.

Two reasons dictate placing the summary at the very beginning. There, of all places, you have the reader's undivided attention. Second, readers want to know, quickly, the meaning or significance of the memo.

Obviously, a summary cannot provide all the facts (Question 1, above) but it should capsule their meaning, and highlight a course of action.

When conclusions and recommendations are not applicable, forget them. When they are, however, you can insert them either right after the abstract or at the end of the memo. Here's one way to decide: If you expect readers to be neutral or favorable toward your conclusions and recommendations, put them up front. If you expect a negative reaction, put them at the end. Then, conceivably, your statement of the problem and your discussion of it may swing readers around to your side by the time they reach the end.

The introduction should give just enough information for the readers to be able to understand the statement of the problem and its discussion.

Literary qualities

A good memo need not be a Pulitzer Prize winner, but it does need to be clear, brief, relevant. LBJ got along poorly with his science adviser, Donald Hornig, because Hornig's memos, according to a White House staffer, "were terribly long and complicated. The President couldn't read through a page or two and understand what Don wanted him to do, so he'd send it out to us and ask us what it was all about. Then we'd put a short cover-memo on top of it and send it back in. The President got mad as hell at long memos that didn't make any sense."

Clarity is paramount. Returning to the asterisked sentence in the second paragraph of the introduction, I could have said: "Memoranda are endowed with the capability of internal perpendicular and lateral deployment." Sheer unadulterated claptrap.

To sum up, be understandable and brief, but not brusque, and get to the point.

Another vitally important trait is a personal, human approach. Remember that your memos reach members of your own organization; that's a common bond worth exploiting. Your memos should provide them with the pertinent information they need (no more and no less) and in the language they understand. Feel free to use people's names, and personal pronouns and adjectives: you-your, we-our, I-mine. Get people into the act; it's they who do the work.

Lastly, a well-written memo should reflect diplomacy or political savvy. More than once, Hornig's memos lighted the fuse of LBJ's temper. One memo, regarded as criticizing James E. Webb (then the head of NASA), LBJ's friend, infuriated the President.

Another example of a politically naive memo made headlines in England three years ago. A hospital superintendent wrote a memo to his staff, recommending that aged and chronically ill patients should not be resuscitated after heart failure. Public reaction exploded so overwhelmingly against the superintendent that shock waves even shook Prime Minister Wilson's cabinet. Result? The Health Ministry torpedoed the recommendation.

Two other courses of action would have been more tactful for the superintendent: make the recommendation orally to his staff or, if he insisted on a memo, stamp it "private" and distribute it accordingly.

Literary style is a nebulous subject, difficult to pin down. Yet if you develop a clear, taut way of writing, you may end up in the same happy predicament as Lawrence of Arabia. He wrote "a violent memorandum" on a British-Arab problem, a memo whose "acidity and force" so impressed the commanding general that he wired it to London. Lawrence noted in his "Seven Pillars of Wisdom" that, "My popularity with the military staff in Egypt, due to the sudden help I had lent . . . was novel and rather amusing. They began to be polite to me, and to say that I was observant, with a pungent style. . . ."

Format of the memo

Except for minor variations, the format to be used is standard. The memo dispenses with the addresses, salutations, and complimentary closes used in letters. Although format is a minor matter, it does rate some remarks.

To and From Lines—Names and departments are enough.

Subject—Capture its essence in ten words or less. Any subject that drones on for three or four lines may confuse or irritate readers.

Distribution—Send the memo only to people involved or interested in the subject matter. If they number less than say, ten, list them alphabetically on page 1; if more than ten, put them at the end.

Text—Use applicable headings listed after the three questions under "*Organization.*"

Paragraphs—If numbering or lettering them helps in any way, do it.

Line Spacing—Single space within paragraphs, and double space between.

Underlines and Capitals—Used sparingly, they emphasize important points.

Number of Pages—Some companies impose a one-page limit, but it's an impractical restriction because some subjects just won't fit on one page. As a result, the half-baked memo requires a second or third memo to beef it up.

Figures and Tables—Use them; they'll enhance the impact of your memos.

Conclusion

Two cautions are appropriate. First, avoid writing memos that baffle people, like the one that Henry Luce once sent to an editor of *Time*. "There are only 30,000,000 sheep in the U.S.A.—same as 100 years ago. What does this prove? Answer???"

Second, avoid "memo-itis," the tendency to dash off memos at the drop of a pen, especially to the boss. In his book, "With Kennedy," Pierre Salinger observed that "a constant stream of memoranda" from Professor Arthur Schlesinger caused JFK to be "impatient with their length and frequency."

Clear writing
means
clear thinking
means...

MARVIN K. SWIFT

When he wrote this article, Marvin K. Swift was
Associate Professor of Communication at the
General Motors Institute.

If you are a manager, you constantly
face the problem of putting words on paper. If you are like most managers,
this is not the sort of problem you enjoy. It is hard to do, and time consuming;
and the task is doubly difficult when, as is usually the case, your words must
be designed to change the behavior of others in the organization.

But the chore is there and must be done. How? Let's take a specific case.

Let's suppose that everyone at X Corporation, from the janitor on up to
the chairman of the board, is using the office copiers for personal matters;
income tax forms, church programs, children's term papers, and God knows
what else are being duplicated by the gross. This minor piracy costs the company a pretty penny, both directly and in employee time, and the general
manager—let's call him Sam Edwards—decides the time has come to lower
the boom.

Sam lets fly by dictating the following memo to his secretary:

```
To: All Employees
From: Samuel Edwards, General Manager
Subject: Abuse of Copiers
```

```
It has recently been brought to my attention that many of the people
who are employed by this company have taken advantage of their
positions by availing themselves of the copiers. More specifically,
these machines are being used for other than company business.
```

Reprinted by permission of the *Harvard Business Review*. "Clear Writing Means Clear Thinking
Means . . ." by Marvin K. Swift (January-February 1973). Copyright © 1973 by the President and
Fellows of Harvard College; all rights reserved.

Obviously, such practice is contrary to company policy and must cease and desist immediately. I wish therefore to inform all concerned —— those who have abused policy or will be abusing it —— that their behavior cannot and will not be tolerated. Accordingly, anyone in the future who is unable to control himself will have his employment terminated.

If there are any questions about company policy, please feel free to contact this office.

Now the memo is on his desk for his signature. He looks it over; and the more he looks, the worse it reads. In fact, it's lousy. So he revises it three times, until it finally is in the form that follows:

To: All Employees
From: Samuel Edwards, General Manager
Subject: Use of Copiers

We are revamping our policy on the use of copiers for personal matters. In the past we have not encouraged personnel to use them for such purposes because of the costs involved. But we also recognize, perhaps belatedly, that we can solve the problem if each of us pays for what he takes.

We are therefore putting these copiers on a pay—as—you—go basis. The details are simple enough . . . . . .

Samuel Edwards

This time Sam thinks the memo looks good, and it *is* good. Not only is the writing much improved, but the problem should now be solved. He therefore signs the memo, turns it over to his secretary for distribution, and goes back to other things.

From verbiage to intent

I can only speculate on what occurs in a writer's mind as he moves from a poor draft to a good revision, but it is clear that Sam went through several specific steps, mentally as well as physically, before he had created his end product:

- He eliminated wordiness.
- He modulated the tone of the memo.
- He revised the policy it stated.

Let's retrace his thinking through each of these processes.

Eliminating wordiness

Sam's basic message is that employees are not to use the copiers for their own
affairs at company expense. As he looks over his first draft, however, it seems
so long that this simple message has become diffused. With the idea of trim-
ming the memo down, he takes another look at his first paragraph:

It has recently been brought to my attention that many of the people
who are employed by this company have taken advantage of their
positions by availing themselves of the copiers. More specifically,
these machines are being used for other than company business.

He edits it like this:

ITEM: "recently"
COMMENT TO HIMSELF: Of course; else why write about the problem? So delete
    the word.

ITEM: "It has been brought to my attention"
COMMENT: Naturally. Delete it.

ITEM: "the people who are employed by this company"
COMMENT: Assumed. Why not just "employees"?

ITEM: "by availing themselves" and "for other than company business"
COMMENT: Since the second sentence repeats the first, why not coalesce?

And he comes up with this:

Employees have been using the copiers for personal matters.

He proceeds to the second paragraph. More confident of himself, he moves in
broader swoops, so that the deletion process looks like this:

Obviously, such practice is contrary to company policy and ~~must~~
~~cease and desist immediately. I wish therefore to inform all~~
~~concerned — those who have abused policy or will be abusing it —~~
~~that their behavior cannot and will not be tolerated. Accordingly~~
~~anyone in the future who is unable to control himself will have his~~
~~employment terminated.~~ will result in dismissal.

The final paragraph, apart from "company policy" and "feel free," looks all
right, so the total memo now reads as follows:

```
To: All Employees
From: Samuel Edwards, General Manager
Subject: Abuse of Copiers

Employees have been using the copiers for personal matters.
Obviously, such practice is contrary to company policy and will
result in dismissal.

If there are any questions, please contact this office.
```

Sam now examines his efforts by putting these questions to himself:

QUESTION: Is the memo free of deadwood?
ANSWER: Very much so. In fact, it's good, tight prose.
QUESTION: Is the policy stated?
ANSWER: Yes—sharp and clear.
QUESTION: Will the memo achieve its intended purpose?
ANSWER: Yes. But it sounds foolish.
QUESTION: Why?
ANSWER: The wording is too harsh; I'm not going to fire anybody over this.
QUESTION: How should I tone the thing down?

To answer this last question, Sam takes another look at the memo.

Correcting the tone

What strikes his eye as he looks it over? Perhaps these three words:

- Abuse . . .
- Obviously . . .
- . . . dismissal . . .

The first one is easy enough to correct: he substitutes "use" for "abuse." But "obviously" poses a problem and calls for reflection. If the policy is obvious, why are the copiers being used? Is it that people are outrightly dishonest? Probably not. But that implies the policy isn't obvious; and whose fault is this? Who neglected to clarify policy? And why "dismissal" for something never publicized?

These questions impel him to revise the memo once again:

```
To: All Employees
From: Samuel Edwards, General Manager
Subject: Use of Copiers

Copiers are not to be used for personal matters. If there are any
questions, please contact this office.
```

Revising the policy itself

The memo now seems courteous enough—at least it is not discourteous—but it is just a blank, perhaps overly simple, statement of policy. Has he really thought through the policy itself?

Reflecting on this, Sam realizes that some people will continue to use the copiers for personal business anyhow. If he seriously intends to enforce the basic policy (first sentence), he will have to police the equipment, and that raises the question of costs all over again.

Also, the memo states that he will maintain an open-door policy (second sentence)—and surely there will be some, probably a good many, who will stroll in and offer to pay for what they use. His secretary has enough to do without keeping track of affairs of that kind.

Finally, the first and second sentences are at odds with each other. The first says that personal copying is out, and the second implies that it can be arranged.

The facts of organizational life thus force Sam to clarify in his own mind exactly what his position on the use of copiers is going to be. As he sees the problem now, what he really wants to do is put the copiers on a pay-as-you-go basis. After making that decision, he begins anew:

```
To: All Employees
From: Samuel Edwards, General Manager
Subject: Use of copiers

We are revamping our policy on the use of copiers . . . . . .
```

This is the draft that goes into distribution and now allows him to turn his attention to other problems.

The chicken or the egg?

What are we to make of all this? It seems a rather lengthy and tedious report of what, after all, is a routine writing task created by a problem of minor importance. In making this kind of analysis, have I simply labored the obvious?

To answer this question, let's drop back to the original draft. If you read it over, you will see that Sam began with this kind of thinking:

- "The employees are taking advantage of the company."

- "I'm a nice guy, but now I'm going to play Dutch uncle."
  ∴ "I'll write them a memo that tells them to shape up or ship out."

In his final version, however, his thinking is quite different:

> • "Actually, the employees are pretty mature, responsible people. They're capable of understanding a problem."

> • "Company policy itself has never been crystallized. In fact, this is the first memo on the subject."

> • "I don't want to overdo this thing—any employee can make an error in judgment."

> ∴ "I'll set a reasonable policy and write a memo that explains how it ought to operate."

Sam obviously gained a lot of ground between the first draft and the final version, and this implies two things. First, if a manager is to write effectively, he needs to isolate and define, as fully as possible, all the critical variables in the writing process and scrutinize what he writes for its clarity, simplicity, tone, and the rest. Second, after he has clarified his thoughts on paper, he may find that what he has written is not what has to be said. In this sense, writing is feedback and a way for the manager to discover himself. What are his real attitudes toward that amorphous, undifferentiated gray mass of employees "out there"? Writing is a way of finding out. By objectifying this thoughts in the medium of language, he gets a chance to see what is going on in his mind.

In other words, *if the manager writes well, he will think well.* Equally, the more clearly he has thought out his message before he starts to dictate, the more likely he is to get it right on paper the first time round. In other words, *if he thinks well, he will write well.*

Hence we have a chicken-and-the-egg situation: writing and thinking go hand in hand; and when one is good, the other is likely to be good.

Revision sharpens thinking

More particularly, rewriting is the key to improved thinking. It demands a real openmindedness and objectivity. It demands a willingness to cull verbiage so that ideas stand out clearly. And it demands a willingness to meet logical contradictions head on and trace them to the premises that have created them. In short, it forces a writer to get up his courage and expose his thinking process to his own intelligence.

Obviously, revising is hard work. It demands that you put yourself through the wringer, intellectually and emotionally, to squeeze out the best you can offer. Is it worth the effort? Yes, it is—if you believe you have a responsibility to think and communicate effectively.

The
legal aspects
of your
business
correspondence

HERTA A. MURPHY and

CHARLES E. PECK

Both Herta A. Murphy and Charles E. Peck
were professors of business administration
at the University of Washington.

W hen you apply integrity, honest
consideration for your reader, and the Golden Rule in your business communications, you should be safe in the eyes of the law. Yet as a cautious, sensible
businessperson—and as a consumer—you need to realize that there are legal
dangers even in some true statements. On the other hand, not all untrue
words that appear to be libelous will lead to a lawsuit.

Thousands of statute laws and decisions have been passed in the 50 states
and federal government. Changing social and business conditions necessitate
changing laws from time to time. Furthermore, the right to freedom of speech
versus the individual right not to be libeled have led to various legal privileges
under various conditions. No single chapter can begin to cover even partially
any specific legal interpretations applied to business writing.

The purpose of this section is to call to your attention some of the legal
risks and complications that may occur in business communications. An overview of pertinent legal concepts should be helpful to you both as the writer
and the recipient of business messages. However, because ignorance of the
law excuses no one, you may need a lawyer to advise you on specific details
that apply to some complicated situations. The discussion here is necessarily a
brief general introduction only; no liability is assumed for its completeness.
Yet if you are aware of the risks discussed here, you can avoid harmful utter-
ances and costly misunderstandings. This section briefs you on:

From *Effective Business Communications,* 2nd ed., by Herta A. Murphy and Charles E. Peck
(New York: McGraw-Hill Book Company, 1976), reprinted by permission of the McGraw-Hill
Book Company.

1. Defamation

2. Invasion of privacy

3. Fraud

4. Other areas of concern

Defamation[1]

The unconsented and unprivileged "publication" of a false idea which tends to injure reputation is defamation. Oral defamation is slander. Written defamation constitutes a libel. You can be sued for defamation if you intentionally "publish" the false idea that injures reputation and for which no legal "privilege" exists. Because the words "publication" and "privilege" have important legal significance, they are discussed first; then follows a sampling of defamatory terms.

Publication

In the legal sense, the unconsented intentional or negligent communication of defamatory matter to a third party is "publication." Any means of communication by which some third party (anyone other than the person attacked) actually receives the defamatory idea can effect a "publication."

If you tell Mr. X to his face privately that you consider him incompetent or a swindler, you are within your legal rights; only he has heard your statement. But if you intentionally communicate the defamatory statement to at least one other person who is not "privileged" (as defined later), you can be in serious trouble. The derogatory qualities that make a statement defamatory are the same for libel and slander. Because libelous statements are more permanent, laws pertaining to libel are more severe than those about slander. The writing (for libel) may be any permanent communication—such as a letter, circular, picture, photograph, cartoon, newspaper, recorded tape, or phonograph record.

Even a sealed letter addressed and mailed to the person you are accusing can result in actionable publication if you knew or should have known that it would be intercepted by or shown to a third person. For this reason, a letter containing unfavorable information about a person (or organization) and any collection message about past-due payments should be mailed only in a sealed envelope and addressed so that it will be read only by the addressee. Adding the words "Personal and Confidential" or "Personal" is a good precaution.

[1] Unless otherwise footnoted, this discussion on defamation is based on Arthur B. Hanson, *Libel and Related Torts*, Vol. I, The American Newspaper Publishers Association Foundation, Inc., New York, 1969, pp. 21–195.

Another precaution is to use an opaque envelope and to fold the message in such a way that it cannot be easily read when held up to a light.

A defamatory telegram also is actionable against the sender if its defamatory meaning is communicated to a third person. In an interstate transmission, governed by federal law, the telegraph company may also be held liable, but only if the message is obviously defamatory and the agents of the company who actually transmit it know the sender is not "privileged" to send it.

Accidental communications to third persons (by eavesdroppers or unauthorized letter readers) are not actionable unless you knew of or should have foreseen such possibilities. A mere possibility that someone may have seen or overheard the statement is not enough.

Dictation to a stenographer is considered by most authorities to be a publication which is conditionally privileged with respect to matters reasonably related to the ordinary conduct of the business.

Privilege

A legal right to communicate defamatory information in certain situations is "privilege." The privilege may be "absolute" or "conditional."

Absolute privilege is mainly limited to three general areas: judicial proceedings, legislative proceedings, and the acts of important government officials, usually executives. Thus judicial officers, attorneys, and all parties participating in a judicial proceeding are absolutely privileged to make defamatory statements during and as part of the trial, if they bear some relationship to the matter under consideration.[2] Letters between parties or attorneys relating to a controversy are also privileged. However, defamatory statements about a case made outside the ordinary course of a judicial proceeding, such as comments to reporters in the hallway, are not entitled to the absolute privilege for judicial proceedings.

Similarly, legislators and government officials are absolutely privileged to make defamatory statements in the performance of their official functions, but not if the statements are irrelevant to the public matter then under consideration. For example, a member of the highway commission in New Mexico made a defamatory statement about a highway contractor at a commission meeting with reporters present. A superintendent of banks in California made libelous statements concerning his former attorney. In each case the Supreme Court of the respective state held that these public officials were protected by an absolute privilege in the exercise of their executive function. In contrast, a public official would not be absolutely privileged to defame his subordinates when publicly explaining why he dismissed them.[2]

A conditional (qualified) privilege applies to several situations in which the interest of either the participants or society dictates that communication in

[2] Paul P. Ashley, *Say It Safely: Legal Limits in Publishing, Radio, and Television,* University of Washington Press, Seattle, 1966, pp. 43–47.

good faith should not be hampered by fear of lawsuits. Thus defamatory statements made in the ordinary commercial activity are qualifiedly privileged, whether they are interoffice messages or sent to persons outside the company, when the recipient has a lawful interest in the topic of discussion. For example, the person who answers an inquiry about the performance of an employee or about the credit record of a customer is obligated to take reasonable precautions to see that the information sent is accurate. And he or she must avoid intentional deceit. If he or she intentionally or carelessly misleads the inquirer who seeks information about another person (for instance, a credit or job applicant), he or she may be sued for damages.

Thus whenever you send requested information to an inquirer (prospective employer or creditor, for instance, who might suffer a loss if he or she employs or lends to an unworthy applicant), make every effort to tell the truth and to reply in good faith without malice. When the truth about an individual or an organization is unfavorable and directly related to a question you are asked to answer, try as much as possible to protect the good name of the one involved. Also indicate in your reply that the information was requested and ask that it be kept confidential. Likewise, when you request someone to send you personal information about another person, show in your letter that you have an interest to protect and promise to keep the received information confidential. You will thus help the informer protect himself against a libel suit. (However, under some of the new public disclosure laws confidentiality may no longer be possible.)

Privilege does not apply to unreasonable disclosure and publication of particulars concerning a debtor to his or her employer, relatives, and to the public by such devices as "deadbeat lists" or obvious communications forms which may be read by others who have not requested the information and have no immediate need of it.

Privilege also does not apply to defamatory statements which are unrelated to the purpose of the particular privilege. If for instance a former employer is requested to recommend an applicant for a new employment, the privilege pertaining to his or her response does not extend to defamatory remarks not related to job qualifications. Also, the former employer may lose the privilege if the response uses such violent or abusive language that the real motive in the reply is evidence of malice or some other improper purpose. Furthermore, if the former employer knows the statement is false, clearly the privilege is defeated. If he or she is negligent or unreasonable in believing it to be true, jurisdictions differ as to whether the privilege is lost.

The risk of liability for criticism of public men has decreased significantly in the United States since the Supreme Court decided the *New York Times* case in 1964. Under the *Times* rule, criticism or comment about the public conduct or fitness for office of public officials, and statements about the public conduct of other voluntary public figures is privileged even if it is based on or includes erroneous material—unless there was actual knowledge of falsity or reckless disregard for whether the material was true or false. Two prongs to the rule are: (1) the inclusion of both fact and opinion within the privilege of fair comment, and (2) the degree of "malice" (intent to injure) necessary to defeat the privilege, constituting knowledge of falsity or reckless disregard for truth. The Supreme Court has included within the public official designation: a city commissioner; a group of parish judges; a county attorney and chief of police; an elected court clerk; a deputy sheriff (and others). The "public figure" to which the rule applies is a person "intimately involved in the resolution of important public questions" or one who by reason of his or her fame shapes events in an area of concern to society at large, and as a result, already has as much access to the mass media "both to influence policy and to counter criticism" of his or her views and activities as does a "public official." The Supreme Court has found a university athletic director and a retired Army General who was actively involved in a federally enforced school integration to be within the class of public figures covered by the *Times* rule.

Defamatory terms

Among the terms that have been judged libelous, the following are a representative (but incomplete) sampling of words to be avoided or used with caution when you refer to a person or an organization:[3]

bankrupt	drug addict	incompetent	quack
blackmailer	faker	inferior	racketeer
Communist	falsified	insolvent	shyster
corrupt	forger	kickbacks	swindler
crook	fraud (fraudulent)	misappropriation	thief
deadbeat	gouged money	misconduct	unchaste
dishonest	grafter	misrepresentation	unworthy of credit
disreputable	hypocrite	profiteer	worthless

In the collection of debts or in attempts to collect any claim alleged to be due or owing, the collector should not unreasonably oppress, harass, or abuse any person. Harassment and abuse includes abusive language, anonymous or repeated telephone calls at odd hours, and anonymous c.o.d. communications.

Some statements are defamatory because they malign a characteristic necessary in a person's work (provided the occupation is legal). Thus, in most jurisdictions it is defamatory to impugn the financial responsibility of a merchant, but not of a teacher, because ability to obtain credit is essential only to the merchant. Also it has been held defamatory to attribute Communist sympathies to a public official, but not to an engineer. And, as already discussed, it is defamatory to impugn the competence of an employee to perform duties required by his or her job. But such statements may be conditionally privi-

[3] Philip Wittenberg, *Dangerous Words—A Guide to the Law of Libel,* Columbia University Press, New York, 1947, pp. 282-308.

leged if made in the ordinary course of business activity, as discussed above under "Privilege."

The truth is usually adequate defense in a libel suit, especially if there is no evidence of malice. But if the writer cannot prove his or her statements to be true or prove that there was adequate reason for writing them, he or she may have to pay large money damages.

Invasion of privacy[4]

The unconsented, unprivileged, and unreasonable intrusion into the private life of an individual is "invasion of privacy." Unlike defamation, privacy can be violated although no publication to third persons takes place and even though the matters delved into are true or not particularly harmful to reputation. The concept of right of privacy is analogous to that of trespass, which gives one the right to keep unwarranted intruders off one's land not because of any resulting emotional distress or loss of rents, but merely to ensure the solitude of landowners.

This section discusses two aspects of invasion of privacy: use of a person's name, photograph, or other identity without permission, and physical surveillance of records, reports, and letters by persons not entitled to examine them.

Use of a person's identity

If a person's name, photograph, or other identity is used without permission on a sales letter or advertisement (or other permanent publication—not word of mouth), that person may have cause for legal action because his or her right of privacy has been violated.

Recovery and monetary awards have also been granted for publication of x-rays and other medical pictures, for pictures of a deformed infant, and for undue .publicity of a delinquent debt.

Yet, not every use of another's likeness or identity is actionable. In some states it must be unreasonable under the circumstances, as well as unprivileged. Using pictures of an All-American football team on a beer company's calendar which also contained advertising was held (in one case) not to be an invasion of team members' privacy because they were public figures and there was no false implication of endorsement. But using a person's picture to illustrate a story about dishonest tactics of cab drivers would shed false and unfavorable imputation on the person and would be an invasion of privacy.

Unreasonable publicity of private life may also result in legal action and costly money awards to the offended person. A classic case (cited in *Libel and Related Torts,* page 203) is one in which the plaintiff, a former prostitute and

[4] Hanson, op. cit., pp. 197–206.

the acquitted defendant in a notorious murder trial had reformed, married, and pursued a respectable life in a new community which knew nothing about her former life until the defendant revealed the whole story in a movie, using her name. She was allowed a cause of action for publication of these true but embarrassing personal facts.

In the "pink letter case" (mentioned in *When You Need a Lawyer*)[5] a suggestive letter bearing a woman's signature was mailed to 1,000 men. Handwritten in a feminine hand, the letter was mechanically reproduced on pink stationery and mailed by a mailing agency. The name signed to the letter was that of the principal character in a motion picture the letter was advertising. Unfortunately, it also turned out to be the name of a woman living in Los Angeles—the only person by that name listed in the City Directory or the telephone directory. When the letters began arriving (in hand-addressed, pink envelopes), many wives must have looked at their husbands with a quizzical eye. But it was worse for the plaintiff, who began getting telephone calls from the men. She also worried for fear that some irate wife might shoot her—for the letter invited the men to meet the signer in front of a certain theater on a certain day and to look for a girl "with a gleam in her eye, a smile on her lips and mischief on her mind." The court felt that the plaintiff should be compensated for invasion of right of privacy.

If you wish to use the picture or identity of an individual for your advertising or sales letters, for instance, be sure first to get previous consent and make clear just how the picture or identity is to be used. An individual may have indicated consent by willfully posing for a photograph, but alteration of the photograph or using it in a way to carry objectionable implications is an invasion of privacy.

Physical surveillance of records, reports, and letters[6]

The right of privacy may also be violated if records, reports, and letters are read by persons not entitled to examine them.

Powerful binoculars, long-range telephoto cameras, and "zoomer"-type television cameras have been used effectively (and illegally) in recent years to look through windows at important papers lying face-up on desks, at models of new products and designs, and at charts displayed at conferences. These techniques have become so common in certain areas of industrial espionage that elaborate security precautions are taken to keep designs and models in windowless rooms and to keep blinds drawn at all times in certain offices.

Modern technology has added to these existing situations the possibility of passing visible light or reflected infrared energy through an envelope and

[5] Kenneth and Irene Donelson, *When You Need a Lawyer,* Doubleday & Company, Inc., Garden City, N.Y., 1964, pp. 245-249.
[6] Alan F. Westin, *Privacy and Freedom,* pp. 78-79; copyright 1967 by The Association of the Bar of the City of New York. Reprinted by permission of Atheneum Publishers, USA.

taking pictures of the contents. These pictures can then be read (deciphered) by persons skilled in reading handwriting or typing where lines are inverted or superimposed. Also available is a needle-thin "flashlight" that can be inserted in a sealed envelope to "light it up" for quick reading by a trained investigator. You can help to greatly reduce or even prevent this type of surveillance by using—when desirable on certain very confidential material—envelopes with a random pattern printed on them to make them opaque and/or inserting more than one sheet of paper in them.

Fraud

The intentional misrepresentation by one party to a contract of a material fact which is relied upon by the other party to his injury is fraud.[7] Both as a seller and a buyer you need to be aware of the elements of fraud as well as the significance of warranties so that you can better detect and avoid fraudulent practices.

Elements

The elements of fraud are: (1) false representation of fact, not opinion, intentionally made; (2) intent that the deceived person act thereon; (3) knowledge that such statements would naturally deceive; and (4) that the deceived person acted to his injury.[8]

The misrepresentation need not be a direct falsehood for fraud to be present. In fact, failing to reveal defects or confirming false impressions by remaining silent can be sufficient. To constitute actionable fraud (for lawsuit), the misrepresentation must be of a *material fact*—a fact that induced the contract. Statements of the seller's opinions and "puffing" (boastful sales talk about the value of the goods) are permissible. The buyer is not justified in relying on such statements; they do not become part of the bargain and are not warranties. The main test for fraud is to ask, "Would the other party have entered into the contract had he known the truth?" Opinions may lead to fraud if they amount to deliberately false statements made by a recognized professional in the field, whose opinions may reasonably be relied upon in the contract. Opinions, however, must be in regard to an existing or past fact and not to forecasts or predictions.[9]

[7] Michael P. Litka, *Business Law*, Harcourt Brace Jovanovich, Inc., New York, 1970, pp. 152–153.
[8] William J. Robert and Robert N. Corley, *Dillavou and Howard's Principles of Business Law*, 8th Edition, Prentice-Hall, Inc., Englewood Cliffs, N.J., 1967, p. 1027.
[9] Litka, loc. cit.

Warranties

In most sales contracts the seller undertakes certain obligations concerning the nature, title, and quality of the goods being sold. When these obligations are expressly stated or implied and when they actually induce the sale, the obligations are called "warranties." They are guarantees by the seller with respect to the goods sold. Warranties may be express or implied.

An express warranty affirms a fact or a promise the seller made to the buyer in bargaining concerning the nature of the goods—description, grade, or model. Such a promise becomes a basis for the contract even though the term "warranty" or "guaranty" is not used.

Implied warranties are considered part of the bargain even though the parties themselves say nothing about them. For instance, the seller warrants that he or she is conveying a good title to the goods. Also, under the Uniform Commercial Code (adopted by all 50 states) if the seller is a merchant with respect to goods of that kind, he or she warrants that the goods are salable and are fit for the ordinary purposes for which such goods are used. If the seller knows the buyer intends the goods for a particular purpose and that the buyer is relying on the seller's judgment as to their suitability, there is an implied warranty of fitness for that particular purpose.[10]

According to the U.S. Postmaster General, in the Post Office Department's informative booklet *Mail Fraud Laws*,[11] fraudulent schemes sent through the mail are costing the American consumers an estimated $500 million a year. Among the many dishonest rackets to trap the unsuspecting consumer are: fake contests, home improvement offers, auto insurance frauds, charity appeals, missing heir schemes, fake business opportunities, worthless medical cures, and fake corresondence-school programs promising "exciting, high-paying jobs."

The U.S. Chief Postal Inspector lists the following ways you can help enforce mail fraud laws:

> To stop a dishonest scheme, inspectors must find that you and others buying a product or service were cheated as a result of claims the seller made in an intentional effort to defraud. Mail fraud violations occur when a general scheme or pattern of fraud exists.

> When you believe mail fraud exists, hold all letters, including envelopes and other evidence related to the questionable scheme. See if your neighbors or business associates have also received similar material.

> Bring such information to the attention of a postal inspector in your area by contacting him directly or through your postmaster.

[10] Litka, op. cit., pp. 470–74.
[11] *Mail Fraud Laws—Protecting Consumers, Investors, Businessmen, Medical Patients, Students;* U.S. Post Office Department, Washington, D.C., 20260, June 1969.

Inspectors cannot investigate a case simply to force a supplier to speed up deliveries, obtain refunds, or to otherwise act as an intermediary in settling unsatisfactory transactions. In such instances the dissatisfied buyer should:

Seek an adjustment or settlement with the seller.

Bring his complaint to the attention of the Better Business Bureau, Chamber of Commerce, Trade Association, or publication which carried the ad.

Seek relief through civil suit if a breach of contract may be involved.

Most states now have consumer protection divisions in the Attorney General's office, and they can be very helpful too.

Other areas of caution in business writing

Among the many other unmailable materials that may violate United States Postal Laws are letters and printed matter concerning lotteries, obscene literature, extortion threats, and solicitation of illegal business. Space does not permit discussion of these items here. You can obtain booklets on most of these subjects through your local postmaster or the U.S. Government Printing Office, Washington D.C., 20402. And if you are in doubt about the mailability of any particular material, you may submit a request to the Office of the General Counsel, Mailability Division, Post Office Department, Washington, D.C., 20260. A ruling will be furnished as promptly as circumstances permit.

The sending of unordered merchandise through the mail does not violate postal laws unless it is sent c.o.d. However, persons receiving such unordered items can:

If the package has not been opened, write "Return to Sender" and put it back into the mails.

If the article is not wanted, set it aside for a reasonable period of time and if unclaimed, destroy.

Treat unordered merchandise as an unconditional gift if living in a state where the laws apply.[12]

The sending of unsolicited credit cards is illegal, as specified in the Consumer Credit Cost Disclosure Act.

Another caution pertains to the copying of certain documents. Congress, by statute, has forbidden the copying of the following documents and items under certain circumstances: United States government obligations or securities, such as Treasury and Federal Reserve Notes, National Bank Currency,

[12] *Mail Fraud Laws,* 1969.

Certificates of Indebtedness, silver and gold certificates, paper money, and others; also U.S. Savings Bonds (except for campaign publicity for their sale), Internal Revenue Stamps (except in copying for lawful purposes a legal document on which there is a cancelled revenue stamp), postage stamps cancelled or uncancelled (except for philatelic purposes provided the reproduction is in black and white and is less than ¾ or more than 1½ times the linear dimensions of the original); postal money orders; bills, checks or drafts for money drawn by or upon authorized officers of the United States; and other representatives of value issued under any act of congress.

Also forbidden is the copying of copyrighted material without permission of the copyright owner; certificates of citizenship or naturalization (except foreign naturalization certificates); passports (except foreign); immigration papers; obligations or securities of any foreign government, bank, or corporation; draft registration cards, selective service induction papers bearing certain information; badges, identification cards, passes or insignia carried by military, naval personnel, or members of the various federal departments and bureaus such as FBI, Treasury (except when ordered by head of such department or bureau). In some states copying auto licenses, automobile certificates of title, and drivers' licenses is also forbidden. For these items—and others not listed here—penalties of fine or imprisonment are imposed on those guilty of making illegal copies.

As a final caution, in general, remember to:

- Be honest and fair in all your business transactions and correspondence.

- Avoid any statements and acts that may be considered defamation, invasion of privacy, or fraud.

- Keep yourself well informed on responsibilities in other legal areas of concern.

- Consult an attorney when in doubt about the handling of any complicated situation that might involve legal risks.

Reports

Audience analysis: the problem and a solution

**J. C. MATHES and
DWIGHT W. STEVENSON**

Both J. C. Mathes and Dwight W. Stevenson are
professors of humanities in the College of
Engineering at the University of Michigan.

Every communication situation involves three fundamental components: a writer, a message, and an audience. However, many report writers treat the communication situation as if there were only two components: a writer and his message. Writers often ignore their readers because writers are preoccupied with their own problems and with the subject matter of the communication. The consequence is a poorly designed, ineffective report.

As an example, a student related to the class her first communication experience on a design project during summer employment with an automobile company. After she had been working on her assignment for a few weeks, her supervisor asked her to jot him a memo explaining what she was doing. Not wanting to take much time away from her work and not thinking the report very important, she gave him a handwritten memo and continued her technical activities. Soon after, the department manager inquired on the progress of the project. The supervisor immediately responded that he had just had a progress report, and thereupon forwarded the engineer's brief memo. Needless to say, the engineer felt embarrassed when her undeveloped and inadequately explained memo became an official report to the organization. The engineer thought her memo was written just to her supervisor, who was quite familiar with her assignment. Due to her lack of experience with organizational behavior, she made several false assumptions about her report audience, and therefore about her report's purpose.

The inexperienced report writer often fails to design his report effectively because he makes several false assumptions about the report writing situation.

From *Designing Technical Reports* by J. C. Mathes and Dwight W. Stevenson. Copyright © 1976 by The Bobbs-Merrill Co., Inc. Reprinted by permission of the publisher.

If the writer would stop to analyze the audience component he would realize that:

1. It is false to assume that the person addressed is the audience.

2. It is false to assume that the audience is a group of specialists in the field.

3. It is false to assume that the report has a finite period of use.

4. It is false to assume that the author and the audience always will be available for reference.

5. It is false to assume that the audience is familiar with the assignment.

6. It is false to assume that the audience has been involved in daily discussions of the material.

7. It is false to assume that the audience awaits the report.

8. It is false to assume that the audience has time to read the report.

Assumptions one and two indicate a writer's lack of awareness of the nature of his report audience. Assumptions three, four, and five indicate his lack of appreciation of the dynamic nature of the system. Assumptions six, seven, and eight indicate a writer's lack of consideration of the demands of day-by-day job activity.

A report has value only to the extent that it is useful to the organization. It is often used primarily by someone other than the person who requested it. Furthermore, the report may be responding to a variety of needs within the organization. These needs suggest that the persons who will use the report are not specialists or perhaps not even technically knowledgeable about the report's subject. The specialist is the engineer. Unless he is engaged in basic research, he usually must communicate with persons representing many different areas of operation in the organization.

In addition, the report is often useful over an extended period of time. Each written communication is filed in several offices. Last year's report can be incomprehensible if the writer did not anticipate and explain his purpose adequately. In these situations, even within the office where a report originated, the author as well as his supervisor will probably not be available to explain the report. Although organizational charts remain unchanged for years, personnel, assignments, and professional roles change constantly. Because of this dynamic process, even the immediate audience of a report sometimes is not familiar with the writer's technical assignment. Thus, the report writer usually must design his report for a dynamic situation.

Finally, the report writer must also be alert to the communication traps in relatively static situations. Not all readers will have heard the coffee break chats that fill in the details necessary to make even a routine recommendation convincing. A report can arrive at a time when the reader's mind is churning with other concerns. Even if it is expected, the report usually meets a reader who needs to act immediately. The reader usually does not have time to read through the whole report; he wants the useful information clearly and succinctly. To the reader, time probably is the most important commodity. Beginning report writers seldom realize they must design their reports to be used efficiently rather than read closely.

The sources of the false assumptions we have been discussing are not difficult to identify. The original source is the artificial communication a student is required to perform in college. In writing only for professors, a student learns to write for audiences of one, audiences who know more than the writer knows, and audiences who have no instrumental interests in what the report contains. The subsequent source, on the job, is the writer's natural attempt to simplify his task. The report writer, relying upon daily contact and familiarity, simply finds it easier to write a report for his own supervisor than to write for a supervisor in a different department. The writer also finds it easier to concentrate upon his own concerns than to consider the needs of his readers. He finds it difficult to address complex audiences and face the design problems they pose.

Audience components and problems they pose

To write a report you must first understand how your audience poses a problem. Then you must analyze your audience in order to be able to design a report structure that provides an optimum solution. To explain the components of the report audience you must do more than just identify names, titles, and roles. You must determine who your audiences are as related to the purpose and content of your report. "Who" involves the specific operational functions of the persons who will read the report, as well as their educational and business backgrounds. These persons can be widely distributed, as is evident if you consider the operational relationships within a typical organization.

Classifying audiences only according to directions of communication flow along the paths delineated by the conventional organizational chart, we can identify three types of report audiences: *horizontal, vertical,* and *external.* For example, in the organization chart in Figure 1, *Part of organization chart for naval ship engineering center,*[1] horizontal audiences exist on each level. The Ship Concept Design Division and the Command and Surveillance Division form horizontal audiences for each other. Vertical audiences exist between levels. The Ship Concept Design Division and the Surface Ship Design Branch form vertical audiences for each other. External audiences exist when any unit

[1] A reference in H. B. Benford and J. C. Mathes, *Your Future in Naval Architecture,* Richards Rosen, New York, 1968.

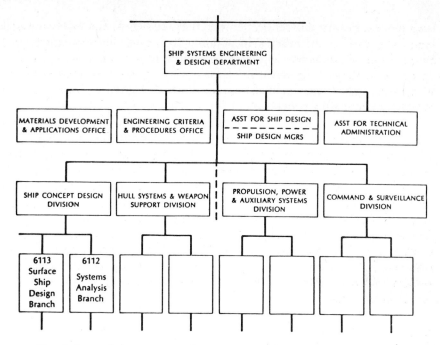

Fig. 1. Part of organization chart for naval ship engineering center.

interacts with a separate organization, such as when the Surface Ship Design Branch communicates with the Newport News Shipbuilding Company.

What the report writer first must realize is the separation between him and any of these three types of audiences. Few reports are written for horizontal audiences within the same unit, such as from one person in the Surface Ship Design Branch to another person or project group within the Surface Ship Design Branch itself. Instead, a report at least addresses horizontal audiences within a larger framework, such as from the Surface Ship Design Branch to the Systems Analysis Branch. Important reports usually have complex audiences, that is, vertical and horizontal, and sometimes external audiences as well.

An analysis of the problems generated by horizontal audiences—often assumed to pose few problems—illustrates the difficulties most writers face in all report writing situations. A systems engineer in the Systems Analysis Branch has little technical education in common with the naval architect in the Surface Ship Design Branch. In most colleges he takes only a few of the same mathematics and engineering science courses. The systems engineer would not know the wave resistance theory familiar to the naval architect, although he could use the results of his analysis. In turn, the naval architect would not know stochastics and probability theory, although he could understand systems models. But the differences between these audiences and writers go well beyond differences in training. In addition to having different educational backgrounds, the audiences will have different concerns, such as budget, production, or contract obligations. The audiences will also be separated from the writer by organizational politics and competition, as well as by personality differences among the people concerned.

When the writer addresses a horizontal audience in another organizational unit, he usually addresses a person in an organizational role. When addressed to the role rather than the person, the report is aimed at a department or a group. This means the report will have audiences in addition to the person addressed. It may be read primarily by staff personnel and subordinates. The addressee ultimately may act on the basis of the information reported, but at times he serves only to transfer the report to persons in his department who will use it. Furthermore, the report may have audiences in addition to those in the department addressed. It may be forwarded to other persons elsewhere, such as lawyers and comptrollers. The report travels routinely throughout organizational paths, and will have unknown or unanticipated audiences as well.

Consequently, even when on the same horizontal organizational level, the writer and his audience have little in common beyond the fact of working for the same organization, of having the same "rank," and perhaps of having the same educational level of attainment. Educational backgrounds can be entirely different; more important, needs, values, and uses are different. The report writer may recommend the choice of one switch over another on the basis of a cost-efficiency analysis; his audiences may be concerned for business relationships, distribution patterns, client preferences, and budgets. Therefore, the writer should not assume that his audience has technical competence in the field, familiarity with the technical assignment, knowledge of him or of personnel in his group, similar value perspectives, or even complementary motives. The differences between writer and audience are distinctive, and may even be irreconcilable.

The differences are magnified when the writer addresses vertical audiences. Reports directed at vertical audiences, that is, between levels of an organization chart, invariably have horizontal audience components also. These complex report writing situations pose significant communication problems for the writer. Differences between writer and audience are fundamental. The primary audiences for the reports, especially informal reports, must act or make decisions on the basis of the reports. The reports thus have only instrumental value, that is, value insofar as they can be used effectively. The writer must design his report primarily according to how it will be used.

In addition to horizontal audiences and to vertical audiences, many reports are also directed to external audiences. External audiences, whether they consist of a few or many persons, have the distinctive, dissimilar features of the complex vertical audience. With external audiences these features invariably are exaggerated, especially those involving need and value. An additional complication is that the external audience can judge an entire organization on the basis of the writer's report. And sometimes most important of all, concerns for tact and business relationships override technical concerns.

In actual practice the writer often finds audiences in different divisions of his own company to be "external" audiences. One engineer encountered this problem in his first position after graduation. He was sent to investigate the inconsistent test data being sent to his group from a different division of the company in another city. He found that the test procedures being used in that division were faulty. However, at his supervisor's direction he had to write a report that would not "step on any toes." He had to write the report in such a manner as to have the other division correct its test procedures while not implying that the division was in any way at fault. An engineer who assumes that the purpose of his report is just to explain a technical investigation is poorly prepared for professional practice.

Most of the important communication situations for an engineer during his first five years out of college occur when he reports to his supervisor, department head, and beyond. In these situations, his audiences are action-oriented line management who are uninterested in the technical details and may even be unfamiliar with the assignment. In addition, his audiences become acquainted with him professionally through his reports; therefore, it is more directly the report than the investigation that is important to the writer's career.

Audience components and the significant design problems they pose are well illustrated by the various audiences for a formal report written by an engineer on the development of a process to make a high purity chemical, as listed in Figure 2, *Complex audience components for a formal report by a chemical engineer on a process to make a high purity chemical.* The purpose of the report was to explain the process; others would make a feasibility study of the process and evaluate it in comparison to other processes.

The various audiences for this report, as you can determine just by reading their titles, would have had quite different roles, backgrounds, interests, values, needs, and uses for the report. The writer's brief analysis of the audiences yielded the following:

He could not determine the nature of many of his audiences, who they were, or what the specifics of their roles were.

His audiences had little familiarity with his assignment.

His report would be used for information, for evaluation of the process, and for evaluation of the company's position in the field.

Some of his audiences would have from a minute to a half hour to glance at the report, some would take the report home to study it, and some would use it over extended periods of time for process analysis and for economic and manufacturing feasibility studies.

The useful lifetime of the report could be as long as twenty years.

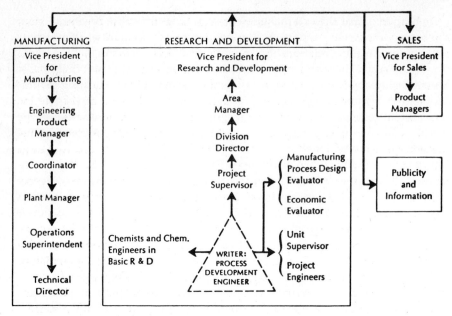

Fig. 2. Complex audience components for a formal report by a chemical engineer on a process to make a high purity chemical.

The report would be used to evaluate the achievements of the writer's department.

The report would be used to evaluate the writing and technical proficiencies of the writer himself.

This report writer classified his audiences in terms of the conventional organization chart. Then to make them more than just names, titles, and roles he asked himself what they would know about his report and how they would use it. Even then he had only partially solved his audience problem and had just begun to clarify the design problems he faced. To do so he needed to analyze his audiences systematically.

A method for systematic audience analysis

To introduce the audience problem that report writers must face, we have used the conventional concept of the organization chart to classify audiences as *horizontal, vertical,* and *external.* However, when the writer comes to the task of performing an instrumentally useful audience analysis for a particular report, this concept of the organization and this classification system for report audiences are not very helpful.

First, the writer does not view from outside the total communication system modeled by the company organization chart. He is within the system himself, so his view is always relative. Second, the conventional outsider's view does not yield sufficiently detailed information about the report audiences. A single bloc on the organization chart looks just like any other bloc, but in fact each bloc represents one or several human beings with distinctive roles, backgrounds, and personal characteristics. Third, and most importantly, the outsider's view does not help much to clarify the specific routes of communication, as determined by audience needs, which an individual report will follow. The organization chart may describe the organization, but it does not describe how the organization functions. Thus many of the routes a report follows—and consequently the needs it addresses—will not be signaled by the company organization chart.

In short, the conventional concept of report audiences derived from organization charts is necessarily abstract and unspecific. For that reason a more effective method for audience analysis is needed. In the remaining portion of this chapter we will present a three-step procedure. The procedure calls for preparing an egocentric organization chart to identify individual report readers, characterizing these readers, and classifying them to establish priorities. Based upon an egocentric view of the organization and concerned primarily with what report readers need, this system should yield the information the writer must have if he is to design an individual report effectively.

Prepare an egocentric organization chart

An egocentric organization chart differs from the conventional chart in two senses. First, it identifies specific individuals rather than complex organizational units. A bloc on the conventional chart may often represent a number of people, but insofar as possible the egocentric chart identifies particular individuals who are potential readers of reports a writer produces. Second, the egocentric chart categorizes people in terms of their proximity to the report writer rather than in terms of their hierarchical relationship to the report writer. Readers are not identified as organizationally superior, inferior, or equal to the writer, but rather as near or distant from the writer. We find it effective to identify four different degrees of distance as is illustrated in Figure 3, *Egocentric organization chart*. In this figure, with the triangle representing the writer, each circle is an individual reader identified by his organizational title and by his primary operational concerns. The four degrees of distance are identified by the four concentric rings. The potential readers in the first ring are those people with whom the writer associates daily. They are typically those people in his same office or project group. The readers in the second ring are those people in other offices with whom the writer must normally interact in order to perform his job. Typically, these are persons in adjacent and management groups. The readers in the third ring are persons relatively more

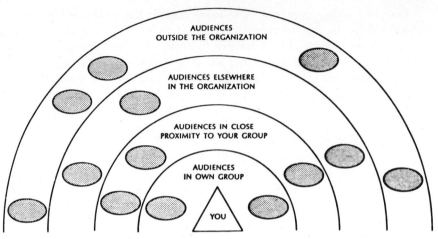

Fig. 3. Egocentric organization chart.

distant but still within the same organization. They are distant management, public relations, sales, legal department, production, purchasing, and so on. They are operationally dissimilar persons. The readers in the fourth ring are persons beyond the organization. They may work for the same company but in a division in another city. Or they may work for an entirely different organization.

Having prepared the egocentric organization chart, the report writer is able to see himself and his potential audiences from a useful perspective. Rather than seeing himself as an insignificantly small part of a complex structure—as he is apt to do with the conventional organizational chart—the writer sees himself as a center from which communication radiates throughout an organization. He sees his readers as individuals rather than as faceless blocs. And he sees that what he writes is addressed to people with varying and significant degrees of difference.

A good illustration of the perspective provided by the egocentric organization chart is the chart prepared by a chemical engineer working for a large corporation, Figure 4, *Actual egocentric organization chart of an engineer in a large corporation.* It is important to notice how the operational concerns of the persons even in close proximity vary considerably from those of the development engineer. What these people need from reports written by this engineer, then, has little to do with the processes by which he defined his technical problems.

The chemical engineer himself is concerned with the research and development of production processes and has little interest in, or knowledge of, budgetary matters. Some of the audiences in his group are chemists concerned with production—not with research and development. Because of this they have, as he said, "lost familiarity with the technical background, and instead

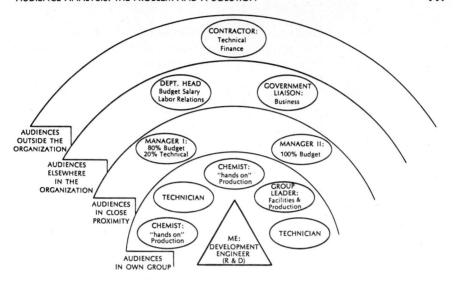

Fig. 4. Actual egocentric organization chart of an engineer in a large corporation.

depend mostly on experience." Other audiences in his group are technicians concerned only with operations. With only two years of college, they have had no more than introductory chemistry courses and have had no engineering courses.

Still another audience in his group is his group leader. Rather than being concerned with development, this reader is concerned with facilities and production operations. Consequently, he too is "losing familiarity with the technical material." Particularly significant for the report writer is that his group leader in his professional capacity does not use his B.S.Ch.E. degree. His role is that of manager, so his needs have become administrative rather than technical.

The concerns of the chemical engineer/report writer's audiences in close proximity to his group change again. Instead of being concerned with development or production operations, these audiences are primarily concerned with the budget. They have little technical contact, and are described as "business oriented." Both Manager I and Manager II are older, and neither has a degree in engineering. One has a Ph.D. degree in chemistry, the other an M.S. degree in technology. Both have had technical experience in the lab, but neither can readily follow technical explanations. As the chemical engineer said, both would find it "difficult to return to the lab."

The report writer's department head and the other persons through whom the group communicates with audiences elsewhere in the organization, and beyond it, have additional concerns as well as different backgrounds. The department head is concerned with budget, personnel, and labor relations.

The person in contact with outside funding units—in this case, a government agency—has business administration degrees and is entirely business oriented. The person in contact with subcontractors has both technical and financial concerns.

Notice that when this writer examined his audiences even in his own group as well as those in close proximity to him, he saw that the natures, the backgrounds, and especially the operational concerns of his audiences vary and differ considerably. As he widened the scope of his egocentric organization chart, he knew less and less about his audiences. However, he could assume they will vary even more than those of the audiences in close proximity.

Thus, in the process of examining the audience situation with an egocentric organization chart, a report writer can uncover not only the fact that audiences have functionally different interests, but also the nature of those functional differences. He can proceed to classify the audiences for each particular report in terms of audience needs.

Preparation of the egocentric organization chart is the first step of your procedure of systematic audience analysis. Notice that this step can be performed once to describe your typical report audience situation but must be particularized for each report to define the audiences for that report. Having prepared the egocentric chart once, the writer revises his chart for subsequent reports by adding or subtracting individual audiences.

Characterize the individual report readers

In the process of preparing the egocentric organization chart, you immediately begin to think of your individual report readers in particular terms. In preparing the egocentric chart discussed above, the report writer mentioned such items as a reader's age, academic degrees, and background in the organization as well as his operational concerns. All of these particulars will come to mind when you think of your audiences as individuals. However, a systematic rather than piecemeal audience analysis will yield more useful information. The second step of audience analysis is, therefore, a systematic characterization of each person identified in the egocentric organization chart. A systematic characterization is made in terms of *operational, objective,* and *personal* characteristics.

The *operational characteristics* of your audiences are particularly important. As you identify the operational characteristics for a person affected by your report, try to identify significant differences between his or her role and yours. What are his professional values? How does he spend his time? That is, will his daily concerns and attitudes enable him to react to your report easily, or will they make it difficult for him to grasp what you are talking about? What does he know about your role, and in particular, what does he know or remember about your technical assignment and the organizational problem that occasioned your report to come to him? You should also consider carefully what he will need from your report. As you think over your entire technical investigation, ask yourself if that person will involve staff personnel in action on your report, or if he will in turn activate other persons elsewhere in the organization when he receives the report. If he should, you must take their reactions into account when you write your report.

In addition, you should ask yourself, "How will my report affect his role?" A student engineer recently told us of an experience he had during summer employment when he was asked to evaluate the efficiency of the plant's waste treatment process. Armed with his fresh knowledge from advanced chemical engineering courses, to his surprise he found that, by making a simple change in the process, the company could save more than $200,000 a year. He fired off his report with great anticipation of glowing accolades— none came. How had his report affected the roles of some of his audiences? Although the writer had not considered the report's consequences when he wrote it, the supervisor, the manager, and related personnel now were faced with the problem of accounting for their waste of $200,000 a year. It should have been no surprise that they were less than elated over his discovery.

By *objective characteristics* we mean specific, relevant background data about the person. As you try to identify his or her educational background, you may note differences you might have otherwise neglected. Should his education seem to approximate yours, do not assume he knows what you know. Remember that the half-life of engineering education today is about five years. Thus, anyone five to ten years older than you, if you are recently out of college, probably will be only superficially familiar with the material and jargon of your advanced technical courses. If you can further identify his past professional experiences and roles, you might be able to anticipate his first-hand knowledge of your role and technical activities as well as to clarify any residual organizational commitments and value systems he might have. When you judge his knowledge of your technical area, ask yourself, "Could he participate in a professional conference in my field of specialization?"

For *personal characteristics,* when you identify a person by name, ask yourself how often the name changes in this organizational role. When you note his or her approximate age, remind yourself how differences in age can inhibit communication. Also note personal concerns that could influence his reactions to your report.

A convenient way to conduct the audience analysis we have been describing and to store the information it yields is to use an analysis form similar to the one in Figure 5, *Form for characterizing individual report readers*. It may be a little time-consuming to do this the first time around, but you can establish a file of audience characterizations. Then you can add to or subtract from this file as an individual communication situation requires.

One final point: This form is a means to an end rather than an end in itself. What is important for the report writer is that he think systematically about the questions this form raises. The novice usually has to force himself to analyze his audiences systematically. The experienced writer does this automatically.

Classify audiences in terms of how they will use your report

For each report you write, trace out the communication routes on your egocentric organization chart and add other routes not on the chart. Do not limit these routes to those specifically identified by the assignment and the addressees of the report. Rather, think through the total impacts of your report on the organization. That is, think in terms of the first, second, and even some third-order consequences of your report, and trace out the significant communication routes involved. All of these consequences define your actual communication.

When you think in terms of consequences, primarily you think in terms of the uses to which your report will be put. No longer are you concerned with your technical investigation itself. In fact, when you consider how readers will use your report, you realize that very few of your potential readers will have any real interest in the details of your technical investigation. Instead, they want to know the answers to such questions as "Why was this investigation made? What is the significance of the problem it addresses? What am I supposed to do with the results of this investigation? What will it cost? What are the implications—for sales, for production, for the unions? What happens next? Who does it? Who is responsible?"

It is precisely this audience concern for nontechnical questions that causes so much trouble for young practicing engineers. Professionally, much of what the engineer spends his time doing is, at most, of only marginal concern to many of his audiences. His audiences ask questions about things which perhaps never entered his thoughts during his own technical activities when he received the assignment, defined the problem, and performed his investigation. These questions, however, must enter into his considerations when he writes his report.

Having defined the communication routes for a report you now know what audiences you will have and what questions they will want answered. The final step in our method of audience analysis is to assign priorities to your audiences. Classify them in terms of how they will use your report. In order of their importance to you (not in terms of their proximity to you), classify your audiences by these three categories:

- *Primary audiences*—who make decisions or act on the basis of the information a report contains.

- *Secondary audiences*—who are affected by the decisions and actions.

- *Immediate audiences*—who route the report or transmit the information it contains.

Figure 5. Form for Characterizing Individual Report Readers.

NAME: TITLE:

A. OPERATIONAL CHARACTERISTICS:
    1. His role within the organization and consequent value system:

    2. His daily concerns and attitudes:

    3. His knowledge of your technical responsibilities and assignment:

    4. What he will need from your report:

    5. What staff and other persons will be activitated by your report
       through him:

    6. How your report could affect his role:

B. OBJECTIVE CHARACTERISTICS:
    1. His education—levels, fields, and years:

    2. His past professional experiences and roles:

    3. His knowledge of your technical area:

C. PERSONAL CHARACTERISTICS:
    Personal characteristics that could influence his reactions—
    age, attitudes, pet concerns, etc.

The *primary audience* for a report consists of those persons who will make decisions or act on the basis of the information provided by the report. The report overall should be designed to meet the needs of these users. The primary audience can consist of one person who will act in an official capacity, or it can consist of several persons representing several offices using the report. The important point here is that the primary audience for a report can consist of persons from any ring on the egocentric organization chart. They may be distant or in close proximity to the writer. They may be his organizational superiors, inferiors, or equals. They are simply those readers for whom the report is primarily intended. They are the top priority users.

In theory at least, primary audiences act in terms of their organizational roles rather than as individuals with distinctive idiosyncrasies, predilections, and values. Your audience analysis should indicate when these personal concerns are likely to override organizational concerns. A typical primary audience is the decision maker, but his actual decisions are often determined by the evaluations and recommendations of staff personnel. Thus the report whose primary audience is a decision maker with line responsibility actually has an audience of staff personnel. Another type of primary audience is the production superintendent, but again his actions are often contingent upon the reactions of others.

In addition, because the report enters into a system, in time both the line and staff personnel will change; roles rather than individuals provide continuity. For this reason, it is helpful to remember the words of one engineer when he said, "A complete change of personnel could occur over the lifetime of my report." The report remains in the file. The report writer must not assume that his primary audience will be familiar with the technical assignment. He must design the report so that it contains adequate information concerning the reasons for the assignment, details of the procedures used, the results of the investigation, and conclusions and recommendations. This information is needed so that any future component of his primary audience will be able to use the report confidently.

The *secondary audiences* for a report consist of those persons other than primary decision makers or users who are affected by the information the report transmits into the system. These are the people whose activities are affected when a primary audience makes a decision, such as when production supervision has to adjust to management decisions. They must respond appropriately when a primary audience acts, such as when personnel and labor relations have to accommodate production line changes. The report writer must not neglect the needs of his secondary audiences. In tracing out his communication routes, he will identify several secondary audiences. Analysis of their needs will reveal what additional information the report should contain. This information is often omitted by writers who do not classify their audiences sufficiently.

The *immediate audience* for a report are those persons who route the report or transmit the information it contains. It is essential for the report writer to identify his immediate audiences and not to confuse them with his primary audiences. The immediate audience might be the report writer's supervisor or another middle management person. Yet usually his role will be to transmit information rather than to use the information directly. An information system has numerous persons who transmit reports but who may not act upon the information or who may not be affected by the information in ways of concern to the report writers. Often, a report is addressed to the writer's supervisor, but except for an incidental memo report, the supervisor serves only to transmit and expedite the information flow throughout the organizational system.

A word of caution: at times the immediate audience is also part of the primary audience; at other times the immediate audience is part of the secondary audience. For each report you write you must distinguish those among your readers who will function as conduits to the primary audience.

As an example of these distinctions between categories of report audiences, consider how audiences identified on the egocentric organization chart, Figure 4, can be categorized. Assume that the chemical engineer writes a report on a particular process improvement he has designed. The immediate audience might be his Group Leader. Another would be Manager I, transmitting the report to Manager II. The primary audiences might be Manager II and the Department Head; they would ask a barrage of nontechnical questions similar to those we mentioned a moment ago. They will decide whether or not the organization will implement the improvement recommended by the writer. The Department Head also could be part of the secondary audience by asking questions relating to labor relations and union contracts. Other secondary audiences, each asking different questions of the report, could be:

> The person in contact with the funding agency, who will be concerned with budget and contract implications.
> The person in contact with subcontractors, determining how they are affected.
> The Group Leader, whose activities will be changed.
> The "hands on" chemist, whose production responsibilities will be affected.
> The technicians, whose job descriptions will change.

In addition to the secondary audiences on the egocentric organization chart, the report will have other secondary audiences throughout the organization— technical service and development, for example, or perhaps waste treatment.

At some length we have been discussing a fairly detailed method for systematic audience analysis. The method may have seemed more complicated than it actually is. Reduced to its basic ingredients, the method requires you, first, to identify all the individuals who will read the report, second, to characterize them, and third, to classify them. The *Matrix for audience analy-*

Characteristics / Types of audiences	Operational	Objective	Personal
Primary	①	④	⑦
Secondary	②	⑤	⑧
Immediate	③	⑥	⑨

Fig. 6. Matrix for audience analysis.

sis, Figure 6, is a convenient device for characterizing and classifying your readers once you have identified them. At a glance, the matrix reveals what information you have and what information you still need to generate. Above all, the matrix forces you to think systematically. If you are able to fill in a good deal of specific information in each cell (particularly in the first six cells), you have gone a long way towards seeing how the needs of your audiences will determine the design of your report.

We have not introduced a systematic method for audience analysis with the expectation that it will make your communication task easy. We have introduced you to the problems you must account for when you design your reports—problems you otherwise might ignore. You should, at least, appreciate the complexity of a report audience. Thus, when you come to write a report, you are less likely to make false assumptions about your audience. To develop this attitude is perhaps as important as to acquire the specific information the analysis yields. On the basis of this attitude, you now are ready to determine the specific purpose of your report.

What
to
report

RICHARD W. DODGE

Richard W. Dodge is a staff writer for
Westinghouse Engineer.

Technical reports *can* be a useful tool for management—not only as a source of general information, but, more importantly, as a valuable aid to decision making. But to be effective for these purposes, a technical report must be geared to the needs of management.

Considerable effort is being spent today to upgrade the effectiveness of the technical report. Much of this is directed toward improving the writing abilities of engineers and scientists; or toward systems of organization, or format, for reports. This effort has had some rewarding effects in producing better written reports.

But one basic factor in achieving better reports seems to have received comparatively little attention. This is the question of audience needs. Or, expressed another way, *"What does management want in reports?"* This is an extremely basic question, and yet it seems to have had less attention than have the mechanics of putting words on paper.

A recent study conducted at Westinghouse sheds considerable light on this subject. While the results are for one company, probably most of them would apply equally to many other companies or organizations.

The study was made by an independent consultant with considerable experience in the field of technical report writing. It consisted of interviews with Westinghouse men at every level of management, carefully selected to present an accurate cross section. The list of questions asked is shown in Table 1. The results were compiled and analyzed and from the report several conclusions are apparent. In addition, some suggestions for report writers follow as a natural consequence.

Richard W. Dodge, "What to Report," reprinted from *Westinghouse Engineer,* 22 (July–September 1962), pp. 108-11, by permission of the Westinghouse Electric Corporation.

Table 1. Questions asked of managers

---

1. What types of reports are submitted to you?
2. What do you look for *first* in the reports submitted to you?
3. What do you want from these reports?
4. To what depth do you want to follow any one particular idea?
5. At what level (how technical and how detailed) should the various reports be written?
6. What do you want emphasized in the reports submitted to you? (Facts, interpretations, recommendations, implications, etc.)
7. What types of decisions are you called upon to make or to participate in?
8. What type of information do you need in order to make these decisions?
9. What types of information do you receive that you don't want?
10. What types of information do you want but not receive?
11. How much of a typical or average report you receive is useful?
12. What types of reports do you write?
13. What do you think your boss wants in the reports you send him?
14. What percentage of the reports you receive do you think desirable or useful? (In kind or frequency.)
15. What percentage of the reports you write do you think desirable or useful? (In kind or frequency.)
16. What particular weaknesses have you found in reports?

What management looks for in engineering reports

When a manager reads a report, he looks for pertinent facts and competent opinions that will aid him in decision making. He wants to know right away whether he should read the report, route it, or skip it.

To determine this, he wants answers fast to some or all of the following questions:

- What's the report about and who wrote it?
- What does it contribute?
- What are the conclusions and recommendations?
- What are their importance and significance?
- What's the implication to the Company?
- What actions are suggested? Short range? Long range?
- Why? By whom? When? How?

The manager wants this information in brief, concise, and meaningful terms. He wants it at the beginning of the report and all in one piece.

For example, if a summary is to convey information efficiently, it should contain three kinds of facts:

1. What the report is about;
2. The significance and implications of the work; and
3. The action called for.

To give an intelligent idea of what the report is about, first of all the problem must be defined, then the objectives of the project set forth. Next, the reasons for doing the work must be given. Following this should come the conclusions. And finally, the recommendations.

Such summaries are informative and useful, and should be placed at the beginning of the report.

The kind of information a manager wants in a report is determined by his management responsibilities, but how he wants this information presented is determined largely by his reading habits. This study indicates that management report reading habits are surprisingly similar. Every manager interviewed said he read the *summary* or abstract; a bare majority said they read the *introduction* and *background* sections as well as the *conclusions* and *recommendations;* only a few managers read the *body* of the report or the *appendix* material.

The managers who read the *background* section, or the conclusions and recommendations, said they did so ". . . to gain a better perspective of the material being reported and to find an answer to the all-important question: What do we do next?" Those who read the *body* of the report gave one of the following reasons:

1. Especially interested in subject;
2. Deeply involved in the project;
3. Urgency of problem requires it;
4. Skeptical of conclusions drawn.

And those few managers who read the *appendix* material did so to evaluate further the work being reported. To the report writer, this can mean but one thing: If a report is to convey useful information efficiently, the structure must fit the manager's reading habits.

The frequency of reading chart in Fig. 1 suggests how a report should be structured if it is to be useful to management readers.

Subject matter interest

In addition to what facts a manager looks for in a report and how he reads reports, the study indicated that he is interested in five broad technological areas. These are:

1. Technical problems;

2. New projects and products;

3. Experiments and tests;

4. Materials and processes;

5. Field troubles.

Managers want to know a number of things about each of these areas. These are listed in Table 2. Each of the sets of questions can serve as an effective check list for report writers.

In addition to these subjects, a manager must also consider market factors and organization problems. Although these are not the primary concern of the engineer, he should furnish information to management whenever technical aspects provide special evidence or insight into the problem being considered. For example, here are some of the questions about marketing matters a manager will want answered:

- What are the chances for success?

- What are the possible rewards? Monetary? Technological?

- What are the possible risks? Monetary? Technological?

Section of Report   Frequency of Reading

Summary

Introduction

Body

Conclusions

Appendix

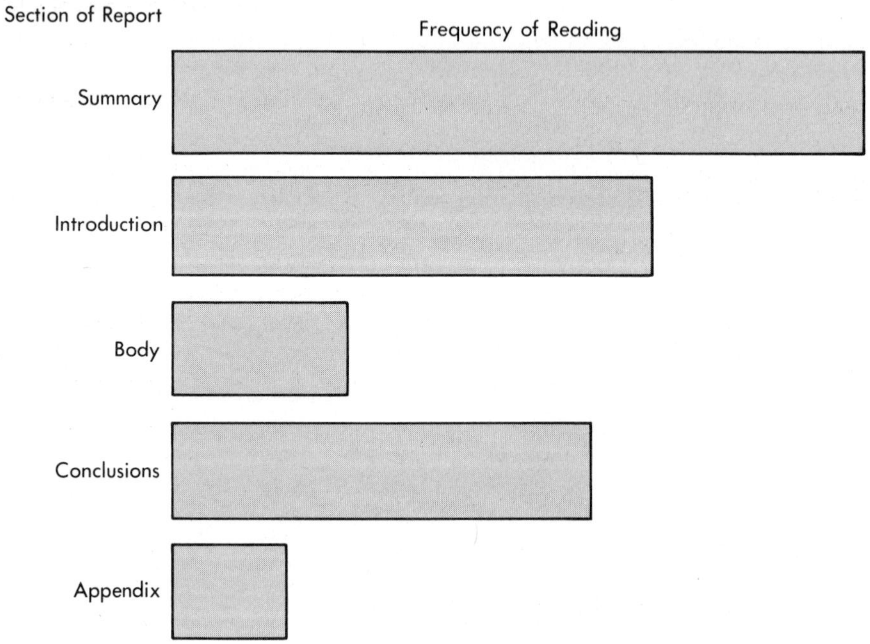

Fig. 1. How managers read reports

Table 2. What managers want to know

Problems	What tested or investigated?
What is it?	Why? How?
Why undertaken?	What did it show?
Magnitude and importance?	Better ways?
What is being done? By whom?	Conclusions? Recommendations?
Approaches used?	Implications to Company?
Thorough and complete?	Materials and Processes
Suggested solution? Best? Consider others?	Properties, characteristics, capabilities? Limitations?
What now?	Use requirements and environment?
Who does it?	Areas and scope of application?
Time factors?	Cost factors?
New Projects and Products	Availability and sources?
Potential?	What else will do it?
Risks?	Problems in using?
Scope of application?	Significance of application to Company?
Commercial implications?	Field Troubles and Special Design
Competition?	Problems
Importance to Company?	Specific equipment involved?
More work to be done? Any problems?	What trouble developed? Any trouble history?
Required manpower, facilities and equipment?	How much involved?
Relative importance to other projects or products?	Responsibility? Others? Westinghouse?
Life of project or product line?	What is needed?
Effect on Westinghouse technical position?	Special requirements and environment?
Priorities required?	Who does it? Time factors?
Proposed schedule?	Most practical solution? Recommended action?
Target date?	Suggested product design changes?
Tests and Experiments	

- Can we be competitive? Price? Delivery?

- Is there a market? Must one be developed?

- When will the product be available?

And, here are some of the questions about organization problems a manager must have answered before he can make a decision:

- Is it the type of work Westinghouse should do?

- What changes will be required? Organization? Manpower? Facilities? Equipment?

- Is it an expanding or contracting program?

- What suffers if we concentrate on this?

These are the kinds of questions Westinghouse management wants answered about projects in these five broad technological areas. The report writer should answer them whenever possible.

Level of presentation

Trite as it may sound, the technical and detail level at which a report should be written depends upon the reader and his use of the material. Most readers—certainly this is true for management readers—are interested in the significant material and in the general concepts that grow out of detail. Consequently, there is seldom real justification for a highly technical and detailed presentation.

Usually the management reader has an educational and experience background different from that of the writer. *Never* does the management reader have the same knowledge of and familiarity with the specific problem being reported that the writer has.

Therefore, the writer of a report for management should write at a technical level suitable for a reader whose educational and experience background is in a field different from his own. For example, if the report writer is an electrical engineer, he should write his reports for a person educated and trained in a field such as chemical engineering, or mechanical engineering, or metallurgical engineering.

All parts of the report *should preferably* be written on this basis. The highly technical, mathematical, and detailed material—if necessary at all—can and should be placed in the appendix.

Management responsibilities

The information presented thus far is primarily of interest to the report writer. In addition, however, management itself has definite responsibilities in the reporting process. These can be summed up as follows:

1. Define the project and the required reports;

2. Provide proper perspective for the project and the required reporting;

3. See that effective reports are submitted on time; and

4. See that the reports are properly distributed.

An engineering report, like any engineered product, has to be designed to fill a particular need and to achieve a particular purpose within a specific situation. Making sure that the writer knows what his report is to do, how it is to be used, and who is going to use it—all these things are the responsibilities of management. Purpose, use, and reader are the design factors in communications, and unless the writer knows these things, he is in no position to design an effective instrument of communication—be it a report, a memorandum, or what have you.

Four conferences at selected times can help a manager control the writing of those he supervises and will help him get the kind of reports he wants, when he wants them.

Step 1—At the beginning of the project. The purpose of this conference is to define the project, make sure the engineer involved knows what it is he's supposed to do, and specify the required reporting that is going to be expected of him as the project continues. What kind of decisions, for example, hinge upon his report? What is the relation of his work to the decision making process of management? These are the kinds of questions to clear up at this conference.

If the project is an involved one that could easily be misunderstood, the manager may want to check the effectiveness of the conference by asking the engineer to write a memorandum stating in his own words his understanding of the project, how he plans to handle it, and the reporting requirements. This can assure a mutual understanding of the project from the very outset.

Step 2—At the completion of the investigation. When the engineer has finished the project assignment—but before he has reported on it—the manager should have him come in and talk over the results of his work. What did he find out? What conclusions has he reached? What is the main supporting evidence for these conclusions? What recommendations does he make? Should any future action be suggested? What is the value of the work to the Company?

The broader perspective of the manager, plus his extensive knowledge of the Company and its activities, puts him in the position of being able to give the engineer a much better picture of the value and implications of the project.

The mechanism for getting into the report the kind of information needed for decision making is a relatively simple one. As the manager goes over the material with the engineer, he picks out points that need to be emphasized, and those that can be left out. This is a formative process that aids the engineer in the selection of material and evidence to support his material.

Knowing in advance that he has a review session with his supervisor, the chances are the engineer will do some thinking beforehand about the project and the results. Consequently, he will have formed some opinions about the significance of the work, and will, therefore, make a more coherent and intelligent presentation of the project and the results of his investigation.

This review will do something for the manager, too. The material will give him an insight into the value of the work that will enable him to converse intelligently and convincingly about the project to others. Such a preview may, therefore, expedite decisions influencing the project in one way or another.

Step 3—After the report is outlined. The manager should schedule a third conference after the report is outlined. At this session, the manager and the author should review the report outline step-by-step. If the manager is satisfied with the outline, he should tell the author so and tell him to proceed with the report.

If, however, the manager is not satisfied with the outline and believes it will have to be reorganized before the kind of report wanted can be written, he must make this fact known to the author. One way he can do this is to have the author tell him why the outline is structured the way it is. This usually discloses the organizational weakness to the author and consequently he will be the one to suggest a change. This, of course, is the ideal situation. However, if the indirect approach doesn't work, the more direct approach must be used.

Regardless of the method used to develop a satisfactory outline, the thing the manager must keep in mind is this: It's much easier to win the author's consent to structural changes at the outline stage, i.e., *before* the report is written, than afterward. Writing is a personal thing; therefore, when changes are suggested in organization or approach, these are all too frequently considered personal attacks and strained relations result.

Step 4—After the report is written. The fourth interview calls for a review and approval by the manager of the finished report and the preparation of a distribution list. During this review, the manager may find some sections of the report that need changing. While this is to be expected, he should limit the extent of these changes. The true test of any piece of writing is the clarity of the statement. If it's clear and does the job, the manager should leave it alone.

This four-step conference mechanism will save the manager valuable time, and, it will save the engineer valuable time. Also, it will insure meaningful and useful project reports—not an insignificant accomplishment itself. In addition, the process is an educative one. It places in the manager's hands another tool he can use to develop and broaden the viewpoint of the engineer. By eliminating misunderstanding and wasted effort, the review process creates a more helpful and effective working atmosphere. It acknowledges the professional status of the engineer and recognizes his importance as a member of the engineering department.

The writing of abstracts

CHRISTIAN K. ARNOLD

Christian K. Arnold was an instructor in English and a technical writer and editor before becoming Associate Executive Secretary of the Association of State Universities and Land-Grant Colleges.

The most important section of your technical report or paper is the abstract. Some people will read your report from cover to cover; others will skim many parts, reading carefully only those parts that interest them for one reason or another; some will read only the introduction, results, and conclusions; but everyone who picks it up will read the abstract. In fact, the percentage of those who read beyond the abstract is probably related directly to the skill with which the abstract is written. The first significant impression of your report is formed in the readers' mind by the abstract; and the sympathy with which it is read, if it is read at all, is often determined by this first impression. Further, the people your organization wants most to impress with your report are the very people who will probably read no more than the abstract and certainly no more than the abstract, introduction, conclusions, and recommendations. And the people you should want most to read your paper are the ones for whose free time you have the most competition.

Despite its importance, you are apt to throw your abstract together as fast as possible. Its construction is the last step of an arduous job that you would rather have avoided in the first place. It's a real relief to be rid of the thing, and almost anything will satisfy you. But a little time spent in learning the "rules" that govern the construction of good abstracts and in practicing how to apply them will pay material dividends to both you and your organization.

The abstract—or summary, foreword, or whatever you call the initial thumbnail sketch of your report or paper—has two purposes: (1) it provides

Christian K. Arnold, "The Writing of Abstracts," © 1961 The Institute of Radio Engineers, Inc. (now The Institute of Electrical and Electronics Engineers, Inc.). Reprinted, with permission, from *IRE Transactions on Engineering Writing and Speech*, December 1961, Vol. EWS-4, pp. 80–82.

the specialist in the field with enough information about the report to permit him to decide whether he could read it with profit, and (2) it provides the administrator or executive with enough knowledge about what has been done in the study or project and with what results to satisfy most of his administrative needs.

It might seem that the design specifications would depend upon the purpose for which the abstract is written. To satisfy the first purpose, for instance, the abstract needs only to give an accurate indication of the subject matter and scope of the study; but, to satisfy the second, the abstract must summarize the results and conclusions and give enough background information to make the results understandable. The abstract designed for the purpose can tolerate any technical language or symbolic shortcuts understood at large by the subject-matter group; the abstract designed for the second purpose should contain no terms not generally understood in a semitechnical community. The abstract for the first purpose is called a *descriptive abstract;* that for the second, an *informative abstract.*

The following abstract, prepared by a professional technical abstracter in the Library of Congress, clearly gives the subject-matter specialist all the help he needs to decide whether he should read the article it describes:

> Results are presented of a series of cold-room tests on a Dodge diesel engine to determine the effects on starting time of (1) fuel quantity delivered at cranking speed and (2) type of fuel-injection pump used. The tests were made at a temperature of $-10°F$ with engine and accessories chilled at $-10°F$ at least 8 hours before starting.

Regardless of however useful this abstract might be on a library card or in an index or an annotated bibliography, it does not give an executive enough information. Nor does it encourage everyone to read the article. If fact, this abstract is useless to everyone except the specialist looking for sources of information. The descriptive abstract, in other words, cannot satisfy the requirements of the informative abstract.

But is the reverse also true? Let's have a look at an informative abstract written for the same article:

> A series of tests was made to determine the effect on diesel-engine starting characteristics at low temperatures of (1) the amount of fuel injected and (2) the type of injection pump used. All tests were conducted in a cold room maintained at $-10°F$ on a commercial Dodge engine. The engine and all accessories were "cold-soaked" in the test chamber for at least 8 hours before each test. Best starting was obtained with 116 cu mm of fuel, 85 per cent more than that required for maximum power. Very poor starting was obtained with the lean setting of 34.7 cu mm. Tests with two different pumps indicated that, for best starting characteristics, the pump must deliver fuel evenly to all cylinders even at low cranking speeds so that each cylinder contributes its maximum potential power.

This abstract is not perfect. With just a few more words, for instance, the abstracter could have clarified the data about the amount of fuel delivered; do the figures give flow rates (what is the unit of time?) or total amount of fuel injected (over how long a period?). He could easily have defined "best" starting. He could have been more specific about at least the more satisfactory type of pump: what is the type that delivers the fuel more evenly? Clarification of these points would not have increased the length of the abstract significantly.

The important point, however, is not the deficiencies of the illustration. In fact, it is almost impossible to find a perfect, or even near perfect, abstract, quite possibly because the abstract is the most difficult part of the report to write. This difficulty stems from the severe limitations imposed on its length, its importance to the over-all acceptance of the report or paper, and, with informative abstracts, the requirement for simplicity and general understandability.

The important point, rather, is that the informative abstract gives everything that is included in the descriptive one. The informative abstract, that is, satisfies not only its own purpose but also that of the descriptive abstract. Since values are obtained from the informative abstract that are not obtained from the descriptive, it is almost always worth while to take the extra time and effort necessary to produce a good informative abstract for your report or memo. Viewed from the standpoint of either the total time and effort expended on the writing job as a whole or the extra benefits that accrue to you and your organization, the additional effort is inconsequential.

It is impossible to lay down guidelines that will lead always to the construction of an effective abstract, simply because each reporting job, and consequently each abstract, is unique. However, general "rules" can be established that, if practiced conscientiously and applied intelligently, will eliminate most of the bugs from your abstracts.

1. *Your abstract must include enough* specific *information about the project or study to satisfy most of the administrative needs of a busy executive.* This means that the more important results, conclusions, and recommendations, together with enough additional information to make them understandable, must be included. This additional information will most certainly include an accurate statement of the problem and the limitations placed on it. It will probably include an interpretation of the results and the principal facts upon which the analysis was made, along with an indication of how they were obtained. Again, *specific* information must be given. One of the most common faults of abstracts in technical reports is that the information given is too general to be useful.

2. *Your abstract must be a self-contained unit, a complete report-in-miniature.* Sooner or later, most abstracts are separated from the parent report, and the abstract that cannot stand on its own feet independently must then either be rewritten or will fail to perform its job. And the rewriting, if it is done, will be done by someone not nearly as sympathetic with your study as you are. Even if it is not separated from the report, the abstract must be written as a complete, independent unit if it is to be of the most help possible to the executive. This rule automatically eliminates the common deadwood phrases like "this report contains . . ." or "this is a report on . . ." that clutter up many abstracts. It also eliminates all references to sections, figures, tables, or anything else contained in the report proper.

3. *Your abstract must be short.* Length in an abstract defeats every purpose for which it is written. However, no one can tell you just how short it must be. Some authorities have attempted to establish arbitrary lengths, usually in terms of a certain percentage of the report, the figure given normally falling between three and ten per cent. Such artificial guides are unrealistic. The abstract for a 30-page report must necessarily be longer, percentagewise, than the abstract for a 300-page report, since there is certain basic information that must be given regardless of the length of the report. In addition, the information given in some reports can be summarized much more briefly than can that given in other reports of the same over-all dimensions. Definite advantages, psychological as well as material, are obtained if the abstract is short enough to be printed entirely on one page so that the reader doesn't even have to turn a page to get the total picture that the abstract provides. Certainly, it should be no longer than the interest span of an only mildly interested and very busy executive. About the best practical advice that can be given in a vacuum is to make your abstract as short as possible without cutting out essential information or doing violence to its accuracy. With practice, you might be surprised to learn how much information you can crowd into a few words. It helps, too, to learn to blue-pencil unessential information. It is perhaps important to document that "a meeting was held at the Bureau of Ordnance on Tuesday, October 3, 1961, at 2:30 P.M." somewhere, but such information is just excess baggage in your abstract: it helps neither the research worker looking for source material nor the administrator looking for a status or information summary. Someone is supposed to have once said, "I would have written a shorter letter if I had had more time." Take the time to make your abstracts shorter; the results are worth it. But be careful not to distort the facts in the condensing.

4. *Your abstract must be written in fluent, easy-to-read prose.* The odds are heavily against your reader's being an expert in the subject covered by your report or paper. In fact, the odds that he is an expert in your field are probably no greater than the odds that he has only a smattering of training in any technical or scientific discipline. And even if he were perfectly capable of following the most obscure, tortured technical jargon, he will appreciate your sparing him the necessity for doing it. T. O. Richards, head of the Laboratory Control Department, and R. A.

Richardson, head of the Technical Data Department, both of the General Motors Corporation, have written that their experience shows the abstract cannot be made too elementary: "We never had [an abstract] . . . in which the explanations and terms were too simple." This requirement immediately eliminates the "telegraphic" writing often found in abstracts. Save footage by sound practices of economy and not by cutting out the articles and the transitional devices needed for smoothness and fluency. It also eliminates those obscure terms that you defend on the basis of "that's the way it's always said."

5. *Your abstract must be consistent in tone and emphases with the report proper, but it does not need to follow the arrangement, wording, or proportion of the original.* Data, information, and ideas introduced into the abstract must also appear in the report or paper. And they must appear with the same emphases. A conclusion or recommendation that is qualified in the report proper must not turn up without the qualification in the abstract. After all, someone might read both the abstract and the report. If this reader spots an inconsistency or is confused, you've lost a reader.

6. *Your abstract should make the widest possible use of abbreviations and numerals, but it must not contain any tables or illustrations.* Because of the space limitations imposed upon abstracts, the rules governing the use of abbreviations and numerals are relaxed for it. In fact, all figures except those standing at the beginning of sentences should be written as numerals, and all abbreviations generally accepted by such standard sources as the American Standards Association and "Webster's Dictionary" should be used.

By now you must surely see why the abstract is the toughest part of your report to write. A good abstract is well worth the time and effort necessary to write it and is one of the most important parts of your report. And abstract writing probably contributes more to the acquisition of sound expository skills than does any other prose discipline.

Displaying data: types of graphic aids

CHARLES W. STRONG and DONALD EIDSON

The authors are both Professors of English: Charles W. Strong at California Polytechnic State University, San Luis Obispo, and Donald Eidson at Central Methodist College, Fayette, Missouri, where he is chairman of the department.

This chapter discusses the basic types of graphic aids: tables, graphs, charts, maps, drawings, and photographs. Tables and graphs are used for displaying numeric data. Charts show the organization of something by representing its subdivisions or a sequence of steps. Maps are used to show some fact about a geographical area, or to show the geography associated with some fact. Drawings show the appearance of something, either in its entirety, in cross section, as if some parts were transparent or as if it were disassembled. Photographs are used to show the actual appearance of something (they are evidence, but a drawing is not). You must decide how much information is to be conveyed by any graphic aid: In general, try to make each aid convey a single idea, and eliminate all extraneous detail.

Although a sufficiently well-designed picture may sometimes be worth a thousand words, it is the text that provides the context and draws the conclusion. It comments on the graphic aids, explaining the significance of important points, giving information on the interpretation of complex aids, and referring the reader to the aids that will help him to visualize the concepts involved or the conclusions drawn. Graphic aids should always be used with intelligence and discretion.

From *A Technical Writer's Handbook* by Charles W. Strong and Donald Eidson. Copyright © 1971 by Holt, Rinehart and Winston, Inc. Reprinted by permission of Holt, Rinehart and Winston.

Tables

Tables are used to present original numeric data and derived statistics; therefore, they fall naturally into the results section of a paper. See Fig. 1. The rows and columns of the table provide a system of classification; the *box head* (or column head) identifies the items in the columns, and the *stub* (first column) identifies the items in the rows under the box heads. A *rule* is usually drawn under the table number and title, another under the box heads, and another at the bottom of the table. The table numbers are often roman numerals rather than the arabic numerals used for other graphic aids. If tables are numbered in arabic numerals, the number and title may be placed below the table, just as they are for illustrations.

The title, box heads, and stubs should be concise but descriptive, and the units of measurement must be specified. Any additional information such as sources of the data and levels of significance might be put in footnotes to the table, appearing just below the closing rule. Lowercase letters are customarily used to designate footnotes. The columns should be of equal width: Do not proportion columns according to the width of the heading. All items are centered in the appropriate column unless they are of different length, in which case the longest is centered and the others are aligned on the ± or the decimal points, in that order. Organize the rows and columns to make significant aspects of the data apparent; if items are to be compared, place them in adjacent rows or columns. A pad of ruled paper may be useful for experimenting with table design.

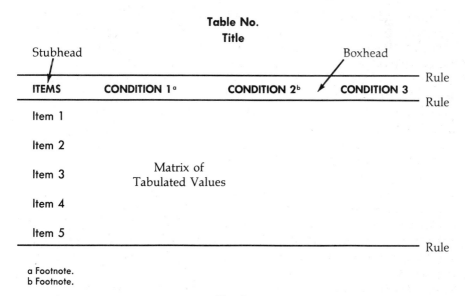

Fig. 1.

Graphs

Graphs provide a kind of shorthand presentation of the same kinds of data that appear in tables. You will want to use tables instead of graphs if you are interested in precise values, but graphs are much more effective in showing comparisons, trends, and distributions. They may show absolute values, percentages, or index numbers. One of the concepts most important to the user of graphs is that of continuous and discrete series. In a continuous series, the variable may take any value between the limits of the series. In a discrete series, the variable is limited to certain discrete values. The heights of American college men are represented by a continuous series, but the distribution of men in various American colleges is discrete. The distinction is important because certain graphs are more appropriate for one kind of datum than for another. Bar graphs best represent discrete data and line graphs continuous data.

Bar graphs

Bar graphs . . . are the simplest, commonest, and most adaptable form of graph. The distinguishing characteristic of bar graphs is the use of parallel horizontal bars to designate the quantities of an item in different periods or the quantities of different items in the same period. The bars are usually arranged in chronological sequence or in order of their length. The space between the bars is conveniently set at one-half the bar width.

One advantage of the bar graph is that it is the only type of graph that can be executed entirely at the typewriter. See Fig. 2. Typewritten graphs are not suitable for material submitted for publication, but they are suitable for

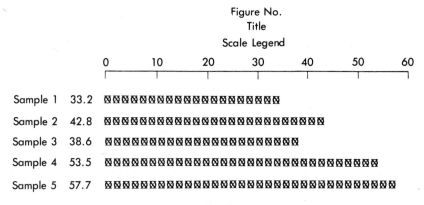

Fig. 2.

many relatively informal reports. Bars can be made by superimposing the capitals X, O, and M (like this: ⊗ ⊗ ⊗ ⊗ ⊗ ⊗), or by using such symmetrical symbols as MMMMM, XXXXX, and OOOOO for bars representing different values. Typewritten graphs necessarily round off the length of the bars. The exact value may be typed in at the left end of the bar. The scale is typed with the underline, and the scale numbers should be typed in before the platen is turned down one space and the ticks are put in with the apostrophe. The basic kinds of bar graphs are the simple bar graph, the subdivided bar graph, the subdivided 100 percent bar graph, the multiple bar graph, the paired bar graph, and the sliding bar graph.

Simple Bar Graph. In the simple bar graph, the bars begin at the left end of the scale and all bars represent the same kind of datum. This type of graph stresses the difference in magnitude of the items graphed.

Subdivided Bar Graph. The subdivided bar graph is constructed in the same way as the simple bar graph except that the bars are subdivided to represent the magnitude of the component items; the different parts of the bar are crosshatched or stippled in different patterns. See Fig. 3. This type of graph is useful when each bar represents the sum of several different classes. The lengths of the bars can be easily compared, but the roles played by each of the components is not so clear.

Subdivided 100 Percent Bar Graph. In the subdivided 100 percent bar graph the scale is marked in percentages and each bar extends the full length of the scale. See Fig. 4. The percentage change of the components of each bar is easily followed, but the magnitude of each bar is lost. This type of chart complements the subdivided bar graph described above.

Multiple Bar Graph. In multiple bar graphs each item is represented by several bars, each showing the value of a different variable. See Fig. 5.

Paired Bar Graph. Paired bar graphs show related data by bars extending from either side of the category or period label. The paired bars may be measured by scales marked off in the same units (plus and minus values,

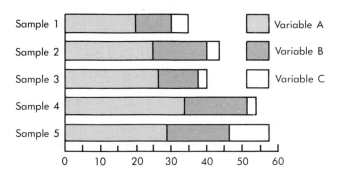

Fig. 3.

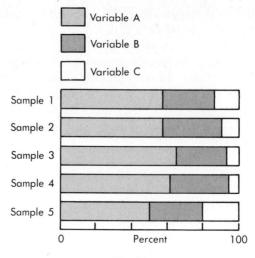

Fig. 4.

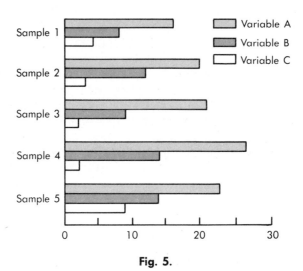

Fig. 5.

percentages, quantities, and so on) or different ones. This type of graph is particularly useful for comparing such related data as temperature and activity at different periods of time.

Sliding Bar Graph. The bars of the sliding bar graph are moved along the X axis so that the relation of the bars to a vertical reference line becomes the most significant feature of the graph. See Fig. 6. The scale may be marked off in absolute numbers or in percentages, and the two halves of the scale may represent any opposed values or main components of an item: hot and cold, strong and weak, activity and passivity, and so forth.

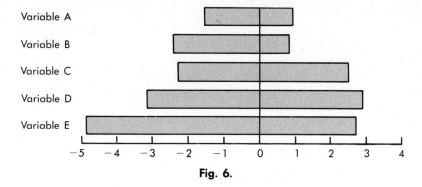

Fig. 6.

Combining forms

The foregoing different types of bar graphs can be combined in different ways to form subdivided sliding-bar graphs, multiple paired-bar graphs, or other useful combinations.

Column graph

Column graphs . . . are bar graphs turned on edge so that the bars become vertical columns. See Fig. 7. Every type of bar graph has a parallel form of column graph. Column graphs are especially useful for depicting time series, for which the time scale is placed on the X axis at the bottom of the chart.

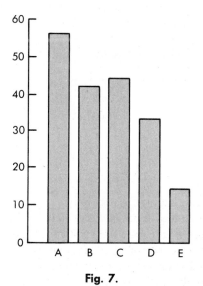

Fig. 7.

Pie graph

Pie graphs are, by their very nature, 100 percent graphs. See Fig. 8. A pie graph is much like a single subdivided 100 percent bar. The actual values of pie slices are not so easily compared as are the values of bars because it is difficult to compare areas by eye, because the slices are not linear, and because there is no base line. Moreover, pie graphs are not well suited to comparisons of more than five items.

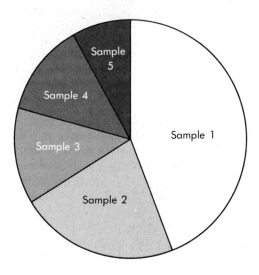

Fig. 8.

Pie graphs are constructed by measuring off the values to be plotted around the margin of the pie. There are 360 deg in a circle and therefore each percent is equal to 3.6 deg. The slices should be laid out beginning with 12 o'clock and proceeding clockwise. The slices should be put in sequence from the largest to the smallest, and they should be shaded from light to dark in the same sequence.

Pictorial graph

The only type of pictorial graph that is not misleading is the graph in which the symbol represents a single unit (which, if it is rectilinear, may serve as a subdivided 100 percent graph). See Fig. 9. These symbols can be repeated in a line to form column or bar graphs. A stack of coins, for example, may serve to represent an amount of money, as shown in Fig. 9.

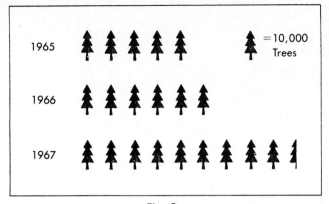

Fig. 9.

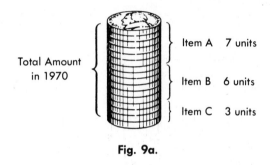

Fig. 9a.

Area graph

If the columns of a subdivided column graph are positioned side by side without spacing, the result is an area graph (see Fig. 10), but they cannot be so positioned unless the categories on the X axis form a continuous sequence of class intervals, either of time or amount. If subdivided 100 percent columns are positioned like this, the entire surface of the chart is used. Connected column graphs are related to other graphs that depict continuous variables, such as the histogram, frequency polygon, and line graph, and line graphs can be used to construct area graphs.

Histogram

The histogram . . . differs from a column graph in that the frequency of occurrence of the event is represented by the area formed by each class interval and its upper boundary, not by the vertical dimension of the area. Frequency distributions approximate ideal curves such as the normal curve, and

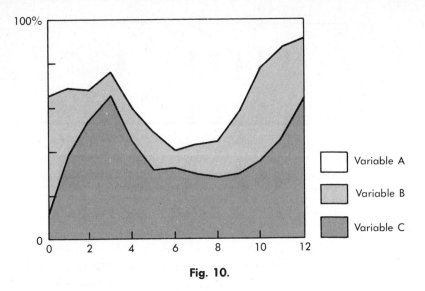

Fig. 10.

because the frequencies are analogous to probabilities, the parallel lines mark-
ing the limits to the class intervals may be erased to give a *step frequency
chart.* This continuous, stair-step line shows the probability of occurrence of
the event charted as it varies with the class intervals. If the histogram is used
to plot discrete data, the curve must not be smoothed.

Frequency polygon

The frequency polygon (Fig. 10a)—the graph obtained by connecting the midpoints of each class interval of the histogram—is a line graph and is related to
the step frequency chart.

Cumulative frequency graph

The cumulative frequency graph, or *ogive,* is the graph obtained by adding the
frequency of each class interval to the sum of the frequencies of all of the
preceding class intervals to get the successive values. See Fig. 11. Such a graph
can begin at either end of the class-interval scale. If it begins at the high end
of the scale, it is of the "more than" type, and frequencies are cumulated
toward the low end. If it begins at the low end, it is of the "less than" type and
frequencies are cumulated toward the high end. "More than" graph frequencies are entered at the lower end of the interval, not at the midpoint; "less
than" frequencies are entered at the upper end.

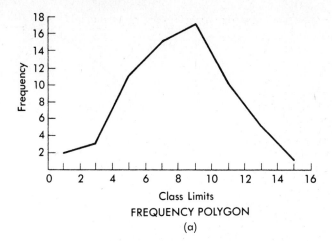

FREQUENCY POLYGON
(a)

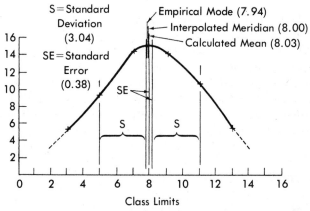

FREQUENCY CURVE
(Smoothed by moving average method)
(b)

Fig. 10a.

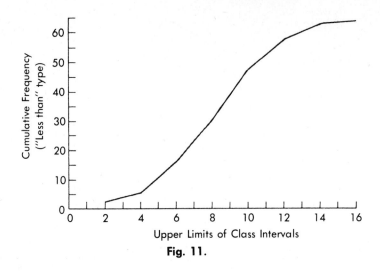

Fig. 11.

Ogives are most useful because they give the number of instances above or below any given point. If the frequency scale is marked in percentages, the percentage above or below any point can be read directly, and the quartiles and median can be found by drawing horizontal lines to the curve from the 25, 50, and 75 percent scale markings, and by projecting these points of inter-section down to the scale on the X axis. Such an ogive is called a *centile curve*.

Probability graph

Probability graphs use a special graph paper, probability paper, to convert the S-shaped centile curve into a straight line. See Fig. 12. Probability paper reverses the axes of the ogive so that the cumulative frequency percentage is on the X axis and the class intervals are on the Y axis.

If the frequency distribution is that of a normal curve, the resulting graph is a straight line running from the lower-left corner to the upper-right corner of the graph. This is of importance in analysis, because deviations from the normal distribution are easily spotted as divergences from the straight line.

Other line graphs

Line graphs are among the most common types of graph. See Fig. 13. They are particularly useful for plotting time series, and they are better than bar or column graphs for this purpose when continuous change with time is being stressed rather than a comparison of the amount of change for given time periods. Line graphs should not be used to present discrete data.

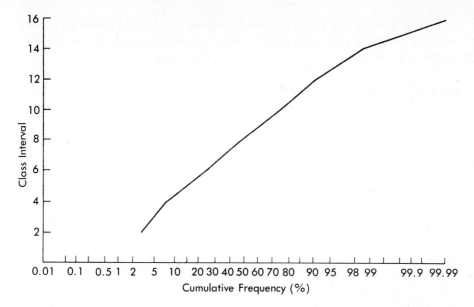

Fig. 12.

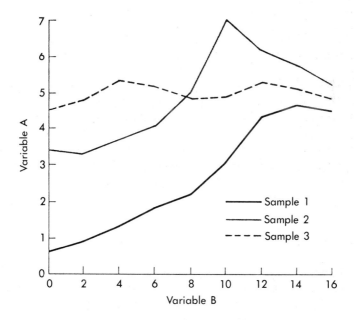

Fig. 13.

If the data for a line graph relate to periods of time and not to points in time, the data should be plotted at the midpoints of the periods. Curves representing different data can be plotted on the same graph. . . .

Lines indicating the trend can be calculated by the moving average or some other method and superimposed on the graph. If the graph approximates a straight line, the semiaverage method may be useful. In this method the data are divided into two equal groups, and each of these is averaged separately to give the two points necessary to draw a line.

Semilogarithmic graph

If a graph appears to follow the curve of a geometric progression, it can be plotted as a straight line on semilogarithmic graph paper. See Fig. 14.

The scale on the Y axis of semilogarithmic graph paper represents logarithmic rather than arithmetic distances. The X axis is divided into the usual arithmetic divisions. The logarithmic scale may have one cycle or more. Each cycle takes up the same portion of the Y axis, even though the first cycle of a three-cycle graph goes up to 10, the second to 100, and the third to 1000.

This property of the semilogarithmic scale makes it easy to compare curves expressed in different units—hundreds may be compared with tens and thousands. If three variables are all increasing by a constant rate, their

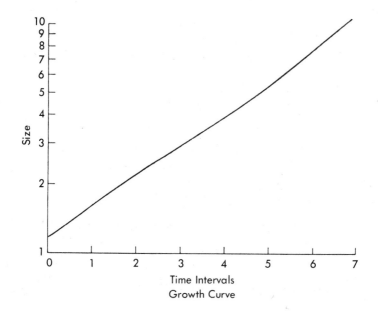

Time Intervals
Growth Curve

Fig. 14.

curves will have the same slope even though one increases from 10 to 100 and another increases from 1000 to 10,000.

Trilinear graph

The trilinear graph enables one to plot the properties of anything with three components or characteristics. See Fig. 15. It is based on the fact that the sum of the lengths of the three perpendiculars drawn from a point in an equilateral triangle to the sides is equal to the altitude. The altitude is given the value 100 percent and each side of the triangle is made the zero point for one of the three properties.

Scatter graph

The scatter graph is a square graph on which dots are plotted to represent agreement of two variables, one on each axis. See Fig. 16. If the dots are largely confined to the diagonal running from lower left, the correlation of the two variables is positive. If the diagonal extends from the upper left, the correlation is negative. If there does not seem to be any clustering, there is no correlation. Double logarithmic paper will spread out the data if the range of both variables is very great.

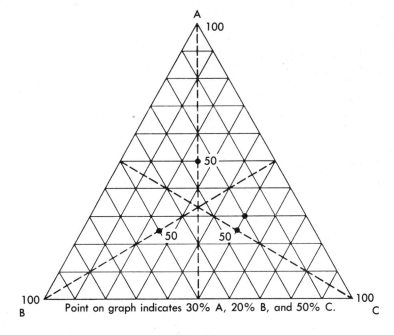

Point on graph indicates 30% A, 20% B, and 50% C.

Fig. 15.

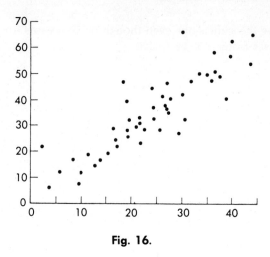

Fig. 16.

Graphic fallacies

Areas are difficult to judge by eye. It is much better to have one rectangle twice as tall as another than to have one of twice the area of another. Never, in pictorial graphs, draw one object twice as tall as another to indicate a twofold increase in *value*. It may be twice as tall, but it is also four times the visible area and eight times the implied volume: each of these is as legitimate a measure of value as height. This is the reason for the limitations mentioned under *pictorial graphs*.

If you do not show the zero mark on the Y-axis scale, break the graph just above the X axis, drawing a double zigzag line across its width as if the graph had been torn in two. See Fig. 17. To neglect this is to be guilty of the *fallacy of the suppressed zero*.

The shape of a curve can be exaggerated by choosing scale values to suit your purpose. It is dishonest to deliberately misrepresent your data in this way.

Charts

Charts symbolically depict the organization of something.

Block charts

Block charts represent the major groups of components of any complex by means of blocks. See Fig. 18. These may be drawn in projection or in an isolated plane view. The electrical or mechanical connections between the blocks are indicated by means of lines.

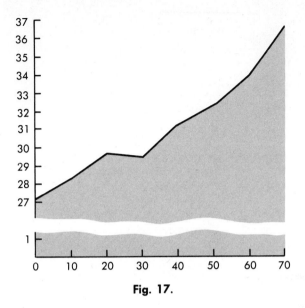

Fig. 17.

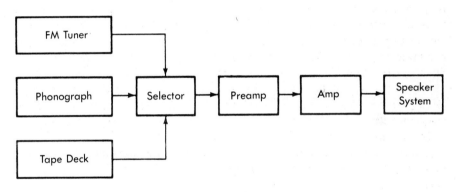

Fig. 18.

Organization charts

Organization charts show the "chain of command" in an organization by means of connected, labeled blocks. See Fig. 19. . . .

Flow charts

Flow charts are also closely related to block charts. They show the sequence of operations in a process as symbols connected by arrows. See Fig. 20. The symbols may be blocks or pictorial representations of the devices at each step.

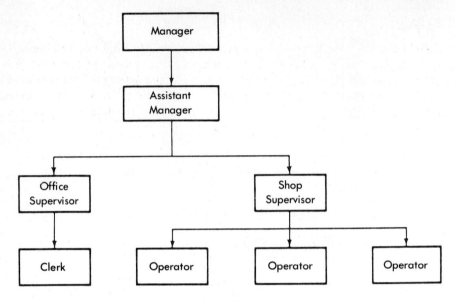

Fig. 19.

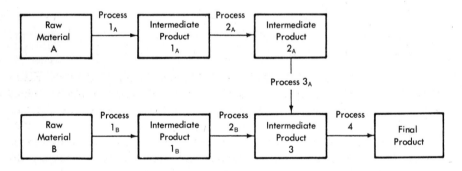

Fig. 20.

Schematics

Schematics are, like block charts, simplified representations of something, but the individual components are not lumped together into groups but are depicted separately. See Fig. 21. Exact proportions and fine detail are sacrificed for clear representation of interrelationships. The simplification may reduce all components to symbols, as in Fig. 21, or it may be somewhat pictorial.

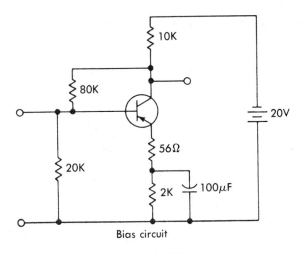

Bias circuit

Fig. 21.

Maps

Maps can be used to advantage whenever data have geographical applications. The important point to remember is that all extraneous detail must be omitted from the base map upon which the data are plotted. If roads are the only important feature, omit rivers, mountains, parks, cities, state and county boundaries, and all other details. If rivers are the important feature, then rivers only should appear on the base map. Data can be plotted on maps in the form of dots, of shaded areas, of lines, and of graphs.

Dot maps

Dot maps may depend upon the number, shape, or size of dots to transmit the data. The number of the dots in any area may represent the number of items in any area. A map of the United States showing each post office as a dot would clearly indicate the distribution of post offices in this country. Dots of different shapes may indicate different items. The distribution of one item in relation to that of another can be easily seen from such a map. Different values of an item may be indicated by dots of different sizes. Road maps generally use dots of different sizes to represent cities of different sizes. Dot maps best represent absolute values.

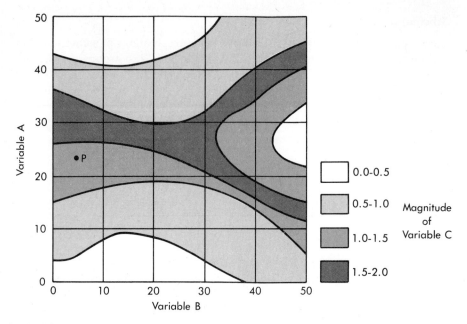

Variables A and B may be longitude and latitude in the case of a map, or may be any two related continuous variables. The value of variable C for point P is between 1.0 and 1.5.

Fig. 22.

Shaded maps

Different shading densities can be used to show the differing numbers of an item in different areas. See Fig. 22. Because large areas are covered, shaded maps are best used to represent averages, rates, percentages, and other ratios. The lighter shades are used to represent the smaller values; the darker shades, greater values.

Line maps

Line maps are of two types: those in which the lines connect points of equal value (such as the isobars of barometric pressure or the contour lines of a topographic map), and those in which the lines connect points of equal ratios. See Fig. 23. In the first type, the location of the points and the determination of the values are simple matters of sampling. In the second type, the values are determined from base areas and the points are base points located in these areas. The base areas must be of the same size and shape, and they must be large enough to be significant as samples and small enough that meaningful variations are not obscured. The values within each area are summed, averaged, or similarly treated, and the base point is located. Base points may be

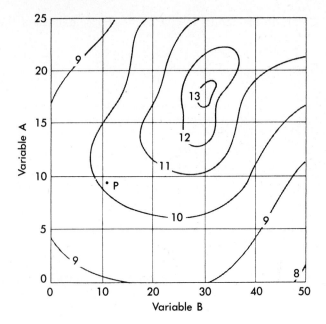

Variable C is indicated by contours (isolines). Variables A and B may be latitude and longitude (in the case of maps) or any other pair of related continuous variables. The value of variable C at point P is between 10 and 11.

Fig. 23.

taken to be the geographical center of the base area, or they may be established at the center of gravity of the area, the point on which the area would balance if the area were cut out, weighted to correspond with the distribution of values, and balanced on the point of a pin. The lines are interpolated between the base points to connect equal ratios.

Map-Graph combinations

Column, bar, and pie graphs can be superimposed on a map to show the values of the variables at given geographic locations.

Drawing views

Drawings can be prepared in various ways to show different aspects of a device: overall, action, phantom, cutaway, and exploded views.

Overall

Overall views, as the name suggests, show the outside of some mechanism. They are usually fully shaded perspective drawings that are placed at the

beginning of a report or manual to give the reader some idea of the appearance of the object.

Action

Action views show the different steps in the operation of some mechanism or show an operator or repairman working with it. The first type may be combined with the phantom and cutaway illustrations discussed below. Perspective projection is most suitable for such drawings.

Phantom

Phantom views show the outside parts of some mechanism as if they were transparent. See Fig. 24. Often, the inner parts are shown as cutaway views. The transparent portions can be represented by a light rendering in brush-and-ink wash. Perspective and isometric projections are both suitable for this kind of drawing.

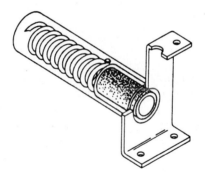

Fig. 24.

Cutaway

Cutaway views show a mechanism as if some external portion has been cut away. See Fig. 25. These drawings are usually made in isometric or perspective projection. Shading is often used to define the different internal levels of a mechanism in outline drawing. The cuts should be made in such a way that they preserve the outside form.

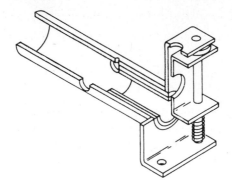

Fig. 25.

Exploded

Exploded views are isometric or perspective drawings of a mechanism with the parts spread out in the proper sequence for reassembly. See Fig. 26. To construct an exploded view, a line representing the axis of disassembly is drawn on tracing paper and superimposed over an assembled view. Then, as the tracing paper is moved along this axis, the pieces are drawn one by one in the proper sequence.

Photographs

Photographs are of limited use in technical illustration. Because they are objective, they can serve as evidence of the extent of wear or damage to a mechanism or to show accurately the size and markings of an animal; but, also because they are objective, they cannot emphasize the important detail, separate a confused welter of lines, or show cutaway, phantom, and other views. Because the camera is not selective, you must choose camera views carefully and crop the negatives to eliminate unwanted detail.

Glossy photographs with sharp contrast should be used in preference to those with a matte finish. The important points in a photograph may be identified by labeling them with white ink on dark areas and black ink on light areas, by typing labels on pieces of paper which are then glued to the photograph, or (preferably) by placing labels on an overlay mounted to the photograph. If only a part of a photograph is to be printed, the desired object can be outlined with opaque-white gouache paint; only that object will be included on the plate.

It is possible to make a drawing from a photograph by printing it very lightly on matte paper. Waterproof drawing ink is then used to draw on the

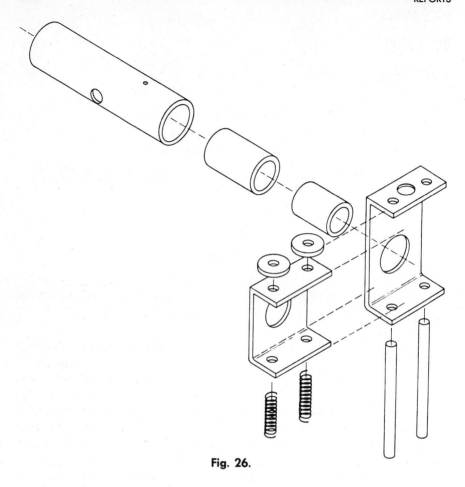

Fig. 26.

surface of the photograph, and the drawing is bleached in a sodium hypo-sulphite and potassium ferricyanide mixture made by dissolving each chemi-cal (obtainable from photographic supply houses) with water in a 1:4 ratio and then mixing the two solutions. After being bleached, the photograph must be washed thoroughly—leave it in slowly running water for at least a half-hour.

How to lie with statistics

DARRELL HUFF

Darrell Huff, a free-lance writer, expanded this article into a book with the same title (Norton, 1954).

"The average Yaleman, Class of '24," *Time* magazine reported last year after reading something in the New York *Sun,* a newspaper published in those days, "makes $25,111 a year."

Well, good for him!

But, come to think of it, what does this improbably precise and salubrious figure mean? Is it, as it appears to be, evidence that if you send your boy to Yale you won't have to work in your old age and neither will he? Is this average a mean or is it a median? What kind of sample is it based on? You could lump one Texas oilman with two hundred hungry free-lance writers and report *their* average income as $25,000-odd a year. The arithmetic is impeccable, the figure is convincingly precise, and the amount of meaning there is in it you could put in your eye.

In just such ways is the secret language of statistics, so appealing in a fact-minded culture, being used to sensationalize, inflate, confuse, and oversimplify. Statistical terms are necessary in reporting the mass data of social and economic trends, business conditions, "opinion" polls, this year's census. But without writers who use the words with honesty and understanding and readers who know what they mean, the result can only be semantic nonsense.

In popular writing on scientific research, the abused statistic is almost crowding out the picture of the white-jacketed hero laboring overtime without time-and-a-half in an ill-lit laboratory. Like the "little dash of powder, little pot of paint," statistics are making many an important fact "look like what she ain't." Here are some of the ways it is done.

The sample with the built-in bias. Our Yale men—or Yalemen, as they say in the Time-Life building—belong to this flourishing group.The exagger-

Reprinted from *How to Lie with Statistics* by Darrell Huff. Pictures by Irving Geis. By permission of W. W. Norton & Company, Inc. Copyright 1954 by Darrell Huff and Irving Geis.

ated estimate of their income is not based on all members of the class nor on a random or representative sample of them. At least two interesting categories of 1924-model Yale men have been excluded.

First there are those whose present addresses are unknown to their class-mates. Wouldn't you bet that these lost sheep are earning less than the boys from prominent families and the others who can be handily reached from a Wall Street office?

There are those who chucked the questionnaire into the nearest waste-basket. Maybe they didn't answer because they were not making enough money to brag about. Like the fellow who found a note clipped to his first pay check suggesting that he consider the amount of his salary confidential: "Don't worry," he told the boss. "I'm just as ashamed of it as you are."

Omitted from our sample then are just the two groups most likely to depress the average. The $25,111 figure is beginning to account for itself. It may indeed be a true figure for those of the Class of '24 whose addresses are known and who are willing to stand up and tell how much they earn. But even that requires a possibly dangerous assumption that the gentlemen are telling the truth.

To be dependable to any useful degree at all, a sampling study must use a representative sample (which can lead to trouble too) or a truly random one. If *all* the Class of '24 is included, that's all right. If every tenth name on a complete list is used, that is all right too, and so is drawing an adequate number of names out of a hat. The test is this: Does every name in the group have an equal chance to be in the sample?

You'll recall that ignoring this requirement was what produced the *Literary Digest's* famed fiasco.* When names for polling were taken only from telephone books and subscription lists, people who did not have telephones or *Literary Digest* subscriptions had no chance to be in the sample. They possibly did not mind this underprivilege a bit, but their absence was in the end very hard on the magazine that relied on the figures.

This leads to a moral: You can prove about anything you want to by letting your sample bias itself. As a consumer of statistical data—a reader, for example, of a news magazine—remember that no statistical conclusion can rise above the quality of the sample it is based upon. In the absence of infor-mation about the procedures behind it, you are not warranted in giving any credence at all to the result.

The truncated, or gee-whiz, graph. If you want to show some statistical information quickly and clearly, draw a picture of it. Graphic presentation is the thing today. If you don't mind misleading the hasty looker, or if you quite clearly *want* to deceive him, you can save some space by chopping the bottom off many kinds of graph.

* Ed.'s note: *The Literary Digest* predicted that Alfred Landon would defeat Franklin Roosevelt in the 1936 presidential election. Landon carried only two states.

Suppose you are showing the upward trend of national income month by month for a year. The total rise, as in one recent year, is 7 per cent. It looks like this:

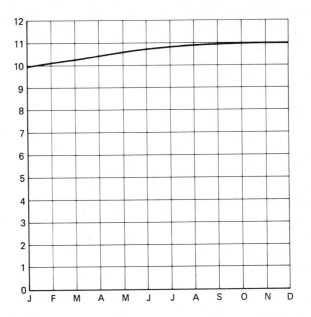

That is clear enough. Anybody can see that the trend is slightly upward. You are showing a 7 per cent increase and that is exactly what it looks like.

But it lacks schmaltz. So you chop off the bottom, this way:

The figures are the same. It is the same graph and nothing has been falsified—except the impression that it gives. Anyone looking at it can just feel prosperity throbbing in the arteries of the country. It is a subtler equivalent of editing "National income rose 7 per cent" into ". . . climbed a whopping 7 per cent."

It is vastly more effective, however, because of that illusion of objectivity.

The souped-up graph. Sometimes truncating is not enough. The trifling rise in something or other still looks almost as insignificant as it is. You can make that 7 per cent look livelier than 100 per cent ordinarily does. Simply change the proportion between the ordinate and the abscissa. There's no rule against it, and it does give your graph a prettier shape.

But it exaggerates, to say the least, something awful:

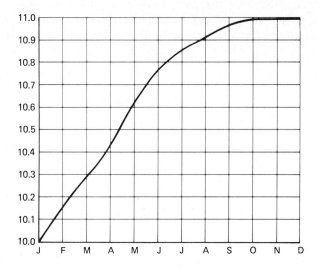

The well-chosen average. I live near a country neighborhood for which I can report an average income of $15,000. I could also report it as $3,500.

If I should want to sell real estate hereabouts to people having a high snobbery content, the first figure would be handy. The second figure, however, is the one to use in an argument against raising taxes, or the local bus fare.

Both are legitimate averages, legally arrived at. Yet it is obvious that at least one of them must be as misleading as an out-and-out lie. The $15,000-figure is a mean, the arithmetic average of the incomes of all the families in the community. The smaller figure is a median; it might be called the income of the average family in the group. It indicates that half the families have less than $3,500 a year and half have more.

Here is where some of the confusion about averages comes from. Many human characteristics have the grace to fall into what is called the "normal" distribution. If you draw a picture of it, you get a curve that is shaped like a bell. Mean and median fall at about the same point, so it doesn't make very much difference which you use.

But some things refuse to follow this neat curve. Income is one of them. Incomes for most large areas will range from under $1,000 a year to upward of $50,000. Almost everybody will be under $10,000, way over on the left-hand side of that curve.

One of the things that made the income figure for the "average Yaleman" meaningless is that we are not told whether it is a mean or a median. It is not that one type of average is invariably better than the other; it depends upon what you are talking about. But neither gives you any real information—and either may be highly misleading—unless you know which of those two kinds of average it is.

In the country neighborhood I mentioned, almost everyone has less than the average—the mean, that is—of $10,500. These people are all small farmers, except for a trio of millionaire week-enders who bring up the mean enormously.

You can be pretty sure that when an income average is given in the form of a mean nearly everybody has less than that.

The insignificant difference or the elusive error. Your two children Peter and Linda (we might as well give them modish names while we're about it) take intelligence tests. Peter's IQ, you learn, is 98 and Linda's is 101. Aha! Linda is your brighter child.

Is she? An intelligence test is, or purports to be, a sampling of intellect. An IQ, like other products of sampling, is a figure with a statistical error, which expresses the precision or reliability of the figure. The size of this probable error can be calculated. For their test the makers of the much-used Revised Stanford-Binet have found it to be about 3 per cent. So Peter's indicated IQ of 98 really means only that there is an even chance that it falls between 95 and 101. There is an equal probability that it falls somewhere else—below 95 or above 101. Similarly, Linda's has no better than a fifty-fifty chance of being within the fairly sizeable range of 98 to 104.

You can work out some comparisons from that. One is that there is rather better than one chance in four that Peter, with his lower IQ rating, is really at least three points smarter than Linda. A statistician doesn't like to consider a difference significant unless you can hand him odds a lot longer than that.

Ignoring the error in a sampling study leads to all kinds of silly conclusions. There are magazine editors to whom readership surveys are gospel; with a 40 per cent readership reported for one article and a 35 per cent for another, they demand more like the first. I've seen even smaller differences given tremendous weight, because statistics are a mystery and numbers are impressive. The same thing goes for market surveys and so-called public-opinion polls. The rule is that you cannot make a valid comparison between two such figures unless you know the deviations. And unless the difference between the figures is many times greater than the probable error of each, you have only a guess that the one appearing greater really is.

Otherwise you are like the man choosing a camp site from a report of mean temperature alone. One place in California with a mean annual temperature of 61 is San Nicolas Island on the south coast, where it always stays in the comfortable range between 47 and 87. Another with a mean of 61 is in the inland desert, where the thermometer hops around from 15 to 104. The deviation from the mean marks the difference, and you can freeze or roast if you ignore it.

The one-dimensional picture. Suppose you have just two or three figures to compare—say the average weekly wage of carpenters in the United States and another country. The sums might be $60 and $30. An ordinary bar chart makes the difference graphic.

That is an honest picture. It looks good for American carpenters, but perhaps it does not have quite the oomph you are after. Can't you make that difference appear overwhelming and at the same time give it what I am afraid is known as eye-appeal? Of course you can. Following tradition, you represent these sums by pictures of money bags. If the $30 bag is one inch high, you draw the $60 bag two inches high. That's in proportion, isn't it?

The catch is, of course, that the American's money bag, being twice as tall as that of the $30 man, covers an area on your page four times as great. And since your two-dimensional picture represents an object that would in fact have three dimensions, the money bags actually would differ much more than that. The volumes of any two similar solids vary as the cubes of their heights. If the unfortunate foreigner's bag holds $30 worth of dimes, the American's would hold not $60 but a neat $240.

You didn't say that, though, did you? And you can't be blamed, you're only doing it the way practically everybody else does.

The ever-impressive decimal. For a spurious air of precision that will lend all kinds of weight to the most disreputable statistics, consider the decimal.

Ask a hundred citizens how many hours they slept last night. Come out with a total of, say, 781.3. Your data are far from precise to begin with. Most people will miss their guess by fifteen minutes or more and some will recall five sleepless minutes as half a night of tossing insomnia.

But go ahead, do your arithmetic, announce that people sleep an average of 7.813 hours a night. You will sound as if you knew precisely what you are talking about. If you were foolish enough to say 7.8 (or "almost 8") hours it would sound like what it was—an approximation.

The semi-attached figure. If you can't prove what you want to prove, demonstrate something else and pretend that they are the same thing. In the daze that follows the collision of statistics with the human mind, hardly anybody will notice the difference. The semi-attached figure is a durable device guaranteed to stand you in good stead. It always has.

If you can't prove that your nostrum cures colds, publish a sworn laboratory report that the stuff killed 31,108 germs in a test tube in eleven seconds. There may be no connection at all between assorted germs in a test tube and the whatever-it-is that produces colds, but people aren't going to reason that sharply, especially while sniffling.

Maybe that one is too obvious and people are beginning to catch on. Here is a trickier version.

Let us say that in a period when race prejudice is growing it is to your advantage to "prove" otherwise. You will not find it a difficult assignment.

Ask that usual cross section of the population if they think Negroes have as good a chance as white people to get jobs. Ask again a few months later. As Princeton's Office of Public Opinion Research has found out, people who are most unsympathetic to Negroes are the ones most likely to answer yes to this question.

As prejudice increases in a country, the percentage of affirmative answers you will get to this question will become larger. What looks on the face of it like growing opportunity for Negroes actually is mounting prejudice and nothing else. You have achieved something rather remarkable: the worse things get, the better your survey makes them look.

The unwarranted assumption, or post hoc *rides again.* The interrelation of cause and effect, so often obscure anyway, can be most neatly hidden in statistical data.

Somebody once went to a good deal of trouble to find out if cigarette smokers make lower college grades than non-smokers. They did. This naturally pleased many people, and they made much of it.

The unwarranted assumption, of course, was that smoking had produced dull minds. It seemed vaguely reasonable on the face of it, so it was quite widely accepted. But it really proved nothing of the sort, any more than it proved that poor grades drive students to the solace of tobacco. Maybe the relationship worked in one direction, maybe in the other. And maybe all this is only an indication that the sociable sort of fellow who is likely to take his books less than seriously is also likely to sit around and smoke many cigarettes.

Permitting statistical treatment to befog casual relationships is little better than superstition. It is like the conviction among the people of the Hebrides that body lice produce good health. Observation over the centuries had taught them that people in good health had lice and sick people often did not. *Ergo,* lice made a man healthy. Everybody should have them.

Scantier evidence, treated statistically at the expense of common sense, has made many a medical fortune and many a medical article in magazines, including professional ones. More sophisticated observers finally got things straightened out in the Hebrides. As it turned out, almost everybody in those circles had lice most of the time. But when a man took a fever (quite possibly carried to him by those same lice) and his body became hot, the lice left.

Here you have cause and effect not only reversed, but intermingled.

There you have a primer in some ways to use statistics to deceive. A well-wrapped statistic is better than Hitler's "big lie": it misleads, yet it can't be pinned onto you.

Is this little list altogether too much like a manual for swindlers? Perhaps I can justify it in the manner of the retired burglar whose published reminiscences amounted to a graduate course in how to pick a lock and muffle a footfall: The crooks already know these tricks. Honest men must learn them in self-defense.

Ten report writing pitfalls: how to avoid them

VINCENT VINCI

Vincent Vinci is Director of Public Relations for
Lockheed Electronics.

The advancement of science moves on a pavement of communications. Chemists, electrical engineers, botanists, geologists, atomic physicists, and other scientists are not only practitioners but interpreters of science. As such, the justification, the recognition and the rewards within their fields result from their published materials.

Included in the vast field of communications is the report, a frequently used medium for paving the way to understanding and action. The engineering manager whose function is the direction of people and programs receives and writes many reports in his career. And therefore the need for technical reports that communicate effectively has been internationally recognized.

Since scientific writing is complicated by specialized terminology, a need for precision and the field's leaping advancement, the author of an engineering report can be overwhelmed by its contents. The proper handling of contents and communication of a report's purpose can be enhanced if the writer can avoid the following 10 pitfalls.

Pitfall 1: Ignoring your audience

In all the forms of communications, ignoring your audience in the preparation of a report is perhaps the gravest transgression. Why? All other forms of communication such as instruction manuals, speeches, books and brochures, are directed to an indefinable or only partially definable audience. The report,

Vincent Vinci, "Ten Report Writing Pitfalls: How to Avoid Them," reprinted by special permission from *Chemical Engineering*, December 22, 1975. Copyright © 1975 by McGraw-Hill, Inc., New York, N.Y. 10020.

on the other hand, is usually directed to a specific person or group and has a specific purpose. So, it would certainly seem that if one knows both the "who" and the "why," then a report writer should not be trapped by this pitfall.

But it is not enough to know the who and why, you need to know "how." To get to the how, let's assume that the reader is your boss and has asked you to write a trip report. You are to visit several plants and report on capital equipment requirements. Before you write the first word you will have to find out what your boss already knows about these requirements. It is obvious that he wants a new assessment of the facilities' needs. But, was he unsatisfied with a recent assessment and wants another point of view, or is a new analysis required because the previous report is outdated—or does he feel that now is the time to make the investment in facilities so that production can be increased over the next five years? That's a lot of questions, but they define both the who and why of your trip and, more importantly, your report.

By this time you may get the feeling that I suggest you give him exactly what he wants to read. The answer is yes and no. No, I don't mean play up to your boss's likes and dislikes. I do mean, however, that you give him all the information he needs to make a decision—the pros and the cons.

I mean also that the information be presented in a way that he is acclimated to in making judgments. For example, usually, a production-oriented manager or executive (even the chief executive) will think in terms of his specialty. The president of a company who climbed the marketing ladder selling solvents will think better in marketing terms. Therefore, perhaps the marketing aspects of additional equipment and facilities should be stressed. You should also be aware that if you happen to be the finance director, your boss will expect to see cost/investment factors too.

A simple method for remembering, rather than ignoring, your audience is to place a sheet of paper in front of you when you start to write your report. On the paper have written in bold letters WHO, WHY and HOW, with the answers clearly and cogently defined. Keep it in front of you throughout the preparation of your report.

Pitfall 2: Writing to impress

Nothing turns a reader off faster than writing to impress. Very often reports written to leave a lasting scholarly impression on top management actually hinder communication.

Generally, when a word is used to impress, the report writer assumes that the reader either knows its meaning or will take the trouble to look it up. Don't assume that a word familiar to you is easily recognized by your reader. I recall a few years ago, there was a word "serendipity" which became a fashionable word to impress your reader with. And there was "fulsome," and "pejorative," and more. All are good words, but they're often misused or misapplied. They were shoved into reports to impress, completely disregarding the reader. Your objective is that your reader comprehend your thoughts, and there should be a minimum of impediments to understanding—understanding with first reading, and no deciphering.

Unfortunately, writing to impress is not merely restricted to use of obscure words but also includes unnecessary detail and technical trivia. Perhaps the scientist, chemist, chemical engineer and others become so intrigued with technical fine points that the meaningful (to your audience) elements of a report are buried. And quite often the fault is not so much a lack of removing the chaff from the grain but an attempt to technically impress the reader. Of course there exist reports that are full of technical detail because the nature of the communication is to impart a new chemical process, compound or technique. Even when writing this kind of report, you should eliminate any esoteric technical facts that do not contribute to communication, even though you may be tempted to include them to exhibit your degree of knowledge in the field.

Pitfall 3: Having more than one aim

A report is a missile targeted to hit a point or achieve a mission. It is not a barrage of shotgun pellets that scatter across a target indiscriminately.

Have you ever, while reading a report, wondered where or what it was leading to—and even when you finished you weren't quite sure? The writer probably had more than one aim, thereby preventing you from knowing where the report was heading.

Having more than one aim is usually the sign of a novice writer, but the pitfall can also trip up an experienced engineer if he does not organize the report toward one objective.

It is too easy to say that your report is being written to communicate, to a specific audience, information about your research, tests, visit, meeting, conference, field trip, progress or any other one of a range of activities that may be the subject. If you look at the first part of the sentence, you will see that "specific audience," and "information" are the key words that have to be modified to arrive at the goal of your report. For instance, you must define the specific audience such as the "members of the research council," "the finance committee" or "the chief process engineer and his staff."

Secondly, you need to characterize the information, such as "analysis of a new catalytic process," "new methods of atomic absorption testing" or "progress on waste treatment programs." You should be able to state the specific purpose of your report in one sentence: e.g., "The use of fibrous material improves scrubber efficiency and life—a report to the product improvement committee."

When you have arrived at such a definition of your purpose and audience, you can then focus both the test results and analysis toward that purpose, tempered with your readers in mind.

The usual error made in writing reports is to follow the chronology of the research in the body of the report with a summary of a set of conclusions and recommendations attached. The proper procedure to follow is to write (while focusing on your report goal) the analysis first (supported by test essentials or any other details), then your introduction or summary—sort of reverse chronology. But be sure that your goal and audience are clearly known, because they become the basis of organizing your report.

Pitfall 4: Being inconsistent

If you work for an international chemical firm, you may be well aware of problems in communicating with plant managers and engineers of foreign installations or branches. And I'm not referring to language barriers, because for the most part these hurdles are immediately recognized and taken care of. What is more significant is units of measure. This problem is becoming more apparent as the United States slowly decides whether or not to adopt the metric system. Until it is adopted, your best bet is to stick to one measurement system throughout the report. Preferably, the system chosen should be that familiar to your audience. If the audience is mixed you should use both systems with one (always the same one) in parentheses. Obviously, don't mix units of measure because you will confuse or annoy your readers.

Consistency is not limited to measurements but encompasses terms, equations, derivations, numbers, symbols, abbreviations, acronyms, hyphenation, capitalization and punctuation. In other words, consistency in the mechanics of style will avoid work for your reader and smooth his path toward understanding and appreciating the contents of the report.

If your company neither has a style guide nor follows the general trends of good editorial practice, perhaps you could suggest instituting a guide. In addition to the U.S. Government Printing Office Style Manual, many scientific and engineering societies have set up guides which could be used.

Pitfall 5: Overqualifying

Chemical engineers, astronomers, geologists, electrical engineers, and scientists of any other discipline have been educated and trained to be precise. As a result, they strive for precision, accuracy, and detail. That tends to work against the scientist when it comes to writing. Add to that the limited training received in the arts, and you realize why written expression does not come easily.

Most reports, therefore, have too many modifiers—adjectives, clauses, phrases, adverbs and other qualifiers. Consider some examples: the single-stage, isolated double-cooled refractory process breakdown, or, the angle of the single-rotor dc hysteresis motor rotor winding. To avoid such difficult-to-comprehend phrases, you could in the first example write "the breakdown of the process in single-stage, isolated double-cooled refractories," and in the second, "the angle of the rotor winding in single-rotor dc hysteresis motors can cause . . . ," and so on. This eliminates the string of modifiers and makes the phrase easier to understand.

Better still, if your report allows you to say at the beginning that the following descriptions are only related to "single-stage, isolated double-cooled refractories" or "single-rotor dc hysteresis motors," you can remove the cumbersome nomenclature entirely.

In short, to avoid obscuring facts and ideas, eliminate excessive modifiers. Try to state your idea or main point first and follow with your qualifying phrases.

Pitfall 6: Not defining

Dwell, lake, and barn, are all common words. Right? Right and wrong. Yes, they are common to the non-scientist. To the mechanical engineer, dwell is the period a cam follower stays at maximum lift; to a chemical engineer, lake is a dye compound; and to an atomic physicist, a barn is an atomic cross-sectional area (10^{-24} cm^2).

These three words indicate two points: first, common words are used in science with other than their common meaning; and second, terms need to be defined.

In defining terms you use in a report, you must consider what to define and how to define. Of the two, I consider what to define a more difficult task and suggest that you review carefully just which terms you need define. If you analyze the purpose, the scope, the direction and your audience (reader/user), you will probably get a good handle on such terms.

"How to define" ranges from the simple substitution of a common term for an uncommon one, to an extended or amplified explanation. But whatever the term, or method of definition, you need to slant it both to the reader and to the report purpose.

Pitfall 7: Misintroducing

Introductions, summaries, abstracts and forewords—whatever you use to lead your reader into your report, it should not read like an exposition of a table of contents. If it does, you might as well let your audience read the table of contents.

The introduction, which should be written after the body of the report, should state the subject, purpose, scope, and the plan of the report. In many cases, an introduction will include a summary of the findings or conclusions. If a report is a progress report, the introduction should relate the current report to previous reports. Introductions, then, not only tell the sequence or plan of the report, but tell the what, how and why of the subject as well.

Pitfall 8: Dazzling with data

Someone once said that a good painter not only knows what to put in a painting, but more importantly he knows what to leave out. It's much the same with report writing. If you dazzle your reader with tons of data, he may be moved by the weight of the report but may get no more out of it than that.

The usual error occurs in supportive material that many engineers and scientists feel is necessary to give a report scientific importance. The truth is that successful scientific writing (which includes reports) is heavily grounded in reality, simplicity, and understanding—not quantity.

The simplest way to evaluate the relevancy of information is to ask yourself after writing a paragraph, "What can I remove from this paragraph without destroying its meaning and its relationship to what precedes and what will follow?" Then, ask another question, "Does my reader require all that data to comprehend, evaluate or make a decision with?" If you find you can do without excess words, excess description and excess supportive data, you will end up with a tighter, better and more informative report.

These principles should also be used to evaluate graphs, photographs, diagrams and other illustrations. Remember, illustrations should support or aid comprehension rather than being a crutch on which your report leans. The same should be kept in mind when determining just how much you should append to your report. There is no need to copy all your lab notes to show that detailed experimentation was performed to substantiate the results. A statement that the notes exist and are available will suffice.

Pitfall 9: Not highlighting

Again, I believe the analogy of the painter applies. A good painter also knows what to highlight and what to subdue in a portrait or scene.

If you don't accent the significant elements, findings, illustrations, data, tests, facts, trends, procedures, precedents, or experiments pertinent to the subject and object of your report, you place the burden of doing so on your reader. As a result, he may consider the report a failure, draw his own conclusions, or hit upon the significant elements by chance. In any event, don't leave it up to your reader to search out the major points of your report.

Highlighting is one step past knowing what goes into your report and what to leave out (see Pitfall 8 above). All the key points of your report should define and focus on the purpose of your report. They must be included in your summary or conclusions, but these sections are not the only places to highlight. Attention should be called to key elements needed for the understanding of your material throughout the body of the report. Several methods may be used: you can underline an important statement or conclusion, you can simply point out that a particular illustration is the proof of the results of an experiment, or, as most professional writers do, you can make the key sentence the first or last sentence of a paragraph.

Pitfall 10: Not rewriting

Did you ever hear of an actor who hadn't rehearsed his lines before stepping before an audience? An actor wouldn't chance it—his reputation and his next role depend on his performance. The engineer shouldn't chance it either. Don't expect the draft of your report to be ready for final typing and reproduction without rewriting.

Once you have judged what your report will contain and how it will be organized, just charge ahead and write the first draft. Don't worry about choosing the precise word, turning that meaningful phrase, or covering all the facts in one paragraph or section. Once you have written your first draft (and the quicker you accomplish this the more time you will have to perfect the text), you are in a better position to analyze, tailor, and refine the report as a whole. Now you are also able to focus all the elements toward your purpose and your audience.

As you begin the rewriting process simply pick up each page of your draft, scan it, and ask yourself what role the material on that page plays in the fulfillment of the report's objective and understanding. You will find that this will enable you to delete, add, change and rearrange your material very quickly.

After you have completed this process, then rewrite paragraph by paragraph, sentence by sentence, and word by word. Your final step is to repeat the procedure of examining each page's contents. When you are satisfied with its flow and cohesion, then you will have a good report, one you know will be well received and acted upon.

Techniques of professional report writers

RÄNDI SIGMUND SMITH

Rändi Sigmund Smith lives in Hartford, Connecticut, where she is a management consultant.

Here are the techniques and tips consultants use in preparing better Management Reports.

1. Brevity

Result-oriented reports are a management tool. Brevity enables your reader(s) to use this tool with a minimal investment of time and effort. Be as brief as possible, without sacrificing reader comprehension or your personal credibility.

A. Condense

We all believe we only include what's necessary. I know, however, how possessive I can be about material I worked hard to obtain. Perhaps you feel the same way?

If I have plenty of data, I am tempted to include it all, hoping my reader will be impressed, if not overwhelmed. Can't you hear him saying to himself, "What a fantastic research job she's done"?

Unfortunately, my great research has produced a welter of irrelevant detail which is now obscuring the important points I hoped to make. "Less is more" in any Management Report, and here's a rule of thumb to achieve it almost painlessly:

From *Written Communication for Data Processing* by Rändi Sigmund Smith. © 1976 by Litton Educational Publishing, Inc. Reprinted by permission of Van Nostrand Reinhold Company.

If any piece of data cannot be used to illustrate a specific conclusion or recommendation, throw it out. Interesting as it may be, it's extraneous to your primary objective.

The reverse is also true: If any alternative you hoped to present cannot be supported by facts you've assembled, throw it out. It may be something you've wanted to say for some time. It may even be something that needs to be said, but it does not belong in *this* report.

B. Use graphics

Illustrations of all kinds—charts, tables, graphs—have always been a part of the Management Report. They usually, however, have been relegated to the Appendix.

Now, any simple graphic material *that takes the place of prose,* thereby cutting back verbiage, is placed directly in the body of your report. This keeps reports shorter and makes exhibits less complicated to use.

It is also perfectly acceptable in contemporary business to be creative with your graphics. One example I saw concerned a workspace allocation report. A DP department was moving from one location to another and an individual was assigned to report on space dispersal. If you have ever seen a standard report on this subject, you know how impossible it can be.

"Two feet beyond the terminal and up six feet is wall clock X . . . ." Or, they present squared-off boxes, representing floor space with X's and Y's—all out of scale—indicating people and equipment placement.

Not this report. The person involved took his camera to the new location and took pictures. On each picture, he noted exact arrangement of work areas and equipment. Every reader could *visualize* exactly what the new location looked like and how it could be used. Movement of the entire department was fast and smoothly organized. That report was "workable"—our prime criterion for judging a business document—and it earned its author a Performance Bonus.

I do have one caution concerning the use of illustrative material, however. If you are not artistically inclined, leave the preparation of your graphics to someone who is. Nothing detracts from the professionalism of a Management Report any faster than a lopsided stick figure or smudged ink sketch. Almost every organization has a graphic arts, audiovisual, advertising, marketing, or printing service area. Use it. If your company does not, enlist the aid of an associate whose artistic talents exceed your own.

C. Use titles and subheadings

We discussed the contribution of titles and subheadings to easy reading and effective document organization. We also considered the importance of making each title or subheading pertinent to the section it describes, avoiding such say-nothing abstractions as *purpose, definition,* and *scope.*

Now, let's impose limits in terms of numbers. I have yet to see a successful result-oriented report that contained more than *five* main headings. More than five, and you are either being redundant or attempting to cover too much ground in one report. The only possible exceptions would be a full-scale Feasibility Study or a major Proposal. Each of these could run up to, but should contain no more than, *ten* main topic listings.

Under each main heading, well-organized reports present only *four* or fewer subheadings. Again, if you wind up with more, you either are being repetitive or you need to more carefully define the main heading involved. Long lists of subheadings are the best indication that a main heading is vague or ill-conceived.

D. Use the Appendix wisely

Don't be afraid of the Appendix, and don't abuse it. Many report writers avoid using an Appendix altogether. Others employ it as a dumping ground for material they couldn't find space for in the body of their report.

Remember, of course, that any complex or highly technical charts or graphs still belong in the Appendix. This is also true of any illustration your reader will expect to use *apart from* your cover report. . . .

Be sure to use your Appendix for any consideration of past studies or any required analysis of data sampling collection techniques. For example, suppose I prepared a report on utilization of available hardware in my organization. I would put descriptive information about the software packages used in my monitoring in the Appendix. Readers who want to know where my figures came from will look for and read such detail there. Other readers may not need to know or wouldn't understand the technical considerations anyway. Why should they be forced to wade through methodology in the body of my report?

2. Encourage reader interest

Most managers approach the reading of a report with a sigh of resignation. No one expects to be caught up in or excited by a report's content.

The only way to change this "necessary evil" attitude is to write reports that involve each reader directly. Any administrator who finds *his* concerns reflected in a report's overall content is going to be interested in the conclusions and recommendations presented. He may not agree with them, but he is certain to pay attention.

A. Start with a "grabber"

We do this with other types of documents. Why not grab the reader in a Management Report, sparking reader curiosity from the beginning? . . .

Traditional business reports have been slow starters. Readers could skim volumes and not miss much of importance. It's no wonder reader attention to most reports has been casual at best.

"Grabbers" change this. For example, I recently saw a Management Report dealing with ineffective assignment of manpower. The opening statement was dynamite:

> "The Data Processing Department does not need to hire any new personnel next year."

The writer, of course, went on to explain. Acquisition of new personnel could not be justified, because the department was not fully utilizing people already available. That's pretty dry material. If you were in that area, however, and screaming for more help, wouldn't you read the report? Consider the difference in your interest level between this writer's opening statement and the *purpose, definition,* and *scope* routine.

I saw another report on the same subject that employed a rhetorical question opener. It began:

> "Are ETAs impossible to meet?"

The writer then proceeded to answer his own question. He demonstrated that target dates were impossible because of failure to allocate manpower properly. His material may have been the same old thing, but his readers were already hooked. Anyone in his department who had blown an ETA read his report carefully and thoroughly. Check that response with the one he would have evoked with

> "The purpose of this report is to investigate personnel allocation over the period covering . . . "

For most readers, there is no comparison.

B. Present the opposing view and drawbacks, if any

Opposition is a strong reader reaction. Certainly, disagreement with the suggested recommendations in a report is better than no response at all. In fact, reader resistance is often the starting point for productive consideration of a problem. It prompts the negotiation necessary to finding a solution.

Where possible, anticipate any negative thinking on the part of your reader(s). Confront it head-on in your original report. Readers are never blasé about their potential veto power. They read carefully to catch your acknowledgment of their involvement. They also look to determine if their reservations concerning your subject received fair play.

Remember, ignoring reader reluctance does not make it go away. Acknowledging it may allow you to answer questions or objections without frustrating follow-up discussion.

C. Use case studies and direct quotes

Case studies have been around a long time in Management Reports. Yet, few newer techniques make a theoretical proposition more relevant to a reader than a factual story illustrating its application. Just be sure your readers know enough detail about the episode to evaluate its pertinence. "My experience with the XYZ system indicates . . ." is not enough. You must explain what experience, for how long, and the incident that actually occurred and influenced your current recommendation.

Direct quotes are a more recent development in result-oriented reporting. Their acceptance grew as people's experience with actual situations became as important to solving DP problems as any verifiable data.

Interviewing is now a basic tool of report writing. When you conduct interviews, you may quote individuals directly. Certainly, you would only quote experts in a given field, and their viewpoint can lend credence and emphasis to your conclusion.

One caution with direct quotation. Always tell the person you plan to quote him *at the time of the initial interview.* Some individuals do not wish to be quoted under any circumstances and they don't like surprises. If possible, allow those you do quote to view your report prior to its distribution. If this is impossible, be sure that each receives an "informational" copy.

3. Avoid writing in the third person

Data processing inherited an objective, third person report style from scientific and academic predecessors. In it, no writer ever intruded his personality into the presentation of material. Facts, and *only* facts, were acceptable.

This approach is no longer possible, given the intended usage of result-oriented reports. By the very act of preparing a Management Report, the writer is participating in the administrative decision-making process. In many instances, his daily activities or future career could be affected by the decision reached, and this has to influence his position. He is not, and cannot pretend to be, an innocent bystander shielded from responsibility by reams of data.

Stepping out of the third person can be uncomfortable. It puts the writer—his analysis and attitudes—on the line. We must do it, however, if result-oriented reports are going to be practical assists to effective management. The easiest way to present your standpoint, without loss of objectivity, is to identify each aspect of the analytical process. Unless you establish these definitions—for yourself as well as your reader—you could find yourself on constantly shifting ground.

A. Carefully distinguish what is data, personal interpretation of data, and writer viewpoint

Everyone, especially statisticians, knows data can be manipulated. Don't do so in a Management Report. Always present quantitative facts and figures in an easily understood and straightforward format.

How, though, does the reader know that what he sees is actual fact? Well, *data,* by definition, are verifiable. Simply *identify your source,* usually in the Appendix. Your reader now knows that the referenced statement is not open to question. If he wishes to perform the same research you did, he will come up with exactly the same information.

On the other hand, *personal interpretation of data* is always subjective. This does not lessen its value to valid analysis, but it must be explained to the reader. A writer's individual interpretation usually is expressed as a conclusion leading to a suggested recommendation. Each reader should recognize that conclusion's dependency on the experience, background, and current responsibility level of the writer or someone he interviewed.

Remember, also, that personal interpretation of data, unlike data itself, is open to reader question or disagreement. Anticipate any such problems in your original presentation.

Writer viewpoint is more difficult to pin down. Generally, it reflects the context in which the topic of the report was evaluated. It also mirrors the writer's values and priorities and the weight he attributes to certain facts. These influencing factors must be distinguished from data, as they are the most common source of "ax grinding" or slanted personal interpretation.

For example, suppose a management committee assigns me a report. The recommendations I come up with are good ones, yet each will increase the responsibility and importance of my unit. Unless I acknowledge these side benefits in my original report, any reader might suspect the recommendations are more *writer viewpoint* than accurate analysis. If I point out my personal involvement, however, without waiting to be challenged on it, my ideas must be evaluated solely on overall merit.

B. Balance facts with personal judgment. Add your own comments where appropriate

When you prepare a Management Report, *you speak as an expert.* With some reports—Feasibility Study or Projected Objectives, for example—you know more than your readers and your opinions are crucial. In fact, your familiarity with a topic will occasionally have more influence on the final decision than any available data.

Here's an illustration. I was once asked to write a report evaluating a particular software package. I had "facts" up to my ears. The vendor had seen to that. I also had demonstrated need. The customers of the DP area were most enthusiastic. Everything—cost, capability, support—looked great.

Unfortunately for the vendor, I had done some work for a firm that had already purchased this package and I knew its failings. The vendor used his customers as testers, compatibility had been exaggerated—you know the routine. Therefore, in my report, I listed the "data," only to follow it with a definitive erasure, *"however . . . ."* My client did not buy.

Which was more important to a good management decision in this instance—available data or my personal judgment?

C. Acknowledge any interpretation of data or viewpoint not your own

It's all too easy to pick up other people's judgments or viewpoints almost through osmosis. This is particularly true if you interview while doing your research. This kind of mental plagiarism is unintentional, but please avoid any suggestion of it in your reports.

Identify the source of any conclusions or recommendations not your own. This supports your objectivity and strengthens your material. Also, giving credit will prevent your reader from asking questions you may not be able to answer adequately.

Of course, any contributors you reference should be notified prior to distribution. They also should receive an "informational" copy of your final report. . . .

4. Convey interest and enthusiasm

Many a legitimate conclusion or valid recommendation has been vetoed because a writer displayed frustration, anger, or impatience. Poor attitudes are catchy.

Conversely, any Management Report is better received when the writer conveys his own interest in his subject and his personal belief in its value. Enthusiasm is also contagious.

Think of your outlook in any report situation as a self-fulfilling prophecy. Let your reader *feel* your conviction. This makes him more highly motivated. It also encourages him to look for the good in your projected end result, if only to see what all the excitement is about.

A. Write a story

The five elements of successful fiction—*situation, characters, problem, solution,* and *resolution*—are also vital to well-written Management Reports. Your reader(s) must know the situation prompting the report, the people concerned, existing problems, proposed solutions, and the end result of implementing the solutions.

Nothing conveys writer involvement in his material better than good story logic. The progression from each story element to another also catches the reader up in the situation. It makes him eager to move to resolution and enthusiastic about his participation in end result.

I am not suggesting that any Management Report will become a book "too good to put down." Taking your reader with you on your analytical journey, however, just might encourage him to find your "story" as absorbing and important as you do.

B. Think in the positive

Occasionally, each of us writes a report where the conclusions we document are negative. We wind up saying something should not be done, rather than recommending positive action.

I have learned, through long experience, that expressing a conclusion in the negative can often evoke a negative response. In fact this frequently occurs even when your reader actually agrees with your basic premise.

Many people in the communications field believe it can take a reader up to six times longer to understand a negative statement than a positive one. We all mentally transpose negative statements into the positive, comprehend them, and then transpose back to negative mode. Naturally, this process slows comprehension and may even prevent it. As we've discussed several times, a reader's instinctive reaction to something he doesn't understand is negative. This is why we elicit unreasonable negative responses to our reasonable negative conclusions.

Where possible, express recommendations in the positive. It's easy to do if you employ one simple rule. Always give reasons why something *should* be done and avoid giving reasons why something *should not* be done.

Take this example:

"Revision of present project control procedures are not recommended because of resulting confusion in manpower assignments."

That's a negative statement and can automatically evoke a negative reaction from many readers. Turn it around:

> "The current project control procedures simplify manpower assignments and should be maintained."

This says the same thing and yet is much more likely to elicit an affirmative response.

There's also an additional advantage to positive expression. The second version is shorter. Check your own writing. Positive statements usually require fewer words. Now, two things are working to help the reader understand and accept your recommendation—no confusing negatives and shorter sentences overall.

C. Avoid formality

The traditional formal approach to report writing is not always the most effective in result-oriented reporting. It can suggest a reserved attitude or total detachment on the part of the writer and probably will elicit the same from each reader.

Wherever possible, give your readers the benefit of a conversational tone. Some formality may be required, depending on the type of report, your subject matter, and your audience. Generally, however, an informal approach conveys greater writer concern and encourages more direct reader participation.

5. Make a convincing presentation

Being objective does not eliminate the need to be convincing in the presentation of recommendations and conclusions. A result-oriented report should *influence* management decisions as well as provide information. Take a stand, but do so skillfully, without obvious politicking or overaggressiveness.

A. Consider climate and past history

Investigate thoroughly the climate in which your recommendation will be circulated. For example, is it a year of financial austerity in your organization? Has there been a shake-up of management, resulting in new policies and priorities? Are you leading from a position of strength—good performance, with minimal time slippage and cost overrun—or has your credibility slipped with your customers and management?

All of these factors influence the preconceived notions and mental attitude of your readers. Determine this "atmosphere" before you write. Knowledge of your readers' orientation allows you to develop recommendations that make sense to their *current* way of thinking.

Also, consider the past history of your report topic. What was the fate of prior recommendations on the same or a similar subject? Why did they succeed, if they did? Which ones failed? How has the situation changed, if at all? In this way, you avoid nonproductive duplication of effort and are prepared, in advance, to counter objections.

B. Provide full information

A reader can properly evaluate conclusions and recommendations only if he knows all the facts and individuals involved. Merge complete informaton with active sentence tone to assist reader understanding and elicit agreement.

Take these sample sentences from reports I reviewed:

"The proposed system was suggested to the Data Processing Department by the Accounting Department."

This statement is passive in tone. It also leaves out essential identification of the responsible individuals in both areas.

"The Accounting Department suggested the system to Data Processing."

This has active tone, but still provides insufficient detail.

"Michael Buckley, supervisor in the Accounting Department, contacted Barbara Jacobs, Director of new projects in Data Processing. He requested development of a system to provide a quarterly corporate income listing."

Now, the reader has all the facts. He understands who originated the request, who received it, and what the request entails.

Please note that when you are providing adequate background, the shortest version is not always the best. Brevity is important, of course, but it should not be attained by omitting information the reader needs.

C. Eliminate bias

It's hard to stay totally objective in result-oriented reporting, particularly if the subject matter is of critical concern to you or your unit. Even a *suggestion* of bias, however, can weaken any Management Report. The best way to avoid conveying a lack of objectivity is to eliminate or modify any section of your report beginning with these sentences:

"While perhaps not directly related to this report. . . ."

This is an immediate tip-off to all readers that you have something you've been wanting to say for a long time. They now also know you are going to use this report as a soapbox and lay it on them.

If material is "not directly related to this report," leave it out. All you can accomplish by including it is to send your readers off on a tangent, distracting them from your actual report objectives.

"As I stressed previously. . . ."

Here is a dangerous approach. It puts any reader on the defensive and, as we have discussed, people on the defensive are incapable of learning anything. In order for your reader now to agree with your premise, he must admit—at least mentally—that he was *wrong* before. How many individuals in your organization are quick to do that? Certainly, the one hold-out on a management committee is not going to do so in the midst of his peers. He'll go to the wall defending his original position.

I know it is occasionally important to point out that a subject has come up before. Do so, however, without provoking rationalization or excuses. "As we discussed previously . . ." at least conveys a cooperative exchange. Only you and perhaps one of your readers will know it was a "bang your shoe on the table" type of discussion.

"Since action was not taken. . . ."

This is the classic, finger-pointing assignment of blame. How productive can it be to aim it directly at those you must "sell" on your recommendations? Believe me, if "action was not taken . . ." before, using this tone to say so practically guarantees it will not be taken this time either.

"When you did not respond. . . ."

No one is comfortable with organizational types who play the martyr. The implication here is: "Oh, *poor me*, having to work with shmucks like you who don't even answer their mail. Let me show you how well I coped with the impossible situation *you* created." I bet you can feel yourself getting angry and impatient already. That's your reader's inevitable reaction also.

Actually, such a sentence should not be necessary. When you do not get a response to a Management Report within a reasonable length of time—call. Ask if your reader(s) need additional material. Perhaps they have questions you can answer. This prompts some sort of verbal reply. You then can ask them to confirm their decision or actions in writing.

D. Restate and reinforce your conclusions and recommendations

Too many Management Reports just seem to drop off into the Appendix. They do not conclude forcefully. Get in the habit of restating, for comprehension, and reinforcing, for motivation, any conclusions and recommendations you've drawn in the context of your material. This summary approach allows you to end your report on the strongest note possible. It gives your reader a handle for the enthusiasm you've generated.

A concise conclusion also can save you considerable writing effort. Most Management Reports are distributed under a cover letter or memorandum. Writing this overview document is difficult, and it doesn't always accurately reflect the full thrust of your analytical judgment. If you conclude with a succinct summary, you can simply lift out that section of your report, making it, with some modification, your cover. No more struggling to compose what needs to be said, without saying too much. Also, you will successfully reach those readers who do not wish to wade through the detail, and read only the introductory letter or memorandum. They now at least are getting a brief exposure to your most critical elements, and staying in tune with readers who review the entire document.

E. Keep your door open

Actions do speak louder than words. Demonstrate your conviction that your ideas are important by offering help to your reader(s). State your availability to clarify or elaborate any point they may question. Volunteer specific assistance in the implementation of any suggestion you propose.

Nothing more quickly convinces a reader that recommendations are worthwhile than the willingness of their author to get involved and stay involved—beyond putting words on a piece of paper.

Annotated
bibliographies

The limitations of this volume and the great quantity of materials that have been published on business and technical writing make any attempt at comprehensiveness in what follows impossible. My purpose in compiling this bibliography has been to provide teachers, students, and business people and technicians additional sources of information on business and technical writing.

My criteria for including materials were several. I was especially interested in including materials that have proved helpful to my students and my colleagues in courses in business and technical writing. I also tried to include materials that dealt with particular problems rather than general theories. Finally, since this anthology was of necessity limited in content, I have annotated items dealing with topics in business and technical writing not fully treated in the essays reprinted here.

For the convenience of its users, I have divided this bibliography into four sections:

1. Bibliographies of materials on business and technical writing
2. Books
3. Business and technical writing anthologies
4. Articles

Bibliographies of Materials on Business and Technical Writing

Balachandran, Sarjoni. *Technical Writing, A Bibliography*. Urbana, Ill.: American Business Communication Association; Washington, D.C.: Society for Technical Communication, 1977. Publications on scientific and technical writing since 1965; annotated.

Blackman, Carolyn M. "A Bibliography for Beginning Teachers of Technical Writing." *Technical and Professional Communication*. Ed. Thomas M. Sawyer. Ann Arbor, Mich.: Professional Communication Press, 1977. Organizations, periodicals, conferences, meetings, institutes, bibliographies, articles, standard works, and general orientation materials on technical writing.

Bowman, Mary Ann. "Books on Business and Technical Writing in the University of Illinois Library." *Journal of Business Communication*, 12 (Winter 1975), 33-67. Books written in English between 1950 and 1973 whose titles appeared in the card catalogue of the University of Illinois library under a variety of subject headings related to business and technical writing.

Carter, Robert. *Communication in Organizations: An Annotated Bibliography and Sourcebook*. Detroit: Gale, 1972. Includes over seventy-five items on business writing.

Cunningham, Donald H. "Bibliographies of Technical Writing Materials." *Technical Writing Teacher*, 1 (Winter 1974), 9-10. Instructional materials.

———. "Books on Police Writing." *College Composition and Communication*, 23 (May, 1972), 199-201. A review of books published between 1957 and 1972 on the fundamentals of police writing.

———, and Vivienne Hertz. "An Annotated Bibliography on the Teaching of Technical Writing." *College Composition and Communication*, 21 (May, 1970), 177-186. Sixty-seven entries; especially designed for beginning teachers of technical writing.

———. "Bibliography: Police Report Writing." *Police Chief*, 38 (August, 1971), 44, 49-50. One hundred and two items including books, parts of books, bound and unbound manuals and bulletins, articles, and materials indirectly related to police reporting.

Fielden, John S. "For Better Business Writing." *Harvard Business Review*, 43 (January, 1965), 164-166, 169-170, 172. References designed to help business people write better.

Larson, Richard L. "Selected Bibliography of Research and Writing about the Teaching of Composition." *College Composition and Communication*, 26 (May, 1975), 187-195; 27 (May, 1976), 171-180; 28 (May, 1977), 181-193; 29 (May, 1978), 181-194; and 30 (May, 1979), 196-213. Some items on business and technical writing; annotated.

Lodge, Frank L. "Specifications and Catalogs Frequently Used in the Presentation of Technical Data." In *Handbook of Technical Writing Practices*. Ed. Stello Jordan, et al. Vol. 2. New York: Wiley, 1971. Specifications and catalogues issued by agencies of the Department of Defense; annotated.

McClure, Lucille. "Two Bibliographies: Technical Writing Books in Print. Photo-typesetting." *IEEE Transactions on Engineering Writing and Speech*," EWS-8 (December, 1965), 65-70. Fifty-nine books on technical writing.

Oslund, R. R. "A Bibliography of Proposals." *STWP Review*, 11 (April, 1964), 13–14. Eighty-four items on proposal writing.

Philler, Theresa, et al. *An Annotated Bibliography on Technical Writing, Editing, Graphics, and Publishing, 1950–1965*. Washington, D.C.: Society for Technical Writers and Publishers; Pittsburgh: Carnegie Library, 1966. Two thousand papers, articles, and books.

Smith, Julian F., et al. "Style Manuals: Guides for Technical Writing." *Journal of Chemical Education*, 42 (July, 1965), 373–375. A review of forty-one style manuals designed for technical writers.

Van Veen, Frederick. "An Index to 500 Papers through 1962 on Engineering Writing and Related Subjects." *IEEE Transactions on Engineering Writing and Speech*, EWS-6 (September, 1963), 50–58. Subject-author index; many of the papers listed have not been published.

Walter, John A. "Basic Recommended Reference Shelf: A Selected Bibliography of Technical and Scientific Writing." In *Handbook of Technical Writing Practices*. Ed. Stello Jordan, et al. Vol. 2. New York: Wiley, 1971. Reference books on grammar, style, usage, and technical writing and communication; annotated.

————. "Style Manuals." In *Handbook of Technical Writing Practices*. Ed. Stello Jordan, et al. Vol. 2. New York: Wiley, 1971. Institutional and instructional style manuals; annotated.

Books

Adelstein, Michael E. *Contemporary Business Writing*. New York: Random House, 1971. A rhetorically based text designed for college students who have already completed basic writing and composition courses.

Andrews, Deborah C., and Margaret D. Blickle. *Technical Writing, Principles and Forms*. New York: Macmillan, 1978. A comprehensive introductory text emphasizing language skills and applied rhetoric.

Angel, Juvenal L. *Specialized Resumes for Executives and Professionals*. New York: Regents, 1967. A guide for resume preparation that includes over forty sample resumes for positions in business and industry.

Atkinson, Philip S., and Helen Reynolds. *Business Writing and Procedures*. New York: American Book Company, 1970. A basic text appropriate for independent use.

Backman, Lon F. *A Digest on the Elements of Proposal Writing*. Olympia, Wash.: State of Washington Planning and Community Affairs Agency, n.d. Detailed guidelines written in the form of an actual proposal.

Barzun, Jacques, and Henry F. Graff. *The Modern Researcher*. Rev. ed. New York: Harcourt Brace Jovanovich, 1970. A scholarly discussion of the principles that should inform any kind of research.

Berenson, Conrad, and Raymond R. Colton. *Research and Report Writing for Business and Economics*. New York: Random House, 1971. A comprehensive guide for writers of business reports and research papers.

Blicq, R. S. *Technically Write!* Englewood Cliffs, N.J.: Prentice-Hall, 1972. A basic text using two engineering firms as the setting for each assignment.

Blumenthal, Lassor A. *The Complete Book of Personal Letter Writing and Modern Correspondence.* Garden City, N.Y.: Doubleday, 1969. A comprehensive guide to social, business, and professional letter writing.

_____. *Successful Business Writing.* New York: Grosset and Dunlap, 1976. A how-to book with sections on letters, proposals, resumes, and oral presentations.

Bostwick, Burdette. *Resume Writing.* New York: Wiley, 1976. A comprehensive guide with discussions and examples of different resume formats.

Brand, Norman, and John O. White. *Legal Writing, The Strategy of Persuasion.* New York: St. Martin's, 1976. A text that applies the principles of advanced composition and persuasion to the specific writing needs of the legal profession; designed for prelaw, paralegal, and law students.

Brennan, Lawrence D., Stanley Strand, and Edward C. Gruber. *Resumes for Better Jobs.* New York: Simon and Schuster, 1973. Model resumes for over two hundred job classifications.

Brown, Harry M., and Karen K. Reid. *Business Writing and Communication.* New York: Van Nostrand Reinhold, 1979. An introductory text with sections on the basic principles of business writing, the kinds of written communication, and the strategies of oral communication.

Brown, James. *Casebook for Technical Writers.* San Francisco: Wadsworth, 1961.

_____. *Cases in Business Communications.* Belmont, California: Wadsworth, 1962. Companion volumes filled with practical assignments for business and technical writing students.

Brusaw, Charles T., and Gerald J. Alred. *Practical Writing.* Boston: Allyn and Bacon, 1973. Introductory text with emphasis on the basic writing process.

_____, and Walter E. Oliu. *The Business Writer's Handbook.* New York: St. Martin's, 1976.

_____. *Handbook of Technical Writing.* New York: St. Martin's, 1976. Easy-to-use, thorough handbooks, each containing over five hundred entries alphabetically arranged.

Cloke, Marjane, and Robert Wallace. *The Modern Business Letter Writer's Manual.* New York: Doubleday, 1974. Handy paperback guide for writers of business letters.

Corwen, Leonard. *Your Resume: Key to a Better Job.* New York: Arco, 1976. Easy-to-follow instructions interspersed with sample resumes.

Crouch, W. George. *Bank Letters and Reports.* New York: American Institute of Banking, 1961. An introductory text for bank employees.

Damerst, William A. *Clear Technical Reports.* New York: Harcourt, 1972. Comprehensive text with emphasis on the elimination of obstacles to clear communication.

Dawe, Jessamon. *Writing Business and Economics Papers, Theses, and Dissertations.* Totowa, N.J.: Littlefield, Adams, 1975. A comprehensive style manual.

Dodds, Robert H. *Writing for Technical and Business Magazines.* New York: Wiley, 1969. Practical discussions of the publishing process from the points of view of writer and editor alike.

Draughton, Clyde O. *Practical Bank Letter Writing.* Boston: Bankers Publishing
    Co., 1971. A guide to the kinds of business letters employees of financial
    institutions are required to write.

Ehrlich, Eugene, and Daniel Murphy. *The Art of Technical Writing.* New York:
    Crowell, 1969. Handy paperback with sections on the various forms of techni-
    cal writing and a handbook on style and usage.

Emerson, Lynn A. *How to Prepare Training Manuals.* Albany: University of the
    State of New York, Department of Education, 1952. Ten chapters that follow
    the order in which the steps of manual preparation should be performed.

Enrick, Norbert L. *Effective Graphic Communication.* Princeton: Auerbach, 1972.
    Guidelines for preparing effective charts and attractive visual and tabular
    forms.

Ewing, David. *Writing for Results in Business, Government, and the Professions.*
    New York: Wiley, 1974. An advanced text for professional writers concerned
    about their impact on readers.

Flesch, Rudolf. *The Art of Readable Writing.* Rev. ed. New York: Harper and
    Row, 1974. A general discussion of writing based on the premise that one
    should as much as possible write the way one talks; includes sections on the
    Flesch Readability Formula.

Gilman, William. *The Language of Science, A Guide to Effective Writing.* New
    York: Harcourt, 1961. A detailed discussion of writing aimed at helping writ-
    ers capture their readers' attention.

Gray, Dwight E. *So You Have to Write a Technical Report.* Washington, D.C.:
    Information Resources Press, 1970. Handy reference based on a series of
    lectures given at Pennsylvania State University; contains brief chapters on the
    important aspects and parts of a technical report.

Gunning, Robert. *New Guide to More Effective Writing in Business and Indus-
    try.* Boston: Industrial Education Institute, 1963. A quick reference designed
    for the technician on the job.

————. *The Technique of Clear Writing.* Rev. ed. New York: McGraw-Hill, 1968.
    A detailed discussion of the author's readability formula, the Fog Index, and
    selected principles of clear writing.

Hafer, W. Keith, and Gordon E. White. *Advertising Writing.* St. Paul: West Pub-
    lishing Company, 1977. A comprehensive text on public relations and adver-
    tising writing.

Harris, John S., and Reed H. Blake. *Technical Writing for Social Scientists.* Chi-
    cago: Nelson Hall, 1976. A brief introductory text applying the rhetoric of the
    scientific method to the social sciences.

Haughney, John. *Effective Catalogs.* New York: Wiley, 1968. Procedures for pro-
    ducing one of today's basic marketing tools—the company catalog.

Herbert, A. J. *The Structure of Technical English.* London: Longman, 1965. A
    grammar book designed to give foreign technicians and engineers practice in
    mastering the skills they need to communicate effectively in English.

Hoover, Hardy. *Essentials for the Technical Writer.* New York: Wiley, 1970. A
    brief text on the writing of reports and specifications.

Houp, Kenneth, and Thomas Pearsall. *Reporting Technical Information.* 3rd ed.
    Beverly Hills, Calif.: Glencoe Press, 1977. Well-illustrated text for basic tech-
    nical writing courses.

Howard, C. Jeriel, and David A. Gill. *Desk Copy: Modern Business Communications*. San Francisco: Canfield, 1971. Basic text designed for students in both business and secretarial programs; emphasizes the business letter.

Jacobi, Ernest. *Writing At Work*. Rochelle Park, N.J.: Hayden Book Company, 1976. A text with emphasis on general principles rather than mechanics; intended for writers on the job.

Janis, J. Harold. *The Business Research Paper*. New York: Hobbs, Dorman, 1967. A compact guide to the formats for and mechanics of business research papers.

――――. *Writing and Communicating in Business*. 3rd ed. New York: Macmillan, 1978. A comprehensive text appropriate for beginning and advanced courses.

――――, and Howard R. Dressner. *Business Writing*. 2nd ed. Barnes and Noble Outline Series. New York: Barnes and Noble, 1972. Self-instruction book on how to write business letters and reports.

Jaquish, Michael P. *Personal Resume Preparation*. New York: Wiley, 1968. Step-by-step instructions for the preparation of resumes.

Johnson, Thomas P. *Analytical Writing: A Handbook for Business and Technical Writers*. New York: Harper and Row, 1966. A self-improvement book that shows how to diagnose and eliminate common stylistic faults.

Katzoff, Samuel. *Clarity in Technical Reports*. Washington, D.C.: NASA, 1964. A pamphlet designed for employees of and anyone seeking contracts with NASA.

Keithley, Erwin M., and Philip J. Schreiner. *A Manual of Style for the Preparation of Papers and Reports*. 2nd ed. Cincinnati: South-Western Publishing Co., 1971. A style guide for undergraduates and graduate students in programs in business and technology.

――――, and Margaret H. Thompson. *English for Modern Business*. 3rd ed. Homewood, Ill.: Irwin, 1977. A basic text for a refresher course in the fundamentals of grammar and writing.

Kleppner, Otto. *Advertising Procedure*. 6th ed. Englewood Cliffs, N.J.: Prentice-Hall, 1973. A standard text on all aspects of advertising.

Krey, Isabelle A., and Bernadette V. Metzler. *Principles and Techniques of Effective Business Communication*. New York: Harcourt, 1976. A basic text-workbook for introductory business writing courses.

Leonard, Donald J. *Shurter's Communication in Business*. New York: McGraw-Hill, 1979. A general text in business communications for undergraduates and those already engaged in business careers; a revision of the third edition of Robert Shurter's *Written Communication in Business* (1971).

Lesikar, Raymond V. *Basic Business Communication*. Homewood, Ill.: Irwin, 1979. A comprehensive introductory text with emphasis on practical applications rather than theory.

――――. *Business Communication, Theory and Application*. 3rd ed. Homewood, Ill.: Irwin, 1976. A comprehensive advanced text discussing all aspects of business communication.

――――. *Report Writing for Business*. 5th ed. Homewood, Ill.: Irwin, 1977. A comprehensive discussion of the process of organizing and writing business reports.

Levine, Norman. *Technical Writing.* New York: Harper and Row, 1979. A brief introductory text with sections on the mechanics of technical writing, technical explanation, and technical reporting.

Locke, Lawrence F., and W. W. Spirduso. *Proposals That Work.* New York: Teachers College Press, 1976. Proposal guidelines for graduate students in the sciences.

Maizell, Robert E., Julian F. Smith, and T. E. R. Singer. *Abstracting Scientific and Technical Literature.* New York: Wiley, 1971. Tips for beginning abstractors, information scientists, and management personnel.

Mandel, Siegfried, and David L. Caldwell. *Proposal and Inquiry Writing.* New York: Macmillan, 1962. An example-filled text that takes the reader through the logical steps of initial inquiry, proposal preparation, and contract.

Menning, J. H., C. W. Wilkinson, and Peter B. Clarke. *Communicating through Letters and Reports.* 6th ed. Homewood, Illinois: Irwin, 1976. A comprehensive text concerned with effective writing.

Menzel, Donald H., Howard Mumford Jones, and Lyle G. Boyd. *Writing a Technical Paper.* New York: McGraw-Hill, 1961. A brief guide for the technician reporting on the research of others.

Mills, Gordon H., and John A. Walter. *Technical Writing.* 4th ed. New York: Holt, Rinehart and Winston, 1978. A comprehensive rhetorically based text.

Mitchell, John N. *Writing for Professional and Technical Journals.* New York: Wiley, 1968. A discussion of the characteristics of and style guides for professional and technical articles.

Monroe, Judson, Carole Meredith, and Kathleen Fisher. *The Science of Scientific Writing.* Dubuque, Iowa: Kendall/Hunt, 1977. A brief guide designed to help students and laboratory researchers write term papers, dissertations, and articles for journals.

Murphy, Herta A., and Charles Peck. *Effective Business Communications.* 2nd ed. New York: McGraw-Hill, 1976. A comprehensive text suitable for both basic and advanced business writing courses.

Nutter, Carolyn F. *The Resume Workbook.* 4th ed. Cranston, R.I.: Carroll Press, 1970. A how-to book for prospective job applicants; includes a series of useful worksheets.

O'Hayre, John. *Gobbledygook Has Gotta Go.* Washington, D.C.: Government Printing Office, 1966. Suggestions about how to write direct and uncluttered reports, memoranda, and letters.

Pauley, Steven E. *Technical Report Writing Today.* 2nd ed. Boston: Houghton Mifflin, 1979. A brief text that asks technical students to write on topics in their specialized fields for an uninformed audience—the instructor.

Payne, Stanley L. *The Art of Asking Questions.* Princeton: Princeton Univ. Press, 1951. A detailed discussion of how to formulate questions.

Pearsall, Thomas E. *Teaching Technical Writing: Methods for College English Teachers.* Washington, D.C.: Society for Technical Communication, 1975. A short booklet for composition teachers who are interested in teaching more specialized courses in technical writing.

————, and Donald H. Cunningham. *How to Write for the World of Work.* New York: Holt, Rinehart and Winston, 1978. Practical, easy-to-use text for business and technical writing courses where the teacher is new to the field.

Pickett, Nell A., and Ann A. Laster. *Writing and Reading in Technical English.* San Francisco: Canfield, 1970. Introductory text for students at two-year colleges.

Rathbone, Robert R. *Communicating Technical Information.* Reading, Mass.: Addison-Wesley, 1966. A self-improvement manual for engineers and scientists who want to write more effective reports, abstracts, and journal articles.

Reid, James M., Jr., and Robert M. Wendlinger. *Effective Letters.* 3rd ed. New York: McGraw-Hill, 1978. A program for self-instruction prepared in collaboration with the New York Life Insurance Company.

Resiman, S. J. *A Style Manual for Technical Writers and Editors.* New York: Macmillan, 1962. A discussion of the types of technical publications; originally designed for employees of the Lockheed Corporation.

Riebel, John. *How to Write Reports, Papers, Theses, Articles.* 2nd ed. New York: Arco, 1972. A brief guide for writers intent upon self-improvement.

Roberts, Louise A. *How to Write for Business.* New York: Harper & Row, 1978. A text designed for introductory courses.

Sandage, Charles H., and Vernon Fryburger. *Advertising Theory and Practice.* 9th ed. Homewood, Ill.: Irwin, 1975. A thorough discussion of all aspects of advertising.

Sherman, Theodore A., and Simon S. Johnson. *Modern Technical Writing.* 3rd ed. Englewood Cliffs, N.J.: Prentice-Hall, 1975. A general text with emphasis on reports and business correspondence.

Shurter, Robert. *Effective Letters in Business.* 2nd ed. New York: McGraw-Hill, 1954. Popular paperback that examines the psychological principles that lie behind effective letters.

Sigband, Norman. *Communication for Management and Business.* 2nd ed. Glenview, Ill.: Scott, Foresman, 1976. A comprehensive text on oral and written business communication.

Smith, Rändi Sigmund, *Written Communication for Data Processing.* New York: Van Nostrand Reinhold, 1976. A brief text specifically designed to meet the writing needs of those in data processing.

Souther, James W., and Myron L. White. *Technical Report Writing.* 2nd ed. New York: Wiley, 1977. An overview of the writing process and a discussion of its application to scientific and technical report writing.

Strong, Charles W., and David Eidson. *A Technical Writer's Handbook.* New York: Holt, Rinehart and Winston, 1971. A comprehensive text designed to meet the different needs of a wide variety of technical writers.

Tichy, Henrietta. *Effective Writing for Engineers, Managers, and Scientists.* New York: Wiley, 1966. A basic text with emphasis on the clear writing style appropriate to business and industry.

Trelease, Sam F. *How to Write Scientific and Technical Papers.* Cambridge, Mass.: M.I.T. Press, 1969. A handy desk manual for technical writers.

Turner, Rufus P. *Grammar Review for Technical Writers.* Rev. ed. San Francisco: Rinehart, 1971. A brief review of practical English grammar for technicians.

Ulman, Joseph N., and Jay R. Gould. *Technical Report Writing.* 3rd ed. New York: Holt, Rinehart and Winston, 1972. Comprehensive text; especially helpful as a reference for technical report writers.

United States Treasury Department, Internal Revenue Service. *Effective Revenue*

Writing. Washington, D.C.: Government Printing Office, Vol. 1, 1961; Vol. 2, 1962. A guide for IRS employees; Volume 1 reviews principles of grammar and punctuation; Volume 2 diagnoses and suggests cures for common writing weaknesses.

Walton, Thomas F. *Technical Manual Writing and Administration.* New York: McGraw-Hill, 1968. A guide for writers of specifications and manuals.

Ward, Ritchie R. *Practical Technical Writing.* New York: Knopf, 1968. An undergraduate text designed around a series of practical and illustrative readings.

Weisman, Herman W. *Technical Correspondence.* New York: Wiley, 1968. Useful handbook for writers of technical letters.

Woodford, F. Peter, ed. *Scientific Writing for Graduate Students.* New York: Rockefeller Univ. Press, 1968. A comprehensive course guide for teachers of scientific writing; prepared by the Council of Biology Editors.

Wyld, Lionel D. *Preparing Effective Reports.* New York: Odyssey, 1967. A handbook for those in business and industry who need quick answers to questions about technical report writing.

Business and Technical Writing Anthologies

Cunningham, Donald H., and Herman A. Estrin, eds. *The Teaching of Technical Writing.* Urbana, Ill.: National Council of Teachers of English, 1975. Twenty-four essays on the teaching of business and technical writing; includes an annotated bibliography.

Effective Communication for Engineers. New York: McGraw-Hill, 1974. More than fifty essays on technical communication reprinted from *Chemical Engineering.*

Estrin, Herman A., ed. *Technical and Professional Writing, A Practical Anthology.* 1963; rpt. New York: Preston, 1976. More than forty articles on important aspects of business and technical writing.

Gieselman, Robert D., ed. *Readings in Business Communication.* Champaign, Ill.: Stipes, 1974. Twenty-two essays on a broad range of topics related to business communication.

Gould, Jay R., ed. *Directions in Technical Writing and Communication.* Farmington, N.Y.: Baywood, 1978. Fourteen essays reprinted from the *Journal of Technical Writing and Communication.*

Jordan, Stello, Joseph M. Kleinman, and H. Lee Shimberg, eds. *Handbook of Technical Writing Practices.* 2 vols. New York: Wiley, 1971. Thirty-two essays offering a complete guide to technical writing and its various support services.

Proposals . . . and Their Preparation. STC Anthology Series No. 1. Washington, D.C.: Society for Technical Communication, 1973. Sixteen essays, all previously published by the society, discussing procedures and guidelines for proposals.

Richards, Jack C., ed. *Teaching English for Science and Technology.* SEAMO Regional English Language Centre Anthology Series No. 2. Singapore: Singapore Univ. Press, 1976. Thirteen essays on the differences among scientific, technological, and technical English and the special problems they create for non-native speakers of English.

Sawyer, Thomas M., ed. *Technical and Professional Communication.* Ann Arbor, Mich.: Professional Communication Press, 1977. Twenty essays on the teaching of business and technical writing.

Shaw, James, ed. *Teaching Technical Writing and Editing—In-House Programs That Work.* STC Anthology Series No. 5. Washington, D.C.: Society for Technical Communication, 1976. Twelve essays, all previously published by the society, discussing the problems of designing and teaching in-house technical writing courses.

Sparrow, W. Keats, and Donald H. Cunningham, eds. *The Practical Craft: Readings for Business and Technical Writers.* Boston: Houghton Mifflin, 1978. Twenty-eight essays on business and technical writing with a brief annotated bibliography of additional sources.

Teaching Scientific Writing. English Journal, 67 (April, 1978). Seventeen articles on the teaching of writing and science.

Weeks, Francis W., ed. *Readings in Communication.* New York: Holt, Rinehart and Winston, 1961. Twenty-eight essays, all previously published in *Fortune,* discussing a variety of topics related to oral and written business communication.

Wilkinson, C. W., J. H. Menning, and C. R. Anderson, eds. *Writing for Business, Selected Articles on Business Communication.* 3rd ed. Homewood, Ill.: Irwin, 1960. More than seventy articles on the theory and practice of business communication.

Articles

Addams, H. Lon. "Preparing Resumes and Letters of Application." *Business Education Forum,* 32 (March, 1978), 29–30. Guidelines for students preparing their first resumes and letters of application.

Adler, Leonard K. "Proposal Writing." *Proceedings of the Annual National STWE Convention,* 7 (1960), 49–60. A general discussion ranging from the establishment of proposal requirements to the physical production of the proposal.

Ammannito, Theresa A. "The Introduction." *STWP Review,* 9 (July, 1962), 11–14. An examination of the correlation between reader expertise and the length and complexity of introductions to technical reports and articles.

Arnold, Christian K. "The Construction of Statistical Tables." *IRE Transactions on Engineering Writing and Speech,* EWS-5 (August, 1962), 9–14. Guidelines for constructing statistical tables, criteria for choosing vertical or horizontal presentations of information, and rules for the use of captions.

Aronson, M. H., and R. C. Nelson. "Technical Reading, Writing, and Editing." *Instruments and Control Systems,* 36 (January, 1963), 71–72; (February, 1963), 75–76; (March, 1963), 75; (April, 1963), 81 and 83; (May, 1963), 81 and 83;

(June, 1963), 73 and 75; (November, 1963), 91–92; and (December, 1963), 73–75. Practical guidelines for beginning writers who need help meeting their readers' needs.

Aziz, Abdul. "Article Titles as Tools of Communication." *Journal of Technical Writing and Communication,* 4 (Winter 1974), 19–21. Suggestions for forming titles that contain as much information in as few words as possible.

Baker, J. R. "English Style in Scientific Papers." *Science,* 123 (April 27, 1956), 713–714. Jargon-filled papers can be clear if writers take care with the words between the technical terms.

Ballard, W. Wesley. "Instruction Manuals for Consumers." In *Proceedings of the 1959 Institute in Technical and Industrial Communication.* Eds. Herman M. Weisman and Roy C. Nelson. Fort Collins, Colo.: Institute in Technical and Industrial Communication, 1960. A discussion of the definitions and purposes of instructional literature and its production and printing; pays particular attention to manuals for commercial products.

Bergwerk, R. J. "Effective Communication of Financial Data." *Journal of Accountancy,* 129 (February, 1970), 47–54. Use tables for comparing several pieces of data and graphs for showing trends over several periods of time.

Biskind, Elliot L. "Writing Right." *New York State Bar Journal,* 42 (October, 1970), 548–554. Suggestions for improving the quality of legal writing.

Booth, Vernon. "Writing a Scientific Paper." *Biochemical Society Transactions,* 3 (1975), 3–26. A simple, practical discussion of prewriting techniques, style, visual aids, and manuscript submission guidelines for scientific papers.

Borko, Harold, and Seymour Chatman. "Criteria for Acceptable Abstracts: A Survey of Abstracters' Instructions." *American Documentation,* 14 (April, 1963), 149–160. Results of a survey of instructions given by 130 services and journals that abstract scientific literature.

Bram, V. A. "Factors Affecting the Readability of Scientific and Engineering Texts." *The Communicator of Scientific and Technical Information,* 33 (October, 1977), 3–5. An author's skill in constructing effective sentences will determine how successfully he communicates with the reader.

Bromage, Mary C. "Gamesmanship in Written Communication." *Management Review,* 61 (April, 1972), 11–15. Suggestions for improving the diction of business writing.

————. "A Matter of Wording." *Journal of Accountancy,* 115 (January, 1963), 59–63. Further comments aimed at improving the diction of business writing.

Butterfield, William H. "Touches of Tact That Take the Sting Out of Adjustments." *Sales Management,* 57 (December 15, 1946), 106–108. Suggestions about how to satisfy readers when making adjustments on claims.

Campbell, H. A. "How to Prepare Technical Reports." *Product Engineering,* 25 (October, 1954), 154–157. An analytic approach to the preparation and writing of technical reports.

Cederborg, Gibson A. "Engineering Writing to Eliminate Gobbledygook." *Machine Design,* 29 (March 7, 1957), 80–82. Recommendations for eliminating common mechanical and stylistic problems in engineering writing.

Christenson, Larry. "How to Write an Office Manual." *American Business,* 25 (July, 1955), 26–27, 33–34. Nine principles for writing effective manuals.

Colman, J. P. "How to Write Market Research Reports." *Industrial Marketing,* 43

(February, 1958), 145–147. An easy-to-follow presentation that will encourage management to act upon the advice of market research.

Cortelyou, Ethaline. "Abstract of the Technical Report." *Journal of Chemical Education,* 30 (October, 1955), 532–533. A discussion of the differences between abstracts and summaries.

Crawford, Donald M. "On Engineering Writing." *Mechanical Engineering,* 67 (September, 1945), 607–609. Suggestions for eliminating weaknesses commonly found in manuscripts prepared by engineers.

DeBakey, Lois. "The Persuasive Proposal." *Journal of Technical Writing and Communication,* 6 (Winter 1976), 5–25. A discussion of the skills needed by investigators who write research proposals.

DeBeaugrande, Robert. "Information and Grammar in Technical Writing." *College Composition and Communication,* 28 (December, 1977), 325–332. Ways in which grammar can help technical writers organize the information in their texts.

Deck, Warren H. "Technical Manuals." *Proceedings of the 1960 Institute in Technical and Industrial Communication.* Eds. Herman M. Weisman et al. Fort Collins, Colo.: Colorado State University, 1961. A guide to successful manual writing.

————. "What Makes a Good Instruction Book." *General Electric Review,* 58 (July, 1955), 40–43. An outline for an instruction book with a discussion of how to meet the different needs of intended audiences.

Deutsch, Arnold R. "Does Your Company Practice Affirmative Action in Its Communication?" *Harvard Business Review,* 54 (November–December, 1976), 16, 186, 188. Suggestions for eliminating sexism in business communication.

Dilley, David R. "A Business Manager Looks at Business Writing." *English Journal,* 50 (April, 1961), 265–270. Suggestions for making the hard work of business writing a little easier.

Dodge, W. J. "Writing the Appropriation Request." *Chemical Engineering,* 73 (March 14, 1966), 152–154. Guidelines for requesting funds and for other kinds of written salesmanship.

Dolphin, Robert, Jr., and Robert A. Wagley. "Reading the Annual Report." *Financial Executive,* 45 (June, 1977), 20–22. Suggestions about how to improve the readability of annual reports.

Dover, J. C. "How to Tell Your Profits Story." *Nation's Business,* 48 (May, 1960), 38–39, 117–120. How to avoid harmful confusion about the size and use of profits.

Eden, Brian F. "Preparing a Bibliography." *IRE Transactions on Engineering Writing and Speech,* EWS-4 (December, 1961), 97–100. Guidelines for preparing a bibliography.

Elliott, Colin R. "Must Scientific English Be Dull?" *English Language Teaching Journal,* 31 (October, 1976), 29–34. Suggestions on how to teach students to produce lively scientific and technical writing.

Encke, C. G. "Scientific Writing: One Scientist's Perspective." *English Journal,* 67 (April, 1978), 40–43. A series of comments on the rhetorical problems of and the use of illustrations and figures in scientific writing.

Flesch, Rudolf. "How to Say It with Statistics." *Printers' Ink,* 233 (December 8, 1950), 23–24. Twelve suggestions on how to make statistics readable.

Fox, Mortimer, Jr. "The Annual Report: An Objective Appraisal." *Financial Executive,* 33 (January, 1965), 38–47. Handy checklists designed to improve the attractiveness and effectiveness of annual reports.

Francis, Henry E. "The Literary Aspects of Business Writing." *Journal of Business Communication,* 4 (October, 1966), 13–18. A discussion of form, style, and tone in business writing.

Garay, Paul N. "The Technical Manual." *Consulting Engineer,* 17 (December, 1961), 68–70. Procedures used by industrial consultants in preparing technical manuals.

Gould, Jay R. "Ten Common Weaknesses in Engineering Reports." *Chemical Engineering,* 70 (October 14, 1963), 210–214. A discussion of problems writers of engineering reports often encounter.

Guccione, Eugene. "Preparing Better Flowsheets." *Chemical Engineering,* 73 (March 14, 1966), 155–157. Suggestions about how to design complete, accurate, and easy-to-follow flowsheets.

"Guide for the Preparation and Publication of Synopses." *Franklin Institute Journal,* 270 (September, 1960), 257–258. Fifteen steps for the preparation of abstracts that conform to guidelines established by the Abstracting Board of the International Council of Scientific Unions.

Happ, W. W. "Guidelines and Checklists for Preparing the Planning Report." *IEEE Transactions on Professional Communication,* PC-16 (December, 1973), 209–214. A checklist of over one hundred items for writers of contract planning reports.

Hayes, J. R., and D. Laird. "Letters That Get Results." *Personnel Journal,* 43 (July–August, 1964), 380–381, 388. Guidelines for writing effective letters.

Hine, Edward A. "Write in Style: Be Clear and Concise." *Chemical Engineering,* 82 (December 22, 1975), 41–45. Suggestions about how to achieve clarity in technical reports.

Hudson, Ralph. "Teaching Technical Writing." *College Composition and Communication,* 12 (December, 1961), 208–212. A series of general observations intended for beginning teachers of technical writing.

Hughson, Roy V. "Guidelines for R & D Reports." *Chemical Engineering.* 73 (March 14, 1966), 158–160. Suggestions about how to write more effective project and progress reports.

Issel, C. K. "The Resume—A Sales Tool." *Technical Communication,* 18 (May–June, 1971), 7–9. Suggestions for writing a resume that will sell the job applicant.

Janes, Harold D. "The Cover Letter and Resume." *Personnel Journal,* 48 (September 9, 1969), 732–733. Results of a survey of the 500 largest corporations in the United States about their preferences concerning cover letters and resumes.

Janis, J. Harold. "The Writing Behavior of Businessmen." *Journal of Communication,* 15 (June, 1965), 81–88. A discussion of the problems business behavior presents for business writers.

Johnson, Robert. "Proposals . . . Write Them to Sell." *Aerospace Management,* 5 (May, 1962), 32–35. Suggestions for writing research and development reports that get results.

Johnson, Thomas P. "How Well Do You Inform?" *Chemical Engineering,* 73

(March 14, 1966), 146–151. Four tests designed to help engineers write analytically.

———. "Organize the Report for Fast Writing, Easy Reading." *Chemical Engineering,* 76 (June 30, 1969), 104–110. How to put what readers want to know most at the beginning of reports.

Jordan, Michael P. "As a Matter of Fact." *Journal of Business Communication,* 15 (Winter 1978), 3–11. How to distinguish among facts, opinions, and assumptions.

———. "New Directions in Teaching Technical Report Writing." *Journal of Technical Writing and Communication.* 5 (Fall 1975), 199–205. Suggestions about how to include instruction in the concepts of technical credibility and scientific inference in technical writing courses.

"Keep It Simple." *The Royal Bank of Canada Monthly Letter,* 56 (May, 1975), 4 pp. A discussion of what simplicity in business writing means.

Kendall, R. "Proposal Digest." *IEEE Transactions on Engineering Writing and Speech,* EWS-6 (December, 1963), 79–81. A discussion of the digest and its importance in preparing and presenting a proposal.

Kennedy, Robert A. "Writing Informative Titles for Technical Literature—An Aid to Efficient Information Retrieval." *IEEE Transactions on Engineering Writing and Speech,* EWS-7 (March, 1964), 4–5. Guidelines for choosing report titles, headings, and subheadings.

Keyes, Langley C. "Profits in Prose." *Harvard Business Review,* 39 (January, 1961), 105–112. Tips on how management can save money by paying attention to employee reading and working habits.

Koff, Richard M. "Eight Steps to Better Engineering Writing." *Product Engineering,* 30 (1959); rpt. 36 (March 15, 1965), 117; (March 29, 1965), 88; (April 12, 1965), 102; (April 26, 1965), 88; (May 24, 1965), 64; (June 7, 1965), 107; (June 21, 1965), 89; and (July 5, 1965), 85–86. Detailed suggestions for improving technical prewriting, writing, and rewriting.

Labine, Roland A. "Writing for Publication." *Chemical Engineering,* 73 (March 14, 1966), 160–162. Suggestions from an editor about how to improve engineering manuscripts prior to submission for publication.

Landman, Amos. "Increasing the Effectiveness of Financial Reports to Top Management." *Credit and Financial Management,* 69 (September, 1967), 26–28. Guidelines for writing forceful, clear, and persuasive financial reports.

Lane, J. C. "Digesting for a Multi-Company Management Audience." *Journal of Chemical Documentation,* 1 (1963), 59–63. A discussion of the special problems the physical scientist has in presenting complex technical information to audiences of differing levels of expertise.

"Let's Put Words to Work." *The Royal Bank of Canada Monthly Letter,* 44 (May, 1963), 4 pp. Suggestions for improving the diction of business communications.

Mabbs, Edward C. "How to Write a Proposal That Really Sells." *Modern Materials Handling,* 23 (July, 1968), 84–85. Four suggestions for proposal writers.

MacIntosh, Fred H. "What Customers Want in Proposals." *STWP Convention Proceedings,* 11 (1964), n.p. Results of a survey conducted by Westinghouse to determine customer wants and needs in nongovernment proposals.

Marsh, Robert T. "Basic Guide for Writing Progress Reports." *Machine Design*, 27 (April, 1955), 345. What to put in and what to leave out.

McCauley, D. E., Jr. "Memo on Memos: Write Less, Say More." *Supervisory Management*, 8 (May, 1963), 8-9. Suggestions on how to write more effective memoranda.

McPherson, Cameron. "Ten Things to Keep in Mind When You Sit Down to Write a Report." *American Business*, 27 (April, 1957), 18-19. No-nonsense suggestions for improving written reports.

"On Writing a Sales Letter." *The Royal Bank of Canada Monthly Letter*, 43 (March, 1962), 4 pp. Guidelines for improving the effectiveness of sales letters.

"On Writing Briefly." *The Royal Bank of Canada Monthly Letter*, 37 (July, 1956), 4 pp. A discussion of what brevity means in the writing of business reports.

"On Writing Clearly." *The Royal Bank of Canada Monthly Letter*, 38 (July, 1957), 4 pp. Suggestions about how to write clear business letters.

Orth, Melvin F. "Abstracting for the Writer." *IEEE Transactions on Professional Communication,"* PC-15 (June, 1972), 43-44. A discussion of the value of abstract-writing for writers of business and technical reports.

Palmer, Charles W. "The Written Procedure—Welcome Relief for the Engineer." *STWP Review*, 12 (April, 1965), 10-12. A description of a special-purpose procedure and a discussion of its planning.

Racker, Joseph. "Selecting and Writing to the Proper Level." *IRE Transactions on Engineering Writing and Speech*, EWS-2 (January, 1959), 16-21. Suggestions for determining the proper levels at which technical materials should be presented to readers with varying degrees of expertise.

Reubens, John B. "Challenge: Good Scientific Writing." *IEEE Transactions on Engineering Writing and Speech*, EWS-8 (December, 1965), 48-55. An examination of the major causes of poor scientific and engineering writing.

Rockett, Frank H. "Planning Illustrations First, Simplifies Writing Later." *IRE Transactions on Engineering Writing and Speech*, EWS-2 (June, 1959), 56-61. How to plan illustration to include as much information as possible.

Rogers, Raymond. "How to Organize a Research Report for Management." *Technical Communication*, 20 (First Quarter, 1973), 7-9. A discussion of the application of principles of written journalism to the writing of research reports.

Schindler, George E., Jr. "Why Engineers and Scientists Write as They Do—Twelve Characteristics of Their Prose." *IEEE Transactions on Professional Communication*. PC-18 (March, 1975), 5-10. A discussion of the problems commonly found in the sentences of technical written communication.

Schnitzler, Robert K. "Making Your Technical Proposals More Effective." *STWP Review*, 10 (April, 1963), 2-5; (July, 1963), 7-11. A detailed discussion of the planning and writing of proposals.

Shaw, Howard D. "How to Get Ready to Write a Letter." *Reporter of Direct Mail Advertising*, 10 (February, 1948), 12-15. Prewriting exercises for sales letters.

_____. "How to Start to Write a Letter." *Reporter of Direct Mail Advertising*, 11 (February, 1949), 12-16. Ten tests for opening sentences.

Shelby, Anne. "How to Type Your Paper." *Technical Writing Teacher*, 1 (Winter 1974), 11-22. Easy-to-follow directions for typing a formal report.

Shidle, Norman G. "Why Don't We Always Write Our Best?" *Journal of Business*

Communication, 6 (Summer 1969), 1-4. A discussion of the problems caused by and attitudes behind poor business writing.

Spangler, E. R. "Modern Grammar and Its Application to Technical Writing." *Journal of Chemical Education,* 33 (February, 1956), 61-64. An application of some basic principles of descriptive grammar to technical writing.

Sparrow, W. Keats. "Six Myths about 'Writing for Business and Industry'." *Technical Writing Teacher,* 3 (Winter 1976), 49-59. Practical advice for beginning teachers of business and technical writing.

Storm, A. Allman. "In Search of Money." *Management Accounting,* 53 (August, 1971), 29-32. Guidelines for those seeking capital.

Sullivan, Albert J. "Nine Steps to More Effective Letters." *Printers' Ink,* 229 (October 14, 1949), 48-50, 54. Practical suggestions for writing lively letters that get results.

Tichy, Henrietta. "Engineers Can Write Better." *Chemical Engineering Progress,* 50 (February, 1954), 104-107; (April, 1964), 206-213; and (July, 1954), 365-371. A detailed discussion of the mechanics of engineering and technical writing.

Tilghman, William S. "Building Better Resumes." *Data on Defense and Civil Systems,* 8 (February, 1963), 49-53. A discussion of formats for, differences among, and advantages in using text, chronological, and summary resumes.

Tutt, Charles L., Jr. "Preparation and Evaluation of an Industrial Report." *General Motors Engineering Journal,* 4 (April-June, 1957), 30-33. Guidelines developed at the General Motors Institute for the evaluation of industrial reports.

Uris, A. "How to Communicate with Managers." *Industrial Research,* 12 (April, 1970), 56, 60, 62. Seven steps to help business and technical writers meet the needs of management.

Weil, B. H. "Standards for Writing Abstracts." *ASIS Journal,* 21 (September-October, 1970), 351-357. Guidelines for the preparation of an abstract.

———, I. Zarember, and H. Owen. "Technical Abstracting Fundamentals." *Journal of Chemical Documentation,* 3 (April, 1963), 86-89; (July, 1963), 125-136. A comprehensive analysis of the abstracting needs and practices of engineers and scientists.

Weismantel, G., and J. Matley. "Is Your Resume Junk Mail?" *Chemical Engineering,* 81 (November 11, 1974), 164, 166. Suggestions drawn from Lockheed's *Job Hunting: The Seven Steps to Success* on how to apply the practices of the direct mail industry to the writing of a resume and cover letter.

Welsh, E. Michael. "Teaching the Letter of Application." *College Composition and Communication,* 28 (December, 1978), 374-376. How to teach students to manage tone and exercise their analytic skills in writing letters of application.

Wright, John W. "Instruction Manuals." *Product Engineering,* 24 (August, 1953), 141-148. A discussion of the requirements for acceptable military and commercial manuals and methods for producing them at reasonable cost.

"Writing a Report." *The Royal Bank of Canada Monthly Letter,* 57 (February, 1976), 4 pp. Suggestions on how to write successful informative and research reports.

A 0
B 1
C 2
D 3
E 4
F 5
G 6
H 7
I 8
J 9